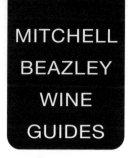

MITCHELL
BEAZLEY
WINE
GUIDES

WINES OF
Spain

Foreword by Hugh Johnson

JAN READ

The Wines of Spain
by Jan Read

Published in Great Britain in 2005 by Mitchell Beazley,
an imprint of Octopus Publishing Group Limited
2–4 Heron Quays, London E14 4JP
First edition published in 1983

A CIP catalogue record for this book is available from the British Library.

ISBN 1 84533 018 8

Commissioning Editor: Hilary Lumsden
Executive Art Editor: Yasia Williams
Senior Editor: Julie Sheppard
Designer: Peter Gerrish
Production: Seyhan Esen

Typeset in Helvetica and Versailles by Cyber Media Services
Printed and bound by Toppan Printing Company in China

Contents

Key to Symbols

r	red
p	rosé
w	white
am	amber
g	generoso
res	reserva
dr	dry
s/sw	semi-sweet
sw	sweet
sp	sparkling
pt	*pétillant*

Where any of the above codes appears in parentheses, it means that the product is a relatively unimportant part of the range.
See page 9 for further information.

☆	everyday wine
☆☆	above average
☆☆☆	excellent quality, highly reputed
☆☆☆☆	the best and most expensive
★	if the star or stars appear black rather than in outline, then the wine is, in addition, usually good value in its class
DO	*denominación de origen* – name and origin controlled (*see* pages 12–14)
DOP	*denominación de origen provisional* (*see* page 12)
VC	*vino comarcal* (*see* pages 12–14)
74, 75	recommended years which may be currently available
DYA	drink the youngest available
NV	vintage not normally shown on label
HARO	a name in small capitals indicates that the word appears as an entry in its own right within that chapter

Foreword

Some wine historian of the future, reviewing the last quarter of the twentieth century, will no doubt enjoy the question of which of the leading wine countries accelerated fastest from being a producer of wine at a fairly primitive, everyday level, to highly organized quality production on a grand scale. It will be surprising if the vote does not go to Spain.

In a quarter of a century, Spain has progressed from what was as dim a start as any winemaking land could have, to being one of the world's most confident, most original, and best-run producers.

Throughout this time, an English film writer and scholar with a passion for Spain has been more than just passively observing the revolution. He has been a much-valued commentator and critic at the heart of it.

Jan Read and his wife Maite (and their son Carlos, too) have been both interpreters and ambassadors for Spain, and at the same time creative inspirations at bodega-floor level.

To its maker, good wine is a very personal thing. It is not just anybody he takes into his confidence. Jan, above all, has been one of the people winemakers can trust to give them a frank opinion, technical advice, encouragement, and friendship. He has also been the same to other writers studying Spanish wine. My own most rewarding journeys in this most rewarding of countries have been with Jan as a guide, philosopher, and friend.

This book condenses more experience than any other writer can claim of one of the most exciting wine countries on earth. Can we ask for more?

Hugh Johnson

Spain

The autonomous regions shown on this map are those used for the chapters of this guide. The definitive boundaries for individual wine-producing areas are shown on the regional maps at the start of each chapter.

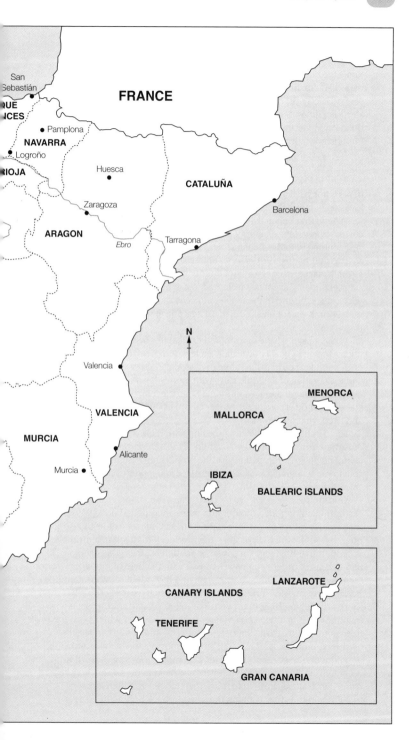

Introduction

Since the time of Sir Francis Drake's "rape of the barrels" in Cádiz (*see* page 151), Spain has been known first and foremost for a single wine: sherry. The sweet dessert málagas achieved a certain vogue in England in Victorian times, but the better beverage wines have been slow to establish themselves in foreign markets. Until recently the image was of sturdy (though often drinkable) "plonk".

The reasons for this are to be found in the drinking habits of the Spanish themselves. What Richard Ford wrote in his *Gatherings from Spain* in 1846 long remained true: "The Spaniard himself is neither curious in port, nor particular in madeira; he much prefers quantity to quality and loves flavour less than he hates trouble…".

When I first began drinking Spanish wine some fifty years ago, the custom was to take an empty bottle to the wine shop and to fill it from a cask marked with the alcoholic degree and some such terse description as *tinto* (full-bodied red), *clarete* (light red), *blanco* (white), *Moscatel,* and so on. It is true, of course, that better wines were available, sometimes of excellent quality like those from La Rioja, which had been bottling its fine wines since the end of the nineteenth century. They were not, however, much drunk except on special occasions and at the more expensive restaurants.

Various factors have contributed to what has been a very remarkable improvement in quality over the past few decades. One of the achievements of General Franco in his latter years was a marked rise in living standards and the creation of a middle class with more sophisticated tastes and the money to indulge them. At the same time, the millions of tourists who started to flood across the Pyrenees began asking for the better wines, and liked what they found.

Hand in hand with this, and starting with Rioja in 1926, the Ministry of Agriculture began the demarcation of the different winemaking areas, laying down strict regulations for the production of better-quality wines sold under a *denominación de origen* (DO) and modernizing the cooperatives.

During the past dozen years there has been an increasing realization among the younger and more enlightened *bodegueros* that Spain's future as a wine producer lies in quality rather than quantity. While the bulk of the wine produced in the vast central plateau is cooperative-made and acceptable enough for everyday drinking, it and dozens of other regions are now – with the help of modern technology – producing characterful and individual growths. Perhaps no other country in Europe makes wine in such a variety of styles: there are the *pétillant* young wines of the north and northwest; a whole gamut of reds, whites, and rosés; excellent sparkling wines produced in larger quantity than Champagne; apéritif and dessert wines such as sherry, montilla, and málaga; and a cupboard full of vermouths and liqueurs. Exports of the better beverage wines have soared in recent years. For example, shipments of Rioja to the UK have increased from 180,000 litres in 1970 to more than nineteen million litres in 2003, and the story is much the same in the USA and in northern

Europe, indicating the growing appreciation of good value, particularly in the mid-price bracket.

A–Z listings in this volume are arranged within broad geographical areas. This reflects the fact that, in Spain, individual labels and house styles are generally of greater significance than minor geographical areas, and the smaller producers tend not to bottle their wine but to sell to large concerns or direct to local restaurants.

The many *bodegueros* and others who have helped me in the preparation of this new edition are too numerous to mention indi-vidually, but I should particularly like to thank Don Bartolomé Vergara of the Asociación de Criadores Exportadores de Sherry, and that brilliant oenologist and leading exponent of Spanish wines, Don Miguel Torres Riera. My wife, Maite Manjón, has made a major contribution to the sections on "Wine and Food", which I hope will add to the enjoyment of visitors to Spain.

How to Read an Entry

Entries are generally of two types: those descriptive of a region or town or of objects or equipment commonly used in Spanish winemaking, and those relating to individual producers (bodegas) and their wines. The top lines of entries referring to producers generally give the following information.

1   The name of the producer.
2   Whether the wine is bottled with a *denominación de origen* (DO) or is a table wine from a specified district (VdT or VdC) – see "Laws and Labels", page 12.
3   The types of wine made by the producer – for example red, rosé, white, sparkling (abbreviated to r, p, w, sp – see "Key to Symbols", page 4).
4   Their general standing as to quality, a necessarily rough-and-ready guide based on the following ascending scale:

☆   everyday wine
☆☆   above average
☆☆☆   excellent quality, highly reputed
☆☆☆☆   the best and most expensive

So much is more or less objective. Additionally, there is a subjective rating; where the stars appear in black rather than in outline (see "Key to Symbols", page 4), this denotes a wine which is, in my experience, particularly good value within its price range, be it luxury or everyday.

Stars have not been used in the sections covering Montilla-Moriles and Málaga; Sherry; Sparkling Wines; and Spirits, Aromatic Wines, and Liqueurs. Here, the producers often make such a vast range of wines or spirits that general judgments become more or less meaningless: one of a sherry house's finos may deserve three stars, while its oloroso is of merely two-star quality, and vice-versa. Some guidance to the quality of such wines will be found in the descriptive notes on each producer.

5   Vintage information. Recommended years which may be available. Most sizeable Spanish bodega*s* make a range of red, white, and rosé wines, the reds varying from young wines to *crianzas* and *reservas*, and the vintages refer to the best of the bodega'*s* red wines.

The text of each of these entries begins with:

1   the town or village in which the bodega is located;
2   the province, in parentheses; and
3   where a bodega makes demarcated wines, the DO is specified – for example, DO Penedès. This is not repeated for the many wines of Rioja and the sherry region, which all fall under their respective single DOs.

The information under "Wine and Food" at the end of each section is intended primarily for visitors, and the dishes which are briefly described are those typical of the region. "International cooking" proliferates in the tourist resorts and large cities. Nouvelle cuisine and its successors have left their mark on Spain as elsewhere – often to the good, in lightening heavy dishes. The current trend among sophisticated chefs is to revive traditional dishes and to cook the best prime ingredients in such a way as to bring out their individual flavours to the fullest extent. Recommended hotels are also detailed here. Where wines are coupled with particular dishes, they are examples of what I myself might choose. However, I do not believe in hard and fast rules about which wine goes with which dish, and suggest that all readers follow their individual preferences.

Suggestions for travelling to and within the regions are made in the introductory paragraphs, and other places to visit appear under the towns in the A–Z listing.

Anatomy of Spanish Wine

Spain has more land under vines than any other country in Europe, but comes third (after Italy and France) in terms of wine production. The reasons for the low yield are various, but include the facts that much of the soil is barren, many of the vines are old and in need of replacement, and the vineyards are often split up among smallholders who have few resources or little technical expertise to draw on.

Criss-crossed by great chains of mountains, Spain is a country of wide geographical contrasts, ranging from the wet and mountainous north to the arid central plateau (with its bitter winters and hot summers) and Andalucía in the south – mild in winter and sun-baked for the rest of the year. It is a pattern giving rise to wines in great variety, and almost every region – apart from the Atlantic coast in the north – produces wines of sorts. The best of the world's beverage wines are produced along a belt lying between 30° and 50° latitude in both hemispheres, and the best Spanish beverage wines come from Rioja, Penedès, Ribera del Duero, Navarra, Somontano, and Galicia, which lie towards the centre of this zone but are somewhat cooler than average because of their altitude. Rioja and Ribera del Duero are predominantly producers of red wines; the Penedès makes both red and white (together with a great deal of sparkling wine), but is better known for its white; Galicia produces elegant and flowery whites.

The great central plateau of La Mancha, which produces a massive thirty-five per cent of Spain's wines, is classified as semi-arid, and much of the wine is cooperative-made and sold in bulk. Ninety per cent is white and the introduction of cold fermentation has resulted in fresher, lighter wines. The best of the reds are from Valdepeñas, where some are now matured in oak. The coastal region of the Levante (the Valencian area and Murcia), bordering the Mediterranean to the east of La Mancha, has traditionally produced earthy, full-bodied wines high in alcohol, both red and white, of which the most attractive are the light and fresh rosés from Utiel-Requena. Here, sweeping improvements in technology have resulted in the large-scale elaboration of lighter and very drinkable wines for export. Andalucía is more or less exclusively a producer of apéritif and dessert wines made in *solera* (*see* page 161) by the progressive blending of older and younger wines. Apart from sherry, the best known are the very similar wines from Montilla-Moriles and the classical but fast-disappearing dessert málagas.

The future looks bright for the Spanish wine industry. With regard to exports, the emphasis was for too long on quantity rather than quality. This has largely been because the heat of the long summers in the central and southerly parts of the country produces very large amounts of sugar in the grapes, and traditional methods of fermentation have led to robust wines which are over-strong in alcohol. With the introduction of earlier picking, stainless-steel vats, and the permitting of fermentation at lower and controlled temperatures, the picture is now changing – and changing fast. The Mediterranean countries (after all, the cradle of winemaking in Europe) may yet be at an advantage over the wetter and colder areas of northern Europe. Further progress will depend on improvement of the vines, either by cloning of the best native varieties – always with a view to quality rather than quantity – or by the acclimatization of noble varieties such as Cabernet Sauvignon and Chardonnay from abroad. Again, a great deal remains to be done: for example, denser planting of the vines and the provision of supports so as to afford more shade and conservation of water in the soil.

The new emphasis on quality has already resulted in a growing number of wines that can stand comparison with the best from elsewhere. This is particularly true of a new generation of Riojas made with hand-sorted grapes from old vines grown in the best terroir. In Spain, these wines have been christened *vinos de alta expresión*, meaning wines made with the utmost care to obtain the maximum concentration and preserve the full flavour of the fruit. Rioja is, of course, far from the only region to make such wines, and a personal choice of the very best from all over Spain for drinking in 2005–6 is listed on pages 18–19.

GRAPE VARIETIES

It would be a Herculean task to list all the grape varieties used in the production of the wines named in this book. Spain claims to have some 600 different varieties – although just twenty cover eighty per cent of the country's vineyards. In Galicia alone there are 136 recognized types of vine. To add to the confusion, the same grape often goes under a different name in different regions of Spain; the Riojan Tempranillo, for example, is the Ull de Llebre in Cataluña and the Cencibel in Valdepeñas. The main grape varieties of each region are discussed in the general introductions, and the entry for each DO zone names the grapes used for its wines.

Laws and Labels

After five years of discussion and consultation a new wine law has been passed in Spain, replacing legislation in the main dating back to the 1970s. Although it took effect from August 2003, it will have little immediate effect, since responsibility for winemaking will now pass to the eighteen different Spanish autonomies, which have yet to incorporate the national law into their own statutes.

Since Spain joined the EU, its wine law was modified to meet European regulations in general. The EU recognizes two broad categories: table wine and quality wine. In Spain, as elsewhere, these have been subdivided and are in ascending order of quality: for Spanish table wines, *vino de mesa* and *vino de la tierra* (VdT), and for quality wine *denominación de origen* (DO) and *denominación de origen calificada* (DOCa). *Vino de mesa* without further qualification is wine grown in unclassified vineyards or blended, while *vino de la tierra* corresponds to the French *vin de pays* and is a table wine with a defined geogaphic description from a large area, often an autonomous region (e.g. Vino de la Tierra de Castilla).

As far as comparisons can be made, Spanish DO corresponds in quality either to the French VDQS (*vin délimité de qualité supérieur*) or AC (*appellation d'origine controlée*) and to the Italian DOC (*denominazione di origine controllata*).

The new legislation adds three additional levels of quality wine to the existing DO and DOCa. *Vino de calidad producio en una region determinada* must originate in a tightly defined area with an overseeing body and may, after a qualifying period of five years, be granted the superior status of DO. Formerly restricted to DO growths, the ageing descriptions of *crianza, reserva,* and *grand reserva* may be used in labelling these wines.

The other new categories of quality wine are *vinos de pago* and *vinos de pago calificada*. These apply to single vineyard sites with a special microclimate and a record of producing wine of exceptional quality, the second applying to a vineyard located within a DOCa. At the time of writing there are only a two *pagos*: the Marqués de Griñon's Dominio de Valdepusa and the Finca de Elez, both in Castilla-La Mancha. Others in regions like Rioja, Penedès, and Priorato are likely to emerge shortly.

As regards DO, the first regions to be demarcated were Rioja in 1926 and Jerez in 1933. The complete list of DOs now runs to:

Abona	Cariñena
Alella	Cataluña
Alicante	Cava
Almansa	Chacolí de Arabaka –
Ampurdán-Empordà-Costa Brava	(Arabaka Txakolina)
Bierzo	Chacolí de Guetería –
Binissalem	(Getariako Txakolina)
Bullas	Chacolí de Vizcaya –
Calatayud	(Bizkaiko Txakolina)
Campo de Borja	Cigales

Conca de Barberà
Condado de Huelva
Costers del Segre
El Hierro
El Monte
Jerez/Xérès/Sherry y Manzanilla-
	Sanlúcar de Barrameda
Jumilla
La Mancha
La Palma
Lanzarote
Málaga
Manchuela
Méntrida
Método Tradicional
Mondéjar
Monte Lentiscal
Monterrei
Montilla-Moriles
Montsant
Navarra
Penedès
Pla de Bages

Plá i Llevant
Priorato Priorat
Rías Baixas
Ribeira Sacra
Ribeiro
Ribera del Duero
Ribera del Guadiana
Ribera del Júcar
Rioja
Rueda
Somontano
Tacoronte-Acentejo
Tarragona
Terra Alta
Toro
Utiel-Requena
Valdeorras
Valdepeñas
Valle de Güímar
Valle de la Orotava
Valencia
Vinos de Madrid
Vinos de Pago

To begin with, cava (sparkling wine made by the Champagne method) was the subject of a *denominación específica*, that related only to quality and the way in which the wine was produced. In addition to this, the DO Cava – like the others – now defines the areas in which it may be made, in Cava's case in several different regions of Spain (*see* "Sparkling Wines", page 176). In similar fashion, a *denominación específica* for wines made with the Albariño grape variety has been replaced by the DO Rías Baixas, demarcating the three principal areas where Albariño is grown (*see* "Galicia", page 93).

All of the above DOs are controlled by a *consejo regulador*, a regulatory body which issues a *reglamento* or set of rules with which DO wines must comply – this is in addition to those of the *Estatuto de la Viña y de los Alcoholes*, a lengthy government decree setting out regulations for the production of wines and spirits in Spain as a whole.

Under the new law of 2003, there are sweeeping changes in the provisions of the *Estatuto* and the functions of the *consejos reguladores*, and as the whole procedure is in a state of transition and likely to remain so for a considerable time, it seems best to quote the Ministry of Agriculture:

> "The biggest change relating to *denominaciones de origen* is the removal of qualitative classification of wines and powers of sanction from the *consejos reguladores* of each DO. The function of the regulatory boards of each DO will now be confined to such activities as improving quality, establishing maximum yield, proposing any variations in the boundaries of the production areas, setting standards for the harvesting and production of wines in their DO, and promoting

sales and marketing. The regulatory councils, which were composed of representatives of the growers and producers, were entrusted with policing themselves, but they will now be governed by independent private or public entities that will enforce quality standards and have the power to regulate the production of wine made within their jurisdiction."

Standards of excellence in the different demarcated regions vary greatly, and the largest production of quality wines is in those like Rioja, Jerez, and Penedès with long-established reputations for making fine wines. At the other end of the scale, no one could possibly maintain that the wines from the DO Méntrida are in any way comparable with French VDQS or AC wines. Indeed, the authoritative *Guide to the Wines of Spain*, published by the Club de Gourmets of Madrid, was long of the opinion that the region barely deserved denomination. Again, it would seem that some other regions, such as Costers del Segre and Binissalem, have been granted DO status on the strength of one or two prestigious producers. Decisions have clearly been taken with the future potential of the region in mind – and the grant of a provisional DO has often induced producers to modernize equipment and improve their wines – but the magic "DO" on a label is currently not a reliable yardstick of quality for the consumer. At one time, the famous firm of Miguel Torres was barred from labelling wines made with acclimatized foreign grapes with the DO Penedès, yet the name "Torres" is the best possible guarantee of quality. The name and reputation of the producer is, in fact, at least as important as DO – and often more so.

Glossary

WORDS USED ON WINE LABELS

3°, 4° año, etc. Bottled in the third, fourth year, etc., after the harvest (*see* "Laws and Labels", page 12). Formerly much used but now virtually discontinued.

Abocado Semi-sweet table wine.

Amontillado A style of sherry made by ageing the fino wine.

Amoroso A light dessert sherry.

Añejo, añejado por Old, aged by.

Blanco White.

Bodega Literally, a wine cellar, but used to describe a concern which may have grown, produced, shipped, or sold the wine. Without further qualification, it normally means that the bodega has made and shipped wine.

Brut Extra-dry, used only of sparkling wine.

Cava a) An establishment making sparkling wines; b) a term used to describe such wines made by the Champagne method, now the subject of the DO Cava.

Cepa Literally, a vine. Its use on labels is not precise (the word itself is not precise), although it sometimes appears coupled with the name of a grape.

Cosecha Vintage; for example: Cosecha 1995.

Cream A sweet sherry or montilla.

Criado por Matured and/or blended by.

Crianza Red wine aged for cñanzas six months in oak cask, followed by eighteen in bottle. White or rosé must be aged for six months in oak cask and twelve months in bottle.

Denominación de origen (DO) The guarantee of the consejo regulador (regulatory body) for a demarcated area. It is often printed on the label in the form of a small stamp or drawing.

Dulce Sweet.

Elaborado por Matured and/or blended by.

Embotellado por Bottled by.

Espumoso Sparkling wine.

Fino A pale, dry, and delicate sherry or montilla.

Generoso A fortified apéritif or dessert wine.

Gran reserva Wine of good quality, aged in the case of *tinto* for at least eighteen months in oak cask, followed by a minimum of forty-two in bottle. White or rosé *gran reservas* must be aged for a minimum period of four years, with at least six months in oak.

Gran-vas Sparkling wine made by the *cuve close* method (*see* "Sparkling Wines", page 180).

Manzanilla One of the driest of *solera* wines, made at Sanlúcar de Barrameda.

Método tradicional Replacement for the term *méthode champenoise* as from August 31, 1994. DO for certain sparkling wines excluded from the DO Cava.

Oloroso A dark, fragrant, full-bodied sherry or montilla.

Palo cortado A rare and superior sherry or montilla, with the nose of an amontillado and the body of an oloroso.

Pasada Used to describe old and superior manzanilla.

Raya a) Term used in classifying musts for sherry; b) a sherry or montilla resembling oloroso, but not of the same quality.

Reserva Wine of good quality. *Tinto* is aged for at least three years in total in oak cask and bottle (and usually for longer) with a minimum one year in cask. White and rosé *reservas* must be aged for at least two years in total in oak cask and bottle, with a minimum of six months in oak.

Rosado Rosé.

Seco Dry.

Semiseco Semi-dry.

Sin crianza Used to denote a young wine that has had little or no maturation in cask.

Solera This denotes (or should denote) that the wine has been aged in a series of butts containing progressively older wine of different vintages (*see* "Sherry and Manzanilla", page 161).

Tinto Red wine.

Vendimia Vintage; for example: Vendimia 1995.

Viña, viñedo Vineyard. Used rather loosely; the name Viña Zaco does not necessarily mean that the wine originated exclusively from a vineyard of this name.

Vino Wine (*see* also "Miscellaneous", page 17).

VOS Very old sherry, more than twenty years old.

VORS Very old sherry, more than thirty years old.

MISCELLANEOUS

Agua Water.

Agua de soda Soda water.

Agua mineral Mineral water:

    con gas sparkling;

    sin gas still.

Aguardiente a) Alcohol of not more than 80° strength distilled from vegetable materials; b) colloquial name for *aguardiente de orujo*, which is akin to the French *marc*.

Anís Aniseed-flavoured liqueur resembling anisette.

Barrica Small cask (usually 225 litres) used for maturing wine.

Bodeguero The person who owns or runs the bodega.

Café Coffee.

Chacolí A green (young) wine from the Biscay coast. Now the subject of the DOs Chacolí (*see* "Navarra", page 110).

Cold fermentation Fermentation in stainless-steel vats over long periods at low temperatures (*see* "Anatomy of Spanish Wine", page 10–11).

Comarca Subdistrict.

Coñac Used colloquially of Spanish brandy.

Crema Liqueur:

    de cacao cocoa-based;

    de café coffee-based;

    de menta crème de menthe;

    de naranja Curaçao.

Flor A film of yeasts which grows on the surface of some wines during maturation in *solera* (*see* "Sherry", page 153).

Ginebra Gin.

Hielo Ice.

Horchata Milky-looking, non-alcoholic drink made from *chufas* or tiger-nuts.

Leche Milk.

Licor Liqueur.

Limonada Lemonade (fizzy).

Orujo Slang name for *aguardiente*.

Parador State tourist hotel of a good standard, often housed in a building of historic interest.

Ponche A herbalized brandy (*see* page 192).

Queimada A punch made from *aguardiente* (*see* above).

Ron Rum

SA *Sociedad Anónima*, an indication of a public company's limited liability, equivalent to Ltd, plc or Inc.

SAT Private company which was formerly a cooperative.

Sangría Cold wine-cup, made by adding sliced orange and lemon, together with ice and a dash of brandy, to red wine.

Sidra Cider.

Sifón Soda water.

Socio A member of a wine cooperative.

Té Tea.

Vermut Vermouth.

Vino Wine:

    corriente inexpensive, everyday wine;

    de aguja slightly sparkling, *pétillant*;

    de alta expresión premium wine made with selected grapes from old vines;

    de Jerez sherry;

    de la tierra table wine of superior quality made in a demarcated region without DO (*see* page 12);

    de lágrima sweet wine made from the juice which has emerged from the grapes under the weight of the fruit only, and without mechanical crushing;

    de mesa table wine, either blended or without indication of origin;

    de pasto an ordinary table wine, often light;

    embotellado a better wine, bottled at the *bodega*;

    gaseoso cheap, carbonated sparkling wine;

    generoso an apéritif or dessert wine, such as sherry or málaga;

    joven/jóvenes young wine/s for immediate drinking, bottled after fining and without ageing in wood;

    rancio an old white wine, maderized and sometimes fortified;

    verde young wine, white or red, with a slight sparkle, prickle, or *pétillance*.

Zumo natural Fruit juice:

    de naranja natural juice from freshly crushed oranges.

ORDERING WINES AND DRINKS

May I see the wine list?
La carta de vinos, por favor.

I should like a bottle/half-bottle of .../a carafe/half-carafe of your house wine.
Por favor traiga una botella/media botella de .../una jarra/media jarra de vino de la casa.

Where does your house wine come from?
¿De dónde es el vino de la casa?

Can you recommend a good local wine?
¿Puede usted recomendar un vino bueno de la región?

Yes, I would like a bottle.
Sí, me gustaría una botella.

I should like to drink a red/dry white/sweet white wine.
Me gustaría beber un vino tinto/vino blanco seco/vino blanco dulce.

Would you please chill the wine?
¿Por favor puede usted enfriar el vino?

The waiter, too, will have something to say, and will probably begin by asking if you would like an apéritif:
¿Quieren ustedes un aperitivo?

Yes, I should like a …
Sí, por favor, un …

No, thank you.
No, gracias.

After you have ordered the wine, he will ask you whether, as is usual in
Spain, you want mineral water:
¿Quieren ustedes agua mineral?

Yes, I should like a bottle/half-bottle of still/sparkling.
Sí, por favor. Me gustaría una botella/media botella sin gas/con gas.

At the end of the meal the waiter will ask you if you want coffee:
¿Quieren tomar café?

Yes, I/we should like black coffee/white coffee/coffee with a little milk.
Sí, por favor, me/nos gustaría café solo/café con leche/café cortado.

Except in expensive restaurants, if you want brandy or a liqueur at the table,
you should ask for it:
I/we should like a brandy/liqueur. What sorts do you have?
Me/nos gustaría tomar un coñac/licor. ¿Qué marcas tienen?

And to ask for the bill:
La cuenta, por favor.

Is service included?
¿Está el servicio incluído?

Staying and Eating at the Bodegas

Many of the larger *bodegas* have operated visitors' centres for a long time.
Some, like that of Miguel Torres at Pachs del Penedès, incorporating
tasting rooms, video displays, exhibits of old agricultural machinery, a
picture gallery, and facilities for buying the wines.

A new trend is for bodegas to attract visitors by opening restaurants
and hotels on the premises or in the vineyards. Bodegas Unidas, for example,
is operating haciendas with hotel accommodation up and down Spain.
Bodegas Palacio offers accommodation and excellent food in its old bodega
in Laguardia. While the most ambitious project is that of the Marqués de
Riscal in Elciego, where Frank Gehry, architect of the Bilbao Guggenheim
Museum, has been commissioned to build a visitors' centre and forty-five-
room hotel (opening in autumn 2005) in similar style.

Details of all these establishments will be found, region by region, in
the "Hotel and Restaurant" sections at the end of each chapter.

A Spanish Selection for 2005–2006

Since this is the ninth edition, and twenty-first birthday, of *Wines of Spain*,
instead of the usual current selection of wines, it seems appropriate to

print a list of bodegas whose wines have regularly been chosen over the past two decades. The same names do, in fact, keep cropping up, whether their wines are traditional or new wave. What matters in the last resort is not whether a wine is oaky or fruit-driven, but that it is well made and a pleasure to drink.

Alión DO Ribera del Duero. Red.

Alejandro Fernández DO Ribera del Duero. Red (Pesquera).

Artadi Cosecheros Alaveses DO Rioja. Red.

Contino DOCa Rioja. Red.

Bodegas de Crianza de Castilla la Vieja DO Rueda. White.

Granxa Fillaboa DO Rias Baixas. White.

Bodegas Guelbenzu Navarra non-DO. Red.

Julián Chivite DO Navarra. Red, white, and rosé.

R. Lopez de Heredia Viña Tondonia DOCa Rioja. Red.

Marqués de Griñón Pago Dominio de Valdepusa. Red.

Marqués de Murrieta DOCa Rioja. Red and white.

Marqués de Riscal DOCa Rioja and DO Rueda. Red and white.

Bodegas Mauro Tudela del Duero non-DO and DO Toro. Red.

Miguel Torres DO Penedès and DO Conca de Barberà. Red, white, and rosé.

Bodegas Muga DOCa Rioja. Red.

René Barbier Clos Mogador, DO Priorato. Red.

Bodegas Roda DOCa Rioja. Red.

Vega Sicilia DO Ribera del Duero. Red.

Viñedos y Crianzas del Alto Aragón Enate, DO Somontano. Red.

Aragón

Aragón ranks fifth in order of area and tenth of the Spanish autonomies as regards production. In the past, it was known for sturdy wine that was high in alcohol and extract, much of it sold outside the area for everyday drinking or blending. There have, however, been marked changes in recent years, beginning with the demarcation of new regions and the accompanying modernization of the cooperatives; the planting of new vine varieties; earlier picking of the grapes so as to lighten the wines; and the emergence of small, sophisticated private firms.

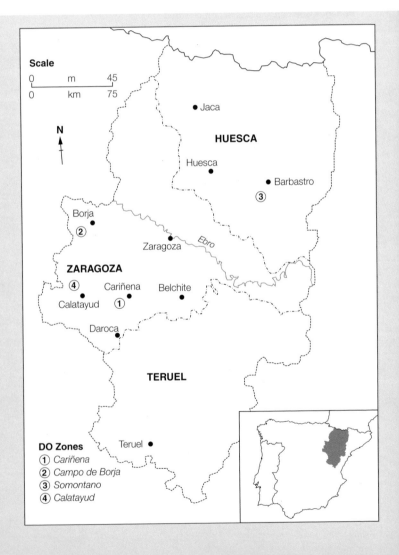

Scale

0 — m — 45
0 — km — 75

N

● Jaca

HUESCA

Huesca ●

● Barbastro

③

Borja ●

②

Zaragoza ●

Ebro

ZARAGOZA

④   Cariñena ●   Belchite ●

Calatayud ●   ①

Daroca ●

TERUEL

DO Zones

Teruel ●

① *Cariñena*
② *Campo de Borja*
③ *Somontano*
④ *Calatayud*

In the early nineteenth century the best-known of the wine regions, Cariñena, made one of the most sought-after Spanish wines. Later, at the height of the phylloxera epidemic, the Bordeaux firm of Violet maintained a large establishment for shipping them to France. With the land lying mostly between 450 and 650 metres above sea level, and in the harsh climatic conditions of freezing winters, hot summers, and strong winds, the vine that does best (and is by far the most prevalent) is the sturdy black Garnacha, though Tempranillo is increasingly being planted for better-quality, oak-aged red wines, and there are also small quantities of white grapes such as the Viura, Garnacha Blanca, and Alcañón (native to Somontano). Oddly enough, the black Cariñena is much more widely grown in Cataluña (the variety also appears in France as the Carignan). As elsewhere in Spain, small amounts of Cabernet Sauvignon and Chardonnay have been introduced on an experimental scale.

Aragón has four DO zones: Cariñena; the more recently demarcated Campo de Borja and Somontano to the north; and to the west Calatayud, demarcated in 1990.

Aragonesas, Bodegas
DO r p w ★→★★

Fuendejalón (Zaragoza). DO Campo de Borja. Large co-op making and exporting worthwhile wines, some of them aged in oak, including young red, white, and rosé Crucillón; red Don Ramón, Duque de Sevilla, and Mosen Cleto *reservas*, made with Garnacha, Tempranillo, and Cabernet Sauvignon. Also a Copa for the UK market.

Belchite
VC r w dr ☆

Small area east of CARIÑENA making sturdy reds and whites.

Blecua
DO r res ☆☆☆☆ 01

Barbastro (Huesca). DO Somontano. Small bodega founded in 2000 by VIÑAS DEL VERO making only a premium and expensive Blecua from Garnacha and Cabernet Sauvignon. The rich and complex wine is already one of the most sought after in Spain.

Bordejé, Bodegas
DO r (w g) ☆→☆☆ 95 98 02

Ainzón (Zaragoza). DO Campo de Borja. A family concern dating from 1770, growing all its own grapes on 100 hectares of vineyards. It is best known for its cherry-red Abuelo Nicolás, made by carbonic maceration, which is not shipped abroad but is delicious when drunk young.

Borruel, Bodegas
DO r w dr ☆☆

Ponzano (Huesca). DO Somontano. Small, old-established (1903) bodega with twenty-four hectares of vineyards. Reliable Osca, red, white, and rosé. The pick of its wines is the characterful red Barón de Eroles *reserva*, made with a blend of Tempranillo, Moristel, and Cabernet Sauvignon.

Borsao, Bodegas
DO r res ☆☆ 98 00 01 02

Borja (Zaragoza). DO Campo de Borja. Founded as a co-op in 1958 and with 1,600 hectares of vineyards and 1,000 oak *barricas*, this winery is a model of its kind. It makes an excellent and modestly priced young Tinto

Joven from a blend of Garnacha, Tempranillo, and Cabernet Sauvignon, and *crianzas* and *reservas* from the same grapes.

Calatayud
DO r p ☆→☆☆

A newly demarcated area embracing 5,939 hectares of DO vineyards and thirteen bodegas, situated in the west of Aragón making honest enough wine in a style that is ideal for everyday drinking. The best are the red wines, which are made with 100 per cent Garnacha.

Campo de Borja
DO r ☆→☆☆

The region takes its name from the small town of Borja in the Ebro Valley west of Zaragoza, the ancestral home of the Borgia family, whose castle still survives. Demarcated in 1977, it now embraces 7,231 hectares of vineyards and fifteen bodegas. Made mainly from the Garnacha Tinta grape, the traditional wine was a very full-bodied red, more astringent and acidic than the wine from CARIÑENA, and containing an average fifteen to sixteen per cent alcohol, and sometimes a hefty eighteen per cent. For this reason it was often used for blending with less robust growths from other regions, much of it being sold in bulk to concerns in Rioja and Cataluña. Lighter rosés and better oak-aged Tempranillo reds are now being produced.

Cariñena
DO r (w dr sw g) ☆→☆☆

A little to the south of Zaragoza, Cariñena – with 17,000 hectares under vine and fifty bodegas – is the most important wine-producing area in Aragón. The vines grow in calcareous clays and the most dominant varieties are the black Garnacha Tinta (sixty per cent) and white Viura (twenty-one per cent). The traditional wine of Cariñena is the red, of a purplish-ruby colour with a bouquet of violets, thirteen to seventeen per cent in strength, full-bodied and deep in flavour. Thanks to fermentation in stainless steel, much lighter, more drinkable *jóvenes* are now being made. Cariñena also produces some everyday white wine from the Viura and Garnacha Blanca, and a fortified dessert wine made in a manner similar to that in which málaga is made (*see* page 98).

Daroca
VdC r ☆

Area in the far south of Aragón on the borders of Teruel. It produces sturdy red wines with thirteen to sixteen per cent alcohol.

Enate
See VIÑEDOS Y CRIANZAS DEL ALTO ARAGÓN.

Grandes Vinos y Viñedos
DO w dr p r res ★→★★

Cariñena (Zaragoza). DO Cariñena. Very large concern with 5,000 hectares of vineyard and 7,500 oak *barricas* making reliable wines for everyday drinking. Main labels are Corona de Aragón and Monasterio de las Viñas.

Lalanne, Bodegas
DO r p w dr res ☆☆ *98 00*

Castillo de San Marcos, Barbastro (Huesca). DO Somontano. This is a small bodega, founded by a French family at the time of the phylloxera epidemic in the nineteenth century, and growing twelve vine varieties on its thirty-seven hectares of vineyards. Some of the wines produced include white and rosé Laura Lalanne, and highly individual oak-aged wines, made from Cabernet Sauvignon blended with Merlot or Tempranillo.

Marqués de Aragón

See VINOS Y VIÑEDOS DEL JALÓN.

Pirineos, Bodega

DO r p w ★★→★★★★ *99 00 01 02*

Barbastro (Huesca). DO Somontano. The large co-op of Somontano de Sobrarbe was re-equipped in 1990 and renamed Bodega Pirineos, since when it has been making quality wines. The best are the splendid Cabernet/Merlot rosé, the Señorío de Lazán *reservas,* and the premium Marboré (99 00) made from Tempranillo and Cabernet Sauvignon.

San Isidro, Bodega Cooperativa del Campo

See VINOS Y VIÑEDOS DEL JALÓN.

San Valero, Bodegas

DO r (p w dr) ☆→☆☆ *96 98 01 02*

Cariñena (Zaragoza). DO Cariñena. Large former co-op on the Zaragoza–Teruel road in the village of CARIÑENA. The bodega produces cold-fermented white and rosé Monte Ducay and oak-aged Monte Ducay, and Marqués de Tosos *crianza* and *reservas.*

Somontano

DO r p w dr ☆☆→☆☆☆☆

This region, which was demarcated in 1984 and is located in the province of Huesca in the foothills of the Pyrenees, has 3,940 hectares of land under vine and fifteen bodegas. It produces wines completely different from the others from Aragón. Made from a profusion of grape varieties, including the traditional Alcañón, Macabeo (Viura), Garnacha Tinta, Mazuelo, and Parraleta, and more recently introduced Tempranillo, Cabernet Sauvignon, Merlot, and Chardonnay, the wines were traditionally ruby-coloured, faintly perfumed, light on the palate, and slightly acidic, ranging in strength from eleven to thirteen per cent alcohol. At the turn of the century these wines were popular in France, and one of the most traditional of the area's wineries, Bodegas LALANNE in Barbastro, is of French origin. It is a region where, thanks to modern technology and fermentation in stainless steel, a dramatic improvement in standards has been achieved.

Valdejalón

VdT r ☆

Large area just west of Zaragoza. The dominant grape variety, Garnacha Tinta, produces wines that are high in alcohol and extract, and are more aligned with the wines of CAMPO DE BORJA than with those of CARIÑENA.

Viñas del Vero

DO r w dr ☆☆→☆☆☆☆ *98 00 01 02*

Barbastro (Huesca). DO Somontano. Founded in 1986, the firm possesses 750 hectares of vineyards and a state-of-the-art winery. Its wines are among the best from the region. There is a lively barrel-fermented 100 per cent Chardonnay (01); a 100 per cent Gewürztraminer (02); a 100 per cent Riesling; and excellent red wines made with 100 per cent Cabernet Sauvignon, 100 per cent Merlot, and the Gran Vos (99 00) containing Merlot, Cabernet Sauvignon, and Pinot Noir. *See* also BLECUA.

Viñedos y Crianzas del Alto Aragón
DO w p r ★★→★★★★ 98 99 00 01

Barbastro (Huesca). DO Somontano. A young bodega, whose fruity, modern-style ENATE wines compete with those from VIÑAS DE VERO as the best from the region. They include excellent barrel-fermented Chardonnay (02), Gewürztraminer (02), Cabernet and Cabernet blends, and the superb Reserva Especial (98) made from Cabernet Sauvignon and Merlot.

Vinos y Viñedos del Jalón
DO r w ★→★★

Maluenda (Calatayud). DO Calatayud. Large cooperative formerly producing only bulk wine, but now making very drinkable red and white Castillo de Maluenda table wines, superior 100 per cent Garnacha Marqués de Aragón, a *reserva* made from a blend of Tempranillo and Garnacha, also branded Poema for the UK and Viña Alarba for the US.

Zaragoza
Capital of the medieval Kingdom of Aragón, Zaragoza is rich in historic remains from Roman times onwards, including the Moorish Aljafería, with its figured plasterwork and beautiful *artesondo* ceilings. The city is dominated by the many-domed Basílica del Pilár, looming above the bridge across the River Ebro, which contains the oldest Marian sanctuary in Europe. The festival of El Pilár in October is the most important date in Spain's religious calendar.

WINE AND FOOD

Aragón is sometimes called the *zona de los chilindrónes*, after the famous *chilindrón* sauce made with onions, garlic, tomatoes, and peppers, and served with chicken and lamb. In Aragón, the young lamb from the mountains is excellent. (*Espárragos montañeses* is a delicious dish rather misleadingly named: this 'mountain asparagus' is actually lambs' tails stewed in tomatoes.) South of Zaragoza in the direction of Teruel, the miles of gardens and orchards produce some of the best fruit in Spain: peaches, plums, apricots, apples, cherries, and strawberries. The vegetables, too, including the white Aragonese cabbage and cardoon, are first rate. The sturdy red wines complement simple dishes and country fare. With a sophisticated meal, try one of the new, lighter growths from Somontano.

Bacalao al ajoarriero Dried salt cod with garlic, paprika, and parsley.

Migas de pastor Breadcrumbs fried until crisp in olive oil, often served as a starter or side dish. Some devotees eat them with hot chocolate or grapes.

Pollo al chilindrón Chicken with *chilindrón* sauce, made from olive oil, garlic, tomatoes, and peppers.

Sopas de ajo Garlic soups with bread, eggs, and a piquant *sofrito* base are a great speciality of Aragón.

Teresicas Small pastries made with butter, flour, and yeast and fried in olive oil.

Ternasco asado Milk-fed kid cooked with white wine, lemon, and garlic.

HOTELS

Zaragoza The best hotels in the district are the five-star *Meliá Zaragoza*, *Palafox*, *NH Gran Hotel*, and *Oriente*.

RESTAURANTS

Huesca *Gaby-Casa Blasquico* at Hecho near Jaca is known for some of the best cooking in the province from Gaby Coarasa, a professor of gastronomy. Inexpensive rooms are also available. *Venta del Sotón* at Esquedas on the Tarragona road provides imaginative cooking from Alto Aragón.

Zaragoza *Gayarre* on the road to the airport serves Aragonese and Basque cuisine. *Goyesco* offers impeccable cooking and an extended table d'hôte. *El Cachirulo* has elegant surroundings, excellent service, and some typical Aragonese dishes, as well as an interesting *menu de degustación*.

Balearics and Canaries

Both these groups of islands, the green and fertile Balearics with their mild, Mediterranean climate and sandy beaches, and the volcanic Canaries, in the wastes of the Atlantic off the coast of North Africa, are favourite tourist resorts for sun-starved northern Europeans. On balance, they consume more wine than they make, so that familiar names from the mainland figure more on their wine lists than the local growths.

Before the depredations of phylloxera there were about 27,000 hectares under vine in Mallorca, the main producer in the Balearics, but in the

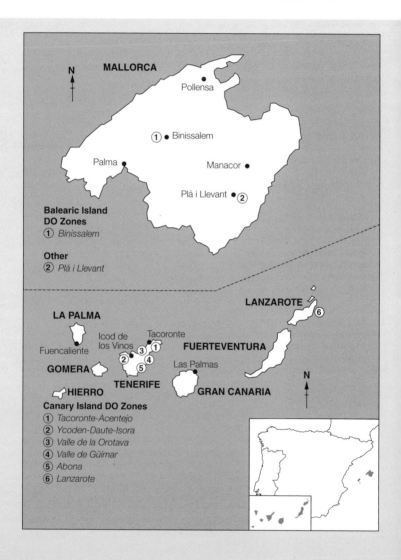

principal vineyard areas of Binissalem and *Plá i* Llevant the area has now shrunk to some 770 hectares qualifying for DO. Tourism aggravated this decline – it proved more profitable to sell the land for holiday villas, and the young people left the villages to work in the hotels of Palma and Pollensa.

The soils of the Balearics are mainly ferruginous clays, and the vines are grown in small plots, which are interspersed with olives and almonds. Most of the grapes are native to Mallorca, the typical varieties being the Manto Negro, Callet, Fogoneu, and Fogoneu Francés. Apart from the superior growths of Franca Roja and tiny bodegas such as Jaume Mesquida, Finca Son Bordils, and Miguel Oliver, the wines are reds or rosés made by the cooperatives or small proprietors for current consumption.

In the Canaries, famous for sack in the sixteenth century, wine production is now mainly confined to the islands of Tenerife, La Palma, and Lanzarote. The soils are volcanic and the principal grape varieties are the white Listán Blanco and Malvasía (Malmsey), and the red Listán and Negramoll.

Until recently the few wines with character were the white Malvasías, but since the mid-1980s – as a result of the planting of better vine varieties and the installation of modern equipment in the wineries – some excellent red and white wines are emerging: especially the young reds made by carbonic maceration.

In 1992 there was a single DO, that of Tacoronte-Acentejo, but the number has now leapt to ten. However, because of the small scale of production, demand much exceeds supply and outside the Islands, even in Spain, the wines are virtually unobtainable.

An Negra Viticultors
Non-DO r ☆☆☆ *00 01*
Felanitx (Mallorca). Small bodega founded in 1994. Its oak-aged 00 An Negra wine made from ninety per cent red Callet grape is fruity and delicate with a concentrated fragrance enhanced by aeration in the glass. The best from Mallorca.

Binissalem
DO r (w dr) ☆→☆☆☆
Binissalem is the traditional producer of the best Mallorcan wines, although the area under cultivation (some 500 hectares) has shrunk to a fraction of its former size. The principal red grape is the Manto Negro, producing full-bodied reds of fourteen to sixteen per cent strength, with pronounced bouquet and high extract; also recommended is the native Callet, while the new regulations additionally permit the use of Tempranillo and Monastrell. The main grape for white wines, made in much smaller amounts, is the Moll or Prensal Blanco.

El Grifo, Bodegas
DO r p w dr g ☆→☆☆
La Geria (Lanzarote). DO Lanzarote. Old-established bodega (1775); with Bodegas MOZAGA, one of the best in the Canaries. It has long been famous for its 14.5 per cent strength Malvasía El Grifo, but it is now making fresh young reds and whites by cold fermentation.

El Hierro
DO w p r ☆→☆☆
Hierro is the smallest of the Canary Islands, and the region, demarcated in 1994, possesses five bodegas. The co-op was one of the first in the

Canaries to install modern equipment and to eliminate the once common defects of unclean odours, high alcoholic degree, oxidation, etc., and the wines now meet the increasingly improved standards of the other modernized wineries in the Canary Islands.

El Lomo

DO r w ☆☆

Tegueste (Tenerife). DO Tacoronte-Acentejo. Founded in 1989, this is one of the new generation of technologically advanced Canarian bodegas. The wines are labelled El Lomo and include a crisp white with ninety per cent Listán Blanco; a fruity red made from a blend of Listán Negro and Negramoll; and an exceptionally fresh and aromatic *maceración carbónica* of 100 per cent Listán Negro.

Felanitx

See PLÁ I LLEVANT DE MALLORCA.

Finca Son Bordils

Non-DO w dr r ☆☆

Inca (Mallorca). Founded in 1998, this small family bodega makes fresh and fragrant white wines from 100 per cent Chardonnay and 100 per cent Moscatel and also worthwhile reds from Cabernet Sauvignon, Syrah, and Merlot.

Flores, Bodegas

DO r ☆☆

La Matanza (Tenerife). DO Tacoronte-Acentejo. Producers of a young, fruity, and deceptively smooth and velvety wine, made with the native Listán Negro, Negramoll, and Listán Blanco, and containing thirteen per cent alcohol.

Franja Roja

DO r (w dr p) res ☆☆→☆☆☆ **98 99 00 01**

Binissalem (Mallorca). DO Binissalem. The bodega was founded in 1931 by the informed and enthusiastic oenologist José L Ferrer and has subsequently been run by his nephews. It is the only concern in Mallorca to export its wines (under the label Franja Roja, the name of the parent company). Its seventy-eight hectares are planted mainly with the indigenous red Manto Negro and Callet, giving rise to smooth and full-flavoured (oak-aged) reds. Over the past years the wines have sometimes seemed tired and a bit sour, but thanks to new oak and improved vinification they are now emerging fresher and more lively.

Fuencaliente

See also LA PALMA DO.

The main production area in the Canary Island of LA PALMA. The principal vines, which were unaffected by phylloxera and are grown ungrafted, are the Listán Blanco and Negra, Vijariego, and Negramoll, and the typical wine is a dry and full-bodied *clarete*. Winemaking progresses; there are now eighteen bodegas and 925 hectares under vine.

Geria, La

See LANZAROTE DO.

Güímar, Valle de

DO w dr (r) ☆

Newly demarcated region of 720 hectares with eighteen bodegas, lying on the east coast of Tenerife to the south of the DO TACORONTE–ACENTEJO. Best are the fruity white wines grown in the higher vineyards at 1,600 metres above sea level.

Icod

DO w dr ☆

Icod de los Vinos, now part of the new DO YCODEN-DAUTE-ISORA in Tenerife, is traditionally one of the areas in the Canaries best known for its vines, notably Listán Blanco and Malvasía.

Insulares Tenerife, Bodegas

DO r w dr ☆☆→☆☆☆ *00 01 02*

Tacoronte (Tenerife). DO TACORONTE-ACENTEJO. Former co-op selling wines produced individually by seventy-one of the region's farmers, under the general name of Viña Norte. One of the best is the fresh and fruity young red *vino joven* from Marcos Guimerá Ravina.

Jaume de Puntiro

DO w dr r ☆→☆☆ *01 02 03*

Santa María del Cami (Mallorca). DO Binissalem. Small bodega producing a pleasant white Daurat fermented in barrel from 100 per cent Prensal Blanco and a decent red *crianza* Buc containing Manto Negro and Callet.

Lanzarote

DO w p r g ☆→☆☆

The principal vine-growing area in Lanzarote – the most desolate of the Canary islands with its 300 volcanoes, blazing volcanic sands, and torrid winds from the Sahara – is La Geria. The vines are sunk into deep pits and surrounded by stone walls to protect them from the wind. The typical wines that result from all this effort are made from a blend of the white Malvasía and Listán, and are amber-coloured and high in alcohol.

La Palma

DO w p r ☆

The main production zone is that of FUENCALIENTE at the southern tip of the island.

Las Palmas

The largest town in the Canaries, with a population of 350,000, Las Palmas is dramatically situated on Gran Canaria beneath an extinct volcano, and possesses good beaches, a colourful promenade, and a bustling port which provides regular ferry services to the other islands.

Manacor

p ☆

Sizeable vine-growing area near Felanitx in Mallorca, making wines of around nine to eleven per cent alcohol from the Fogoneu grape.

Mesquida, Jaume

DO r w dr p ☆☆

Porreres (Mallorca). DO Plá i Llevant. Jaume Mesquida is one of the few makers of quality wines in Mallorca. He believes the future of Mallorcan wines lies with acclimatizing foreign vine varieties, and makes good Cabernet Sauvignon and Pinot Noir.

Monje, Bodegas

DO r w dr ☆☆ *98 01 02*

El Sauzal (Tenerife). DO TACORONTE-ACENTEJO. The young red Monje, made from eighty per cent Listán Negro with a little Listán Blanco and Negramoll, some of it by carbonic maceration, is smooth, full-bodied, and fruity: a *vino joven* for early consumption.

Monte Lentiscal

DO r w ☆

Founded in 1999, this small DO to the northeast of the island of
Gran Canaria comprises ninety-two hectares and twelve bodegas.
The white wines are made from Malvasía, Gual, Listán Blanco, and
Moscatel, *et al.,* and the red from Listán Negro, Negramoll, and
Moscatel Negra.

Mozaga, Bodegas

DO w sw g ☆☆→☆☆☆

La Geria (Lanzarote). DO LANZAROTE. Maker of one of the best wines from
the Canary Island of Lanzarote, the Malvasía Seco. The grapes are picked
when well ripe, they are lightly crushed, and aged in oak for two or three
months after vinification. The wine is further aged in bottle in cellars
excavated beneath the lava. Also a good Moscatel Mozaga of seventeen
per cent strength.

Oliver, Miguel

DO r w dr p ☆☆ 99 00 01 02

Petra (Mallorca). DO Plá i Llevant de Mallorca. Miguel Oliver is one of
the few producers to be making worthwhile wines in the Balearics.
The wines include a good Chardonnay, a luscious Muscat, a 100 per cent
Merlot, and a fifty/fifty Cabernet Sauvignon/Merlot Ses Ferritges
reserva.

Orotava, Valle de la

DO w dr ☆

Small vine-growing area situated between the DOs of TACORONTE-ACENTEJO
and YCODEN-DAUTE-ISORA on the north coast of Tenerife. It produces dry
white wines very similar to those of ICOD.

Palma de Mallorca

Palma is one of the most beautiful cities of the Mediterranean, with its
wide bay and surrounding beaches, and the thirteenth-century cathedral
dominating the port. The narrow streets in the centre have many elegant
shops, good restaurants, and old houses with secret, shaded patios.
Nowhere in Mallorca is very far from Palma, so it is a good base for
visiting the wine areas.

Pere Seda

DO w dr p r ★→★★★ 99 01

Manacor (Mallorca). DO Plá i Levant. Established bodega with a range
of wines, including whites made from Parellada, Prensal, Chardonnay,
and Macabeo; a *rosado* blended from Cabernet Sauvignon and
Tempranillo; and red *crianzas* and *reservas* made from Callet and
Manto Negro.

Plá i Llevant de Mallorca

DO r (p w dr) ★→★★★

In the southeast of the island, the area around FELANITX has some 2,000
hectares under vine, of which 271 are demarcated, and is the largest of the
Mallorcan wine regions. However, only three small bodegas produce a
wine to match those from FRANJA ROJA in BINISSALEM. The typical grape is
the Fogoneu, usually vinified so as to give rosés of nine to eleven per cent.
Most of the wine was made in the co-op at Felanitx serving the small
proprietors; it has, however, now closed down. There are also distilleries in
the town producing grape spirit and alcohol.

Ribas, Hereus de
DO r w dr ☆☆

Consell (Baleares). DO Binissalem. An old bodega reorganized in 1986, it owns some fifty hectares of vineyards planted with both native and foreign varieties. The wines include a decent white made from a blend of native grapes and Chardonnay, and fruity reds containing a proportion of Cabernet Sauvignon.

Tacoronte-Acentejo
DO r (w dr p) DYA ☆→☆☆

Tacoronte, the first region in the Canaries to be accorded the DO in 1992 and now numbering forty-two bodegas, is the most intensely cultivated wine area in Tenerife. The 1,800 hectares lie on the mountain slopes to the west of the island and are planted mainly with the red Listán Negro and Negramoll. Since the installation of stainless steel in some of the bodegas, the varieties are beginning to make fresh and lighter red wines in a modern style, all of them at the moment young.

Timanfaya, Bodegas
DO w sw br ☆☆

Playa Honda (Lanzarote). DO Lanzarote. Young bodega making a fresh Moscatel and a fruity port-like wine. Both are labelled Cenizas de Timanfaya, descriptive of the volcanic ash in which the vines are grown.

Viñatigo, Bodegas
DO w p r ★→★★

La Guancha (Tenerife). DO YCODEN-DAUTE-ISORA. Founded in 1989, this concern sells wines under the labels of Añaterve, Oroval, and Viñatigo. The range includes good whites made with Listán Blanco, one fermented in cask; a rosé; and a fragrant young red produced by carbonic maceration.

Ycoden-Daute-Isora
DO w dr p (r) ☆→☆☆

This DO at the northwestern tip of Tenerife, founded in 1994, comprises 1,200 hectares and includes Icod de los Vinos, long known for its wines. It is now one of the most active and innovative wine areas in the Islands with twenty-six small, well-equipped new bodegas. The best of the wines are the rosés, but there are also reds and whites with good acidity and balance.

WINE AND FOOD

The Balearics, famous for the invention of mayonnaise (from Port Mahón), have a varied regional repertoire. As might be expected, they excel in seafood and rich fish soups. The appetizing *coca mallorquina*, traditionally made in outdoor ovens fired by wood, much resembles the Italian pizza. *Tumbet* is a variation on ratatouille. Most typical of the excellent charcuterie are the delicate white *butifarra* and soft red *sobrasada*. There is a good Mahón cheese and do not miss the fluffy *ensaimadas*, halfway between bun and pastry, for breakfast.

The Canaries are rich in natural resources, such as bananas and tropical fruits; excellent potatoes; abundant fish, tender rabbit, and partridge. There are also some interesting local cheeses – *see* glossary below. However, regional specialities hardly amount to a cuisine and you may find it difficult to find them in holiday hotels where the menus are either mainland Spanish – or "international" for the benefit of visitors from further afield. To find local dishes and wines it is a question of seeking out the smaller restaurants.

Balearics

Acelgas con pasas y piñones Spanish variety of spinach, paler in colour and sweeter than the English equivalent, boiled and served with *sofrito*, a sauce made with pine kernels, raisins, toasted bread, and garlic.

Berenjenas rellenas estilo balear Aubergines stuffed with a mixture of ground beef, chopped ham, onions, eggs, breadcrumbs, and garlic.

Butifarra A delicate white pork sausage, eaten uncooked, or in a stew with *mongetes* (haricot beans).

Caldereta de dátiles de mar Chowder made with small, dark sea dates, fished off the coast.

Caracoles con sobrasada Snails cooked together with ham, onions, tomatoes, garlic, olive oil, milk, brandy, and white wine. They are usually served with *sobrasada*, the soft and spicy Mallorcan pepper sausage, and green vegetables.

Coca mallorquina The Mallorcan version of pizza, which often contains onion, peppers, tomatoes, anchovies, and sardines.

Sopa de pescador formentor Rich fish soup made with garlic, onions, tomatoes, olive oil, and parsley.

Tumbet A Mallorcan egg-and-vegetable pie made with potatoes, red peppers, onions, courgettes, and tomato sauce.

Canaries

Buñuelos de dátiles Sweet fritters made with flour, orange juice, Cointreau, sugar, eggs, and dates.

Gofio A popular form of bread eaten all over the Canaries in country districts, and made in the shape of a big ball from a mixture of flour with water or milk.

Mojo colorado Sauce prepared with olive oil, vinegar, hot paprika, cumin seeds, and chillis.

Papas arrugadas New potatoes, boiled in their skins in sea water or much-salted water, then baked in a hot oven and served with *mojo* sauce.

Platanos canarios fritos Fried bananas, Canary style.

Quesos Cheeses, look out for the goat's milk Flor de Guía and Majorero from Fuerte-Ventura, and the smoked cheeses from La Palma, La Gomera, and El Hierro.

HOTELS

Gran Canaria

Las Palmas *Santa Catalina, AC Gran Canarias, NH Imperial Playa*, and *Cortijo San Ignacio Golf* (all four-star).

Lanzarote

Teguise *Gran Meliá Salinas* with beautiful views, international food, and some local dishes.

Tenerife

Adeje *Gran Hotel Bahía del Duque* is the best hotel in the Canaries.

Playa de las Américas *Hotel Jardín Tropical* is renowned for its cooking (*see* below*).*

Puerto de la Cruz *Botánico* is set in beautiful grounds and conveniently situated as a base for visiting the bodegas in the north of the island. *Tigaiga* is a smaller, family-run hotel with excellent cuisine.

Mallorca

Palma de Mallorca *Castillo Hotel, Son Vida, Gran Meliá Victoria, Palacio Ca Sa Galesa,* and *Arabella Sheraton Golf Hotel Son Vida* are the best of dozens of hotels in Palma, a prosperous town which is home to more than half the inhabitants of the Balearics. There are plenty of hotels in most categories.

RESTAURANTS

Mallorca

Inca, near Binissalem *Monnaber Nou* is the restaurant at the Monnaber Nou hotel, situated among woods and olive groves, and known for its Mediterranean cooking.

Palma de Mallorca The first class *Koldo Royo* specializes in locally caught fish. *Calviá Tristán*, twenty kilometres from Palma de Mallorca, has outstanding cuisine, *e.g. rape salteado con caracoles de mar y tomillo.*

Gran Canaria

Agaete *Casa Pepe*, forty-eight kilometres from Las Palmas, serves home-cooked local dishes with fresh ingredients. Try the *pescado de la Canaria.*

Lanzarote

Teguise *Gran Meliá Salinas. See* "Hotels", above.

Tenerife

Playa de las Américas *Hotel Jardín Tropical* incorporates the restaurant El Patio, which serves some of the best food and wines in the Canaries.

Tacoronte *Casa del Vino* offers local dishes, such as *solomillo al vino de Tacoronte*, and Tenerife wines. *Los Limoneros* serves excellent food, *e.g. ensalada de salmón, angulas y aguacates.*

Tegueste *Mesón el Drago* is fifteen kilometres from Santa Cruz. Highly sophisticated and it is a leading exponent of "New Canarian Cooking". *Los Olivos* is run by a Scot and serves inventive dishes such as scallops with mandarin sauce.

Castilla-La Mancha

Between them, the two Castiles occupy the wide central plateau of
Spain. Old Castile, so called because it was the first part of the area to
be reconquered from the Moors, stretches north from Madrid. South
of the capital the landscape becomes increasingly arid, and the central
and southern parts of New Castile are known as La Mancha. What
was New Castile is now substantially the autonomy of Castilla-La
Mancha, and Old Castile (minus Cantabria) the autonomy of Castilla-
León (*see* page 44). Madrid, although listed in this section, is an
autonomy in its own right.

The climate is Mediterranean-style, with long, hot summers and low
rainfall; for this reason, the grapes contain large amounts of sugar and
have traditionally produced earthy wines with high alcohol and little
acidity, though cold fermentation and earlier picking of the grapes are
changing the picture. Since the land, lying between 500 and 800 metres

Scale

| 0 | m | 40 |
| 0 | km | 65 |

GUADALAJARA

Guadalajara •

MADRID

Madrid •   ⑤   ⑥

Méntrida   Chinchón

① Aranjuéz •   Colmenar   Cuenca •
Toledo •   ② de Oreja

TOLEDO   Quintanar
de la Orden

Villarrobledo •   ⑦

Tomelloso •

• Daimiel   Albacate • Alpera •
Ciudad Real •   ④ Almansa
Valdepeñas •

CIUDAD REAL ③   **ALBACETE**
Santa Cruz •
de Mudela

N

DO Zones
① *Méntrida*
② *La Mancha*
③ *Valdepeñas*
④ *Almansa*
⑤ *Vinos de Madrid*
⑥ *Mondéjar*
⑦ *Manchuela*

above sea level, is mainly flat, the vineyards extend in unbroken expanses – in reality, a patchwork of holdings belonging to small proprietors.

This is the land of the cooperatives *par excellence*, of which there are hundreds in the central region as a whole, and in recent years large firms from other regions have been moving in (*see* CASTILLA-LA MANCHA VINO DE LA TIERRA). Because of its huge size and despite a low yield of sixteen to eighteen hectolitres per hectare, the region supplies about thirty-five per cent of the country's output, much of it going to other, less prolific areas for blending and the surplus being used for distillation.

The typical grape is the white Airén (or Lairén). It has thick skin, which affords it some protection against the blazing sunshine, of which, on average, there are 200 days in the year. Airén is a favourite with the small proprietors because it produces proportionately three times as much must as the other most important grape of the region, the black Cencibel (known in the Rioja as Tempranillo and in Cataluña as Ull de Llebre or Ojo de Liebre).

Ninety per cent of the wine from the central area is white; but perhaps the best is the red Valdepeñas from the extreme south of La Mancha bordering Andalucía. This is made with a proportion of the black Cencibel and has been famous since the days of the Holy Roman Emperor Charles V (King Charles I of Spain), who had the wine sent across Europe on mule-back during his military campaigns in the Low Countries in the sixteenth century.

Apart from Valdepeñas, the other DO regions of the area are Almansa, La Mancha, Manchuela, Méntrida, Mondéjar, Ribera del Júcar, and Vinos de Madrid.

Albali, Viña
DO r w dr (p) ☆☆ *97 98 99 00 02*
Reliable wines from Bodegas Félix *solis*, especially the sturdy red.

Almansa
DO r w dr ☆→☆☆☆
Bordering the Levante and just north of the DO zones of Yecla and Jumilla (*see* "Valencia and Murcia"), this region centres on the town of Almansa, with its story-book castle. The soils here are chalky, and in its 7,000 hectares of vineyards the predominant grape variety is the black Monastrell (43.5 per cent); Garnacha Tinta and Tintorera account for another thirty-three per cent, and there is also some white Forcallat, Airén, and Bobal. Fortunately, the area was little affected by the phylloxera epidemic, and eighty-three per cent of the vines are ungrafted; these produce wines that are high in both alcohol and extract.

The typical wines are deep in colour, full-bodied with little acid, and with an alcoholic strength of between twelve and fifteen per cent. Their quality depends on the proportion of Monastrell in the blend, but most are sold in bulk for blending. Only two concerns in the region, Bodegas PIQUERAS and Tintoralba Cooperative, are entitled to bottle their wines as DO.

Aloque
r ★→★★
The lightest style of VALDEPEÑAS, made with a blend of black and white grapes, usually ten per cent Cencibel and ninety per cent Airén. It's a dry wine, deep-coloured, and between thirteen and fifteen per cent alcohol.

Considering their strength, the wines are surprisingly light and fresh in taste, and they are much drunk in the bars and restaurants of Madrid.

Arganda

DO r w dr ☆☆

One of the sub-zones of the DO VINOS DE MADRID, to the south of the capital. The principal grape varieties grown here are the black Tinto Madrid and Tempranillo, and white Malvar and Jaén – when blended they produce smooth red wines. This area is also home to a pleasant, straw-coloured white of twelve to 13.5 per cent alcoholic strength. The wines were at their most popular during the seventeenth century, when the court transferred from Valladolid to Madrid. At that time, what is now the airport of Barajas was a flourishing vineyard, producing white wines reputedly more fragrant and delicate than those of Rueda, while Carabanchel, now the site of the great prison, made a luscious Moscatel. Today, the best wines from the area are made by Jesús DIAZ E HIJOS, VINOS JEROMIN, and VIÑAS EL REGAJAL.

Ash Tree Estate

r w

Branded wines produced by cava giant Freixenet (*see* "Sparkling Wines" page 17) in the VdT Castilla-La Mancha and according to the makers (but not us) "significantly over-delivering on quality at their price point".

Ayuso Bodegas

DO r p w dr ★→★★

Villarrobledo (Albacete). DO La Mancha. This is a large, well-equipped bodega, selling the best of wines under the Estola label. Red Estola, made with 100 per cent Cencibel, is available as *crianza, reserva,* and *gran reserva.*

Casa de la Viña

DO r p w dr ☆☆ *98 99 00 02*

La Solana (Ciudad Real). DO Valdepeñas. The firm belongs to Bodegas y Bebidas (formerly Savín, *see* "Rioja", page 126) and makes pleasant white, rosé, and red wines, ageing its attractive 100 per cent Cencibel *reservas* in oak.

Casa Gualda

See NUESTRA SEÑORA DE LA CABEZA, COOPERATIVA.

Castilla-La Mancha Vino de la Tierra

In June 1999 all 600,000 hectares of vineyards in the vast autonomy of Castilla-La Mancha (including the DO regions) producing a third of Spain's wine were given VdT status. This was part of the measures under the Common Agricultural Policy to reinstate 100,000 hectares lost during the droughts of 1991–5. In recent years, dozens of large firms from other regions such as Faustino and Martínez Bujanda from Rioja (*see* "Rioja", pages 129 and 133), Osborne from Jerez (*see* "Shervy", page 157), and FREIXENET from Cataluña (*see* "Sparkling Wines", page 179) have set up large-scale operations in the area for making branded table wines.

Centro Españolas, Bodegas

DO r p w ☆☆ *97 98 99 00 02*

Tomelloso (Ciudad Real). DO La Mancha. Large, modern winery selling wines under the Allozo, Rama Corra, and Verdial labels. Ed Flaherty has made a name for himself in Chile and produces some fruity, easy-drinking wines, such as the Tempranillo Verdial.

Ciudad Real

Important winemaking town and capital of the province of the same name in LA MANCHA.

Dehesa del Carrizal
r ★★★ *92 94 95*
Retuerta del Bullaque (Ciudad Real). Non-DO. This tiny bodega, with only twenty-two hectares of vineyard and 600 oak *barricas*, shows the potential of this region. Its Cabernet Sauvignon 94 and 95 were among the best in the country.

Don Darius/Don Hugo
r w dr ☆
Huge-selling, modestly priced, sound-quality Rioja lookalikes from the undenominated Bodegas Vitorianas, in the Alto Ebro.

Finca la Antigua
DO r ★→★★ *00 01*
Los Hinojos (Cuenca). DO La Mancha. This very large new winery is an outpost of the Riojan firm of Martínez Bujanda (*see* "Rioja", page 133). There are 295 hectares of vineyard and 5,000 oak *barricas*, and the wines, young and lacking complexity, but excellent value, are made from Tempranillo and Cabernet Sauvignon.

Jesús del Perdón, Cooperativa
DO (r p) w dr ★→★★
Manzanares (Ciudad Real). DO La Mancha. A co-op with a capacity of forty million litres, bottling its wines under the names Lazarillo and Yuntero: good dry whites, and reds made with 100 per cent Cencibel, some cask-aged.

Jesús Díaz, Bodegas
DO r ★★
Colmenar de Oreja (Madrid). DO Vinos de Madrid. The red wines from this bodega were "discovered" by CLUVE (Club de Selección de Vinos) but have recently disappointed.

La Invencible, Cooperativa
DO r p w dr ☆→☆☆
Valdepeñas (Ciudad Real). DO Valdepeñas. Best of the co-ops in VALDEPEÑAS. Its light red is particularly attractive.

La Plazuela
r ★★★→★★★★ *01*
Magnificent, round, and concentrated red made from old-vine Garnacha and Cencibél in Dos Barrios (Toledo) by the tiny non-DO Más Que Vinos Global.

Leganza, Bodegas
DO r p w ☆
Quintanar de la Orden (Toledo). DO La Mancha. Large bodega belonging to Bodegas FAUSTINO (*see* "Rioja", page 129) and producing the inexpensive, branded Condesa de Leganza.

López Tello, Rafael
DO (w dr) r ☆→☆☆
Valdepeñas (Ciudad Real). DO Valdepeñas. One of the oldest firms in VALDEPEÑAS founded in 1893, still making reliable wines, mostly red, some of them now matured in oak *barricas*.

Los Llanos, Bodegas
DO r (p w dr) res ★★ *93 95 97 99*
Valdepeñas (Ciudad Real). DO Valdepeñas. Founded as Bodegas Cervantes in 1875, this was the first concern in VALDEPEÑAS to mature its wines in oak,

and Cosecheros Abastecedores, who acquired it in 1972, scored another first in bottling the wines. The bodega is equipped with stainless-steel fermentation tanks and possesses no fewer than 28,000 American-oak *barricas*; its mature and fruity Señorío de los Llanos red *reservas* and *gran reservas* are fine wines which will surprise those used to the traditional Valdepeñas, which is made for early drinking. There are also a Pata Negra Gran Reserva made from 100 per cent Tempranillo and a young and flowery white, Armonioso.

Madrid

Madrid lies at the centre of the DO VINOS DE MADRID, a vine-growing district of some interest; and in view of the dearth of accommodation in the wide plains of La Mancha, a stopover in the capital is in any case more or less obligatory for a visit to this region. Nevertheless, its main interest on a wine tour is that its hundreds of restaurants offer the widest possible spectrum of regional wines and cooking from the length and breadth of Spain. Apart from wines, if there for the first time one could hardly leave without visiting the magnificent Prado gallery, the arcaded sixteenth-century Plaza Mayor, and the Palacio Real.

Mancha, La

DO (r) w dr ★→★★★

La Mancha, embracing the province of CIUDAD REAL and parts of those of TOLEDO, Albacete, and Cuenca, comprises the larger part of the great central *meseta* of Spain with an average height of 700 metres from the River Tagus in the north to the Sierra Morena, dividing it from Andalucía, in the south. This is Don Quixote country: arid, treeless, bitingly cold in winter, and very hot in summer, with unbroken expanses of wheat, olives, and vines. The DO La Mancha, which is located at the centre of the area, is by far the largest in Spain, with 193,133 hectares under vine and 301 bodegas. The output of wine in 2002, most of it made in co-ops, was 117.5 million litres. The subsoil is chalky with a layer of clay above, and by far the most dominant grape, amounting to some ninety per cent, is the white Airén (or Lairén). The typical wines are light yellow in colour, offering a pleasant enough nose but a shortage of fruit, containing very little acid, and ranging between thirteen and fourteen per cent in strength. Because of their somewhat neutral character these wines are supplied in vast quantities to other regions for blending and further huge amounts are distilled. Recently, earlier picking and cold fermentation have resulted in crisper, fruitier wines.

Manchuela

It was always a puzzle why Manchuela, lying to the east of the DO LA MANCHA and producing bulk wines of no very marked character, was demarcated. The DO was subsequently revoked, but has recently been reinstated. Though some of the wine is now bottled, it is unremarkable.

Marqués de Griñón

VdP r res ☆☆☆→ ☆☆☆☆ 95 96 97 98 99 00 01

Malpica de Tajo (Toledo) Dominio de Valdepusa. At the suggestion of Professor Amerine of Davis University, the adventurous Carlos Falcó, Marqués de Griñón, embarked on the plantation of Cabernet Sauvignon and Merlot on his estate near TOLEDO. With advice from the redoubtable Professor Peynaud and the late Alexis Lichine he proceeded to make Petit Verdot, a Bordeaux-style Cabernet, and outstanding Syrah, the likes of which have never been seen in La Mancha. They have gone from strength to strength since the first vintage in 1981, and lose nothing by comparison with good Bordeaux. Outstanding are Emeritus (00), Domino de Valdepusa Syrah (01), Petit Verdot (01), and Cabernet Sauvignon (01), perhaps at their best within five years of the vintage. The concern now belongs to Bodegas Unidas (*see* "Rioja", page 125); the Marqués also makes good Riojas in collaboration with Bodegas Berberana (*see* page 124) and red Durius in The Alto Duero (*see* page 48).

Megía, Luís
DO r p w ☆→☆☆

Valdepeñas (Ciudad Real). DO Valdepeñas. Owned by the Hispano-Japanese Group Collins, the bodega makes a wide range of reliable wines. Best are the fresh white Marqués de Castañaga, and the superior red Duque de Estrada, made with eighty per cent Cencibel.

Méntrida
DO r p

Méntrida, with 12,500 hectares of vines, forty bodegas, and an output in 2002 of 4.5 million litres, is southwest of MADRID in the north of TOLEDO province. The grapes are eighty-five per cent Garnacha Tinta, producing robust red wines, deep in colour and fourteen to fifteen per cent strength. The bulk go for blending and the quality is so nondescript that in Spain it has been suggested that the DO be suspended. Again, the advent of stainless steel and new technology is improving matters.

Mondéjar
DO ☆

Small, recently demarcated region to the east of the DO VINOS DE MADRID. The climate is continental and the area has in the past supplied bulk wine, mostly red, to the bars of Madrid. Best of its four bodegas is the Sociedad Cooperativa San Donato.

Navalcarnero
DO r ☆

A little to the south of the capital, this is a sub-division of the DO VINOS DE MADRID. Its dark-red and slightly astringent wines have a following locally and in Madrid, but are apt to oxidize rapidly and lose their freshness because of the high content of Garnacha.

Nuestra Señora de la Cabeza, Bodegas
DO r ★★→★★★ *98 99 00 01 02*

Pozoamargo (Cuenca). DO La Mancha. Small, well-equipped ex-cooperative making blends under the label of Casa Gualda of Cencibel (Tempranillo), and Cabernet, Cencibel, and Merlot of unbeatable quality and value. The 98 Selección, 100 per cent Cencibel, was rated by *El País* as one of the twenty-four best wines from Spain.

Nuestra Señora de Manjavacas, Cooperativa
DO r p w dr ☆→☆☆

Mota del Cuervo (Cuenca). DO La Mancha. Large co-op producing improved, fresh young wines under the Zagarrón label using temperature-controlled fermentation in stainless steel.

Osborne Malpica
VdT r ☆→☆☆ *00 01*

Malpica de Tajo (Toledo). VdT Castilla-La Mancha. New, 1,000 hectare estate formed by sherry giant Osborne (*see* "Sherry", page 157) for the large-scale production of its branded Solaz wines, made with a blend of Tempranillo and Cabernet Sauvignon.

Piqueras, Bodegas

DO r res ★★→★★★ *98 00 02*

Almansa (Albacete). DO Almansa. This small family bodega makes some of the best red wines from La Mancha, using Cencibel, Monastrell, and Garnacha grapes. They include the Castillo de Almansa *crianza* and *reserva*, and Marius *gran reserva*.

Ribera del Júcar

DO r ☆☆

Founded in 2001 this small new DO in the province of Cuenca extends to 9,411 hectares and numbers seven bodegas. The best are the Cooperativa Purísima Concepción, selling Tempranillo and Cabernet Sauvignon wines under the Testinos label, and the Sociedad Cooperativa San Ginés, with its worthwhile Cico Almudes wines, a blend of Tempranillo, Bobal, Syrah, and Merlot.

Ricardo Benito, Bodegas

DO w dr p res ☆☆→☆☆☆ *97 98 00 01 02*

Navalcarnero (Madrid). DO Vinos de Madrid. Well-made wines, ranging from a barrel-fermented white and a 100 per cent Tempranillo rosé to a young red Tapón de Oro made by carbonic maceration and a first-rate, but very expensive Divo *reserva* (00).

San Martín de Valdeiglesias

DO r ☆

Sub-zone of the DO VINOS DE MADRID lying between MENTRIDA and Cebreros (*see* "Castilla-León", page 47). Its sturdy red wines, made from a blend of Garnacha Tinta, Tinto Navalcarnero, and white Albillo grapes, resemble those from Cebreros.

Santa Rita S.A.T.

DO w dr r res ★★→★★★ *95 97 99 00 01*

Mota del Cuervo (Cuenca). DO La Mancha. Stars of this bodega and quite untypical of La Mancha are the *crianza* and *reserva* Varones made from 100 per cent Tempranillo. The 01 *reserva* has a three-star rating.

Solís, Bodegas Félix

DO r res w ★★ *93 97 98 99 01 02*

Valdepeñas (Ciudad Real). DO Valdepeñas. Large bodega, best known for its sturdy, reliable red VIÑA ALBALI, aged in oak and made with 100 per cent Cencibel.

Tinajas

These large amphora-shaped vessels are made of the local clay and derived from the Roman *orcae*. Standing three metres high and with an approximate capacity of 1,600 litres, they have traditionally been used in LA MANCHA, Málaga, and Montilla-Moriles for fermenting wines, and are now used for maturing wines in VALDEPEÑAS. *Tinajas* have been progressively replaced by larger cylindrical receptacles of cement reinforced with steel rods, and by stainless-steel tanks.

Toledo

Rising dramatically above the River Tagus, Toledo – with its superb medieval cathedral and collections of paintings by its adopted son, El Greco – is by far the most interesting place to visit in LA MANCHA.

Valdepeñas

Town in the south of the province of CIUDAD REAL, long famous for its red wines, which has given its name to the local DO and is the headquarters of the *consejo regulador*. There are bodegas to be found in almost every street, in the form of courtyards with a high, blank wall pierced by a high arch and double doors. Many are now disused, but the town, an unpretentious place of low houses and sunbaked streets, still boasts establishments of all sizes currently making wine.

Valdepeñas

DO r (w dr) ★★→★★★

The demarcated region lies in the most southerly part of the province of CIUDAD REAL and possesses 18,212 hectares of vineyards and eighty bodegas. The soil is a mixture of gravel, clay, and chalk, and the average annual rainfall is only 400 millimetres. Although the typical wines are red, ninety-three per cent of the grapes are white Airén, the balance consisting of the black Cencibel (or Tempranillo) and Garnacha Tintorera. The red wines often contain a proportion of Airén, but such is the amount of colour and extract in the black grapes that, in spite of the small proportion used, the wines emerge bearing a deep ruby colour.

The tradition was to make and mature the wines in earthenware *tinajas*, from which they were usually sold young in their first or second year. The *tinajas* have been replaced by stainless-steel tanks, allowing for temperature-controlled fermentation. Again, it was not normal practice to age the wines in oak, because Airén musts oxidize easily and, in the past, little wine was made with a large proportion of the scarcer and more expensive Cencibel.

There are now a number of bodegas, notably CASA DE LA VIÑA, LOS LLANOS, and FÉLIX SOLIS, making red *crianza* and *reserva* wines from 100 per cent Cencibel and successfully ageing them in 225-litre oak *barricas*. The Airén contributes a fragrant nose to the finished wine, but also leads to low acidity; the colour, body, and fruity flavour come from the Cencibel. Alcoholic strength lies between 12.5 and fourteen per cent. Valdepeñas also makes white wines similar to those of the DO LA MANCHA.

An increasing number of the bodegas in the DO Valdepeñas bottle their wine – but it must be said that some of the best and freshest examples come unnamed from the jugs of bars and restaurants in MADRID.

Vinícola de Castilla

DO r p w dr sw ★★→★★★ 94 95 96 97 98 00

Manzanares (Ciudad Real). DO La Mancha. This huge, ultra-modern bodega with a storage capacity of fifteen million litres was one of the showpieces of the dispossessed RUMASA group. The bodega is well known for a large range of well-made and reasonably priced wines, such as Selección, Balada, Finca Vieja, and Castillo de Alhambra wines (red, white, and rosé). It also makes superior Señorío de Guadianeja 100 per cent Cencibel and 100 per cent Cabernet Sauvignon *gran reservas* from grapes grown in its own vineyards.

Vinícola de Tomelloso

DO w dr p r res ☆→☆☆☆

Tomelloso (Ciudad Real). DO La Mancha. In the birthplace of Don Quixote's Dulcinea, this well-conducted winery makes a fresh and delicious white

Añil, a 100 per cent Cabernet Sauvignon Torre de Gazate rosé, and worthwhile *crianza* and *reserva* reds.

Vinos de Madrid

DO r ☆→☆☆

Newish DO in the immediate vicinity of MADRID, with 10,800 hectares of vineyards and forty bodegas, long known for its sturdy red wines. It comprises the sub-zones of NAVALCARNERO, ARGANDA, and SAN MARTIN DE VALDEIGLESIAS.

Vinos Jeromín

DO w dr p r ☆☆→☆☆☆ *99 00 02*

Villarejo de Salvanés (Madrid). DO Madrid. Up-and-coming bodega, now one of the best in the MADRID area. The wines are named after famous streets in the capital, but best of the reds is the Manu (99 00), a blend of Tempranillo, Syrah, and other grapes.

Visán

DO r (w dr) ☆☆

Santa Cruz de Mudela, Valdepeñas (Ciudad Real). DO Valdepeñas. The firm makes pleasant white and red wines, selling them under the labels of Castillo de Calatrava, Castillo de la Mancha, and Villa del Duquel. Some of the reds are aged in oak.

WINE AND FOOD

With its roasts, its nourishing *potajes* (thick soups), and *cocidos* or *ollas* (stews), the cooking of New Castile is in many ways similar to that of Old Castile, though, because of its more limited resources, more austere. Drink a good red Valdepeñas with meat dishes (alternatively, treat yourself to a bottle of the Marqués de Griñón's Cabernet Sauvignon or Syrah) and a La Mancha white with lighter fare.

Atascaburras Rabbit stewed with garlic.

Bizcochos borrachos Sponge cakes in the shape of rings then soaked in wine or liqueur.

Caldereta de cordero Lamb ragout prepared with tomatoes and peppers.

Callos a la madrileña Tripe, Madrid style; highly spiced, and a model to other countries' tripe dishes.

Ensalada manchega Salad containing dried cod and tuna, hard-boiled egg, olives, and onions.

Espárragos de Aranjuéz South of Madrid, Aranjuéz with its royal palace, produces some of the most luscious fresh asparagus (and the best strawberries) in Spain.

Gallina en pepitoria Stewed fowl with almonds.

Lágrimas de aldea A stew of pork, potatoes, black pudding, or *chorizo*.

Marmita de verduras A vegetable hot-pot.

Miel con hojuelas Pancakes with honey.

Migas Fried breadcrumbs, often served with fried eggs.

Mojete A vegetable dish resembling ratatouille.

Morteruelo Highly spiced regional version of liver pâté.

Perdices estofadas Partridge stewed in white wine with chopped ham and seasoning.

Pisto manchego A vegetable dish like ratatouille with scrambled eggs.

Queso frito Wedges of cheese, dredged in egg and breadcrumbs before being fried.

Queso manchego Best known of Spanish cheeses, made in large rounds from ewes' milk, either fresh or matured in olive oil.

Tortilla a la magra An omelette made with strips of cooked fillet of pork.

Tortilla española A thick and substantial potato omelette, sometimes including onion.

HOTELS

Madrid *The Ritz Hotel* is one of the most perfect in Europe. The best guides to Madrid's countless other hotels and to its restaurants are the Spanish publication *Gourmetour* and the red *Michelin Guide* Spain .

Toledo *AC Ciudad de Toledo, Doménico, Alfonso VI,* the *Cardenál,* and the four-star *Parador de Turismo* poised on a hill above the city.

Valdepeñas *Tryp El Hidalgo* (outside the town to the north, on the NIV towards Madrid). *Central* is a comfortable new hotel in the centre of Valdepeñas. *Hotel Casa-Palacio Santa Cruz de Mudela* is located fourteen kilometres from Valdepeñas.

RESTAURANTS

Almagro *Parador de Almagro* is a historic *parador* in a fascinating old town. Try aubergines in spicy sauce; rabbit stewed in white wine.

Madrid A vast range. For the ultimate in sophisticated cooking and wines, *Zalacaín* and *Jockey* are outstanding. Among the many others, a few personal favourites are: *Café de Oriente*; *Cabo Mayor* for Cantabrian cooking and fish; *El Bodegón* for Basque-influenced cuisine and a long wine list; *La Trainera*; and *Viridiana,* which has the most interesting wine list in Madrid.

Manzanares *Parador de Manzanares* is a gastronomic oasis.

Toledo *Asador Adolfo* boasts innovative cooking and an extensive wine list; *La Lumbre*; *Casa de los Lopez de Toledo.*

Castilla-León

Old Castile and the ancient Kingdom of León, united in 1230, are the very heart of Catholic Spain. It was their monarchs who planned and carried through the counter-offensive against the Moors; and the very names of their cities – Avila, Segovia, Salamanca, Burgos, Valladolid, and León – seem to echo the "slow old tunes of Spain". They now form the autonomous region of Castilla-León. (The former province of Santander is now the autonomy of Cantabria, *see* page 110.)

Apart from the enclave of Cebreros in the Sierra de Gredos near Avila, only the northern area, especially around the River Duero basin, produces wines in any quantity. The land is often bleak and arid, bitterly cold in winter, and fiery-hot in summer; in areas such as Toro the annual rainfall amounts to only 300 millimetres. In some districts, once famous for their wines, production has declined disastrously because of the difficulty of cultivating vines in such conditions. Nevertheless, Castilla-León produces

DO Zones
1. Rueda
2. Ribera del Duero
3. Toro
4. Bierzo
5. Cigales

Others
6. Valdevimbre, Los Oteros
7. Fermoselle
8. Cebreros

worthwhile wines in great variety, notably the stylish reds from the Ribera del Duero, the refreshing whites from Rueda, and the light reds of Cigales and Bierzo. The wines from León have improved notably with modern methods and Toro, with its concentrated reds, is one of the most up-and-coming regions in Spain.

There is a profusion of vine varieties, but among the best and most typical are the black Tinto Fino (also known as the Tinto del País or Tinto Aragonés), a variant of the Tempranillo grown in the Ribera del Duero; the white Verdejo, native to Rueda; and the Prieto Picudo, a black grape with a white pulp, used for making rosés in León. The white "Jerez" or Palomino is also widely grown, but its musts are not of the same quality as in its native habitat in the south of Spain. In one remote district of León there are even hybrids resulting from the direct crossing of American and native vines, but they are frowned upon by the authorities as containing a toxic alkaloid, the ill-famed *malvina*, and wines of this type may not be exported.

As in most parts of Spain, a great deal of the wine is made in cooperatives; but perhaps nowhere else have these small proprietors making wine for consumption in the immediate locality survived in greater numbers. In districts such as Los Oteros and Valdevimbre near León, the serried peasant bodegas, which are dug deep into the ground and have mounded earth roofs, look like prehistoric earthworks.

There are five *denominaciónes de origen*: RUEDA, instituted in 1980; RIBERA DEL DUERO (1982); TORO (1987); and the even more recently demarcated BIERZO and CIGALES.

Abadía Retuerta

r ★★★→★★★★ *96 97 98 99 00 01 02*

Sardón de Duero (Valladolid). Non-DO. Owned by the Swiss Novartis, this is one of the most modern bodegas in Spain, with 206 hectares of vineyard and 3,200 oak *barricas*. Under the direction of the oenologist from Château Ausone, it is making exceptional 100 per cent Tempranillo; Tempranillo/Cabernet Sauvignon/Merlot; and Tempranillo/ Cabernet Sauvignon. The Pago Valdebellón (99) made from 100 per cent Cabernet Sauvignon and Negralada (99) made from 100 per cent Tempranillo, both aged for two years in *barrica*, are superb.

Agrícola Castellana Sociedad Cooperativa

DO w dr am ★→★★★

La Seca (Valladolid). DO Rueda. This large and well-regulated co-op in the TIERRA DE MEDINA was founded in 1935 and now has a storage capacity of ten million litres. The co-op makes both the traditional *flor*-growing RUEDA from a blend of Verdejo and Palomino – ageing it either in *solera* or in glass carboys in the open – and also fresh, young wines made from Verdejo, Viura, and Sauvignon Blanc. Typical of the first type are the Campo Grande fino and Dorado 61, both sherry-like in flavour and about fifteen per cent strength. Its pleasant, light wines are sold as Azumbre, Pampano, and Veliterra. The splendid Cuatro Rayas, made from 100 per cent Verdejo, is light-greenish in colour, dry, fragrant, fruity, and pleasantly astringent.

Alión, Bodegas y Viñedos

DO r ☆☆☆ *94 95 99 00*

Peñafiel (Valladolid). DO Ribera del Duero. Since discontinuing the three-year-old VALBUENA, VEGA SICILIA has developed this second bodega to make red wines with 100 per cent Tempranillo. The results are impressive; the wines are vigorous and good for medium-term laying down. The 99 vintage is outstanding.

Alta Pavina, Bodegas

r ☆☆

La Parrilla (Valladolid). Castilla y León. Non-DO. This small bodega makes good 100 per cent Cabernet Sauvignon and Tinto Fino, both oak-aged, spicy, dark, and dense. Also variable Pinot Noir.

Alvarez y Díez

DO w dr ★★→★★★ *DYA*

Nava del Rey (Valladolid). DO Rueda. Best of its fresh and intensely fruity white wines are the 100 per cent Mantel Blanco fermented in barrel and the 100 per cent Sauvignon Blanc Mantel Blanco (00).

Antaño, Bodegas

DO w dr (r) ☆☆☆

Rueda (Valladolid). DO Rueda. Ambitious new bodega started by Madrid restaurateurs, making clean and fruity white Viña Mocen, and red Viña Cobranza, a blend of Tempranillo and Cabernet Sauvignon, in Medina del Campo.

Arzuaga Navarro, Bodegas

DO (w dr) r res l ☆→☆☆☆☆ *94 95 96 99 00*

Quintanilla de Onésimo (Valladolid). DO Ribera del Duero. Good red wines made mainly from Tinto Fino. Dense and oaky, they are slow to mature.

Bañeza, La

r ☆

La Bañeza is an area to the west of the city of LEÓN and part of the undemarcated COMARCA DE LEÓN. It was formerly widely known for its *claretes de aguja* (light red wines with slight sparkle), but little wine is now made except in primitive subterranean cellars for local consumption.

Basa

w ☆☆

Brand name for Verdejo white from RUEDA, made by gifted young oenologist TELMO RODRÍGUEZ, formerly of LA GRANJA REMELLURI in RIOJA.

Belondrade y Lurtón SL

DO w dr ☆☆☆ *DYA*

La Seca (Valladolid). DO Rueda. This small bodega founded by the flying winemaker produces some of the best Rueda. The 2001 Verdejo, fragrant, delicate, and elegant, is a triumph.

Benavente

VdC r ☆

Like LA BAÑEZA, Benavente once made good *claretes* with a slight sparkle, but many of its vineyards have now been abandoned.

Bierzo

DO r w p ☆→☆☆☆☆

Bierzo, in the northwest of the province of León bordering Galicia, of which the DO Bierzo forms part, is ideal for the production of quality wines. Its 4,065 hectares of vineyards thrive in a climate which could be described as halfway between the dry heat of Castilla-León and the rain and humidity more typical of Galicia. Vines are thickest on the ground around Villafranca and Ponferrada, and the most dominant vine varieties are the black Mencía and Alicante, and the white Palomino.

The fragrant and fruity red wines age well in cask, developing a good ruby colour, and are smooth and silky, with not more than twelve per cent alcohol. The whites, which average 10.5 to 11.5 per cent, are fruity, flowery on the nose, and better balanced than the traditional acidic wines of Galicia. There are also excellent rosés, produced mainly from the Mencía grape and having a refreshing residual acidity.

The temptation has always been to sell the wines to Galicia and Asturias, where they find a ready market. The co-ops of Cacabelos and Villafranquina bottle worthwhile and representative wines (*see* Sociedad VINOS DEL BIERZO). Among the most sophisticated wines from the region are the 100 per cent Godello whites and red Mencía from PRADA A TOPE. *See also* PEREZ CARAMES, DESCENDIENTES DE J PALACIOS, and LUNA BEBERIDE.

Bornos, Palacio de
See Bodegas de Crianza CASTILLA LA VIEJA.

Callejo, Bodegas Félix
DO r p ☆☆→☆☆☆ *95 99 00 02*
Sotillo de la Ribera (Burgos). DO Ribera del Duero. Young bodega making fruity, well-structured reds from 100 per cent Tinto Fino.

Casar de Valdaiga
DO r p w dr ☆☆
Label for the wines made by PEREZ CARAMES in the DO BIERZO. The fruity red is well worth looking out for.

Castilla la Vieja, Bodegas de Crianza
DO r w p ★★→★★★
Rueda (Valladolid). DO Rueda. Bodegas founded by local growers to elaborate their wines in the best possible fashion, ageing some in oak. Founded by Antonio Sanz and now run by Ricardo Sanz (*see also* Vinos SANZ) it makes first-rate Palacio de Bornos whites, including a barrel-fermented ninety per cent Verdejo Rueda Superior (01); 100 per cent Sauvignon Blanc (01); a red non-DO Almirantazgo de Castilla; and an excellent sparkling Palacio de Bornos Brut conforming to the local *vinos espumosos método tradicional*.

Cebreros
VdT r p ☆
Situated in the province of Avila in the Sierra de Gredos west of Madrid, Cebreros produces wines from the black Garnacha and Tinto Aragonés and the white Albillo. Robust and heady *tintos* and *rosados* with a minimum of thirteen per cent alcohol, they are much in demand for everyday drinking in Madrid and the surrounding area.

Cigales
DO r ☆→☆☆
The 2,780 hectares of the recently demarcated Cigales are planted with white Palomino, Verdejo, and Albillo, and black Garnacha, Tinto del País, and Tinto Madrid. Its *claretes*, famous since medieval times, may no longer be labelled as such thanks to the wisdom of Brussels; they are made by mixing the black and white grapes, destalking them, and fermenting them *en blanc*. Light red wines of this type were, from time immemorial, the most popular in the taverns of VALLADOLID, but what now passes for a light red Cigales is more likely to be a blend of red wine from Zamora with a white from the central plains of La Mancha.

Because much of the wine is made in archaic subterranean bodegas for local consumption, and the production of good Cigales was more or less limited to two sizeable private concerns – those of Pablo Barrigón Tovar and Bodegas FRUTOS VILLAR – demarcation of this small region in 1991 was delayed. The large and modernized co-op at Cigales makes an excellent Torondos rosé.

Con Class
DO w ★★→★★★ DYA

Fresh, fruity white Rueda wines from CUEVAS DE CASTILLA include a Vendimia Excepcional and a 100 per cent Sauvignon Blanc.

Condado de Haza
DO r ☆☆☆ 97 98 01

Pesquera de Duero (Valladolid). Do Ribera del Duero. Alejandro FERNANDEZ's new bodega, producing a pure Tinto Fino aged in oak. Sister ship of PESQUERA, with similar consistently good wines.

Conde de Siruela
DO r ☆☆☆ 95 96 98

Good red RIBERA DEL DUERO wines from Bodegas FRUTOS VILLAR.

Cuevas de Castilla
DO w dr ★→★★★ DYA

La Seca (Valladolid). DO Rueda. Outpost of the Sanz family, making good and reasonably priced Con Class and Palacio de Menade whites from Verdejo, Viura, and Sauvignon Blanc.

Dehesa de los Canónigos, Bodega
DO r res ☆☆→☆☆☆ 96 98 00 01

Pesquera de Duero (Valladolid). DO Ribera del Duero. The grapes from the vineyards of this young firm in the RIBERA DEL DUERO were formerly sold to VEGA SICILIA. It now makes its own stylish and concentrated, if dauntingly expensive, Tinto Fino reds.

Descendientes de J Palacios
DO r ☆☆☆ 01

DO Bierzo. Alvaro Palacios of Priorato fame has revived some old vineyards and is making remarkable and expensive red wines from the native Mencia grape. First vintage of his BIERZO and more sophisticated Corullon was 99.

Dominio de Pingus
DO r ☆☆☆→☆☆☆☆ 99 00

DO Ribera del Duero. Tiny bodega with five hectares of sixty-year-old vines, recently founded by Danish winemaker Peter Sisseck. Its excellent, concentrated wines have already achieved cult status and are absurdly expensive, but there is an affordable second wine named Flor de Pingus.

Durius Alto Duero, Bodegas
VdT r ☆☆ 00

Fermoselle (Zamora). VdT Arribes de Duero. Fruity Tempranillo introduced by the Marqués de Griñón (*see* "Castilla-La Mancha", page 38) and made by Bodegas Unidas (*see* "Rioja", page 125). The estate is also home to the Hacienda Unamuno, a winemaking facility which is also home to a visitors' centre and hotel.

Estefanía, Bodegas
DO r ☆☆☆ 00 02

Ponferrada (Léon). DO Bierzo. Sizeable bodega with thirty-six hectares of vineyards and 1,000 oak *barricas*. Best of its wines, with good balance between fruit and oak, are the Pagos de Posada.

Fariña, Bodegas
DO r res ☆☆→☆☆☆☆ *95 96 97 98*

Casaseca de las Chanas (Zamora). DO Toro. The oldest-established bodega
of the DO TORO, but now being overtaken by younger rivals. Makes dark,
spicy red wines with heavy fruit: Colegiata is unoaked, while the Gran
Colegiata is aged in cask.

Fermoselle
VdT r ☆

Fermoselle lies between the basins of the two rivers Duero and Tormes in
the southwest corner of the province of Zamora, almost within a stone's
throw of the Portuguese border. Its granite and schistous soils, and its
blistering summers and low rainfall, resemble those of the Upper Douro.
That its wines, though in some ways resembling the Portuguese, are not
their equal, is probably because the dominant grape, Juan García, is not
of the same quality as the varieties grown in Portugal. During the sixteenth
century Fermoselle produced an annual one million litres of wine, and the
place seems to be hollow with disused cellars hewn from the granite. Now,
however, it is difficult to find the authentic full-bodied red wine, with its
strange resinous (but not unattractive) nose and flavour, because most of it
is sold in bulk for blending. But *see* DURIUS.

Fernández, Alejandro
DO r res ☆☆☆☆ *91 92 94 95 96 97 00*

Pesquera de Duero (Valladolid). DO Ribera del Duero. The bodega was
founded in 1970. Its wines, intensely fruity in the very best manner of the
RIBERA DEL DUERO, improved dramatically with the installation of stainless-
steel and new-oak barrels. Since the PESQUERA wines were "discovered"
by the foreign press, and Robert Parker put them on a par with those of
Château Pétrus, prices, prestige, and exports have leapt. The premium
Janus (95) is outstanding. *See also* CONDADO DE HAZA.

Frutos Villar, Bodegas
DO r p w dr ☆→☆☆

Cigales (Valladolid). DO Cigales. The largest outfit in Cigales, making the
reliable Viña Calderona *rosado*. The company also makes very drinkable
red Muruve and Gran Muruve in TORO, and has further outposts in RUEDA
and in RIBERA DEL DUERO, where it makes good CONDE DE SIRUELA *crianzas*
and *reservas*.

Grupo Sindical de Colonización No 795
VdT r (p w dr) ☆

Cebreros (Avila). Makers of El Galayo, available in different styles and
perhaps the best of these sturdy wines.

Ismael Arroyo
DO r res ☆☆→☆☆☆☆ *94 95 96 98 00 01*

Sotillo de la Ribera (Burgos). DO Ribera del Duero. Small bodega with
twenty hectares of vineyard and 1,200 oak *barricas*, well known for its
reliable and well-structured wines sold under the labels of Mesoneros
de Castilla and Valsotillo.

Leda Viñas Viejas, Bodegas
Non-DO ☆☆☆☆ *98 99 00 01*

Tudela de Dueo (Valladolid). Non-DO. This small bodega with only fourteen
hectares of Tinto Fino and 200 oak *barricas* produces a red wine which ranks
with the best from Spain – fragrant, luscious, and beautifully balanced.

León

Situated high on the Castilian plateau, the old city of León, capital of the medieval kingdom, is the centre of an increasingly important wine-producing area. The Gothic cathedral, with its airy flying buttresses and magnificent stained-glass windows, is one of the finest in Spain.

León, Comarca de

r p w dr ☆→☆☆

The name is used to describe the wine-producing area to the southeast of the city of León. It comprises, in order of importance, the following sub-divisions: VALDEVIMBRE, LOS OTEROS, LA BAÑEZA, LEÓN, Tierra de Campos, Valderas, La Antique, Payuelos, and RIBERA ALTA DEL CEA.

Los Curros, SAT Grupo Yllera

DO w dr r ★★

Rueda (Valladolid). DO Rueda. Former co-op making the fresh and flowery Viña Cantosán from 100 per cent Verdejo – the house white at Madrid's famous Zalacaín restaurant. The bodega also bottles the rich and oaky red YLLERA, made by a sister establishment in Boada de Roa in RIBERA DEL DUERO.

Luna Beberide, Bodegas y Viñedos

DO w dr r ☆→☆☆

Cacabelos (Leon) DO Bierzo. Drinkable whites made from Gewürztraminer and Chardonnay in the unlikely outpost of BIERZO, and also a 100 per cent Mencia red.

Marqués de Riscal

See VINOS BLANCOS DE CASTILLA.

Mauro, Bodegas

r res ☆☆☆☆ *94 95 96 97 98 99 01*

DO Toro (Valladolid). Small, private bodega whose impeccable round and fruity Tinto Fino reds are made by Mariano García of VEGA SICILIA fame. They do not currently carry the DO RIBERA DEL DUERO, as some of the fruit is grown outside Ribera del Duero. Premium wines are superb: Vendimia Seleccionada (99) and Terreus (99).

Maurados, Bodega y Viñedos

r ☆☆☆☆ *97 99 00*

DO Toro. It is a new departure for Bodegas Mauro to make TORO wines and the operation has been mounted by Mariano García, former oenologist of VEGA SICILIA. San Román 99 is splendidly fruity and concentrated, and tannic in the way of a Toro.

Nava del Rey

Largest of the townships in the TIERRA DE MEDINA southwest of VALLADOLID, and part of the DO RUEDA.

Numancia Termes, SL

DO r ☆☆☆ *98 99 00*

Valdefincas (Zamora) DO Toro. Founded in 1998, this young bodega is already making perhaps the best Toro wine to date in the shape of the 100 per cent Tinta de Toro Numanthia.

Oteros, Los

VdT r p w dr ☆

Los Oteros, east of the León–Benavente road, is second in importance of the sub-divisions of the Comarca de LEÓN. The major grape is the Prieto Picudo, grown in clay soils. Much of the wine is made in tiny peasant bodegas, constructed by digging deep into the ground, installing the simplest of beam presses, mounding up the soil on top, and leaving a chimney for the escape of carbon dioxide. The typical wine made in such cellars is a *clarete* (which may no longer be described as such under EC regulations) of ten to 13.5 per cent, but methods are so archaic that on occasion the volatile acidity is so high the wine tastes of raspberry vinegar. *See* also VALDEVIMBRE.

Pago de Carraovejas

DO r ☆☆☆ 98 00 01

Peñafiel (Valladolid). DO Ribera del Duero. Bodega with sixty hectares of vineyards, planted between 1988 and 1991 with Tinto Fino and Cabernet Sauvignon. Currently earning a reputation for some of the region's most stylish and densely fruity wines.

Palacio de Bornos

See Bodegas de Crianza CASTILLA LA VIEJA.

Peñafiel

Township in RIBERA DEL DUERO surmounted by a magnificent twelfth-century castle, beneath which Bodegas PROTOS maintains cellars for maturing its wines. Another part of its medieval legacy is the extraordinary jousting ground and the houses surrounding it.

Peñalba López, Bodegas

DO r (p) ★★→★★★ 95 96 98 99 00

Aranda de Duero (Burgos). DO Ribera del Duero. Old-established family firm with its own 200 hectares of vineyards, making and ageing in oak good fruity TORREMILANOS reds from the Tinto Fino grape, more Rioja-like than most. *See also* "Hotels".

Pérez Caramés, Bodegas

DO w dr r ☆☆

Villafranca de Bierzo (León). DO Bierzo. This is the largest of the producers in BIERZO, making wine in the northwest corner of the province. It produces some very creditable wines under the labels of Consales de Roma and Casar de Valdaiga.

Pérez Pascuas, Bodegas Hermanos

DO r (p) res ☆☆☆ 94 95 96 97 98 99 01

Pedrosa de Duero (Burgos). DO Ribera del Duero. This tiny and scrupulously kept family bodega makes fruity and complex VIÑA PEDROSA red wines and a magnificent Pérez Pascuas Gran Selección (96), rated by *Club de Gourmets* magazine as among the best in Spain.

Pesquera

r ☆☆☆ 91 92 94 95 96 97 00

Famous wines from Alejandro FERNÁNDEZ.

Prada a Tope, Bodegas

DO (w dr p) r res ★★ 96 98 00 02

Cacabelos (León). DO Bierzo. Tiny modern bodega installed in the Palace of the Señorío de Canedo, where the individualistic José Luís Prada makes small amounts of some of the best Bierzo wines, including a white Godello and reds with the local Mencía grape.

Protos, Bodegas

DO r res ☆☆→☆☆☆ 98 99 00 01 02

Peñafiel (Valladolid). DO Ribera del Duero. This large bodega, formerly a cooperative, was one of the first in the region to age its wines in oak. Its storage capacity runs to 6.5 million litres and it has 8,000 American and French oak casks for maturing the wines, which average 12.5 per cent alcohol. The youngest wine is the *crianza,* with a deep, plummy colour: fresh and tasting of blackberries. The *reserva* spends two years in oak *barricas*; and there are also Protos *gran reservas*, aged for much longer in cask and bottle. The wines, greatly improved by a new oenologist, are shipped to the UK and Germany and have been much admired by connoisseurs for their clean, fruity nose, deep flavour, and long finish.

Ribera Alta del Cea
VdC r

Small winemaking area between LEÓN and Palencia, formerly producing red wines from hybrids obtained by directly crossing European and American vines. As the wines contained small amounts of a toxic alkaloid (*malvina*), they were blended with others from the area. The district now makes pleasant light red wines from a Mencía, Prieto Picudo, and Palomino blend.

Ribera de Burgos
DO r ☆→☆☆

Part of the DO RIBERA DEL DUERO, centred on Aranda de Duero. The predominant grape varieties are Tinto del País, Tinto Madrid, Jaén, Valenciano, Albillo, Tinto Aragonés, and Tempranillo. The area's typical wines are the light reds formerly known as *claretes* or *claros*, most of which are made by small proprietors or in co-ops. Some of the best of them are produced by the Bodegas Santa Eulalia (FRUTOS VILAR) in La Horra and bottled as CONDE DE SIRUELA.

Ribera del Duero
DO r ☆☆→☆☆☆

Demarcated in 1982, this region produces some of the best red wine in Spain. It borders the River Duero for a distance of 110 kilometres, with a maximum width of thirty kilometres, from Tudela de Duero near VALLADOLID to just east of El Burgo de Osma, and covers an area of 17,103 hectares with 166 bodegas. This is one of the fastest-growing and most fashionable wine-growing areas in the country, with bodegas mushrooming and finance flowing in from Madrid. Prices for the wines are correspondingly high.

The larger and central part of the region lies within the province of Burgos; there are small areas within the provinces of Soria to the east and Segovia to the south, but the best of the wines are made around PEÑAFIEL and Valbuena in the province of Valladolid. In these areas the vines grow on chalky, pine-fringed slopes bordering the Duero, and the predominant grape is Tinto Fino or Tinto Aragonés, a variant of the Riojan Tempranillo, whose musts are particularly suitable for maturation in oak. This area is famous for the legendary VEGA SICILIA, but dozens of excellent bodegas, such as Alejandro FERNÁNDEZ and Bodegas Hermanos PEREZ PASCUAS, have now come to the fore.

Rodero, Bodegas
DO r res ☆☆☆ *95 96 98 99 01 02*

Pedrosa de Duero (Burgos). DO Ribera del Duero. Carmelo Rodero is one of the doyens of RIBERA DEL DUERO. The wines are consistently good and the 95 and 98 *reservas* are superb.

Rueda
DO w dr am ★★→★★★

This small region to the southwest of VALLADOLID, with an area of 7,364 hectares, takes its name from the village of Rueda, which, with NAVA DEL

REY, LA SECA, and SERRADA, is a main centre for making the wines. The predominant grape varieties are the native white Verdejo, Viura, and Palomino, grown in calcareous clays. More recently, Sauvignon Blanc has been introduced from France. Until recently the district was demarcated only for white wines, for which it has been famous since the seventeenth century, but the DO has now been extended to include the reds from the Tierra de Medina. The traditional Rueda, amber-coloured and of some fifteen per cent strength, was a *flor*-growing white matured either in loosely stoppered glass carboys or in *solera*, tasting like a rough sherry. Following the lead of the MARQUÉS DE RISCAL, which built a large modern winery near Rueda, the region now produces fresh and attractive cold-fermented white wines, made mainly with Verdejo and Sauvignon Blanc. Their success has, in the manner of Ribera del Duero and Priorato, attracted a host of mercenary outsiders, which has effectively doubled the number of wineries in the region, sending the proces of grapes into hyperspace.

Santo Cristo, Crianzas y Viñedos Soc. Cooperativa

DO r w g res ✩✩→✩✩✩ *96 98 00 01 02*

Ainzón (Zaragoza). DO Campo de Borja. Large co-op making very drinkable wines under the labels of Viña Collado, Viña Ainzón, and Peñazuela.

Sanz, Vinos

DO r p w dr am res ★★→★★★ *DYA*

Rueda (Valladolid). DO Rueda. Large family bodega founded in 1870, and headquarters of the Sanz dynasty of Rueda. It makes wines in various styles, including Sanz Rueda Superior, Sanz Sauvignon, and premium Finca la Colina Sauvignon, and also undertakes the vinification and maturation of wines for a variety of other concerns.

Seca, La

Small village and winemaking centre in the DO RUEDA.

Señorío de Nava, Bodegas

DO r p ✩✩→✩✩✩ *94 96 97 98 99 01*

Nava de Roa (Burgos). DO Ribera del Duero. Controlled since 1986 by VINOS DE LEÓN, the firm owns or controls 300 hectares of vineyard planted with Cabernet Sauvignon, Merlot, and native varieties. The rosé, made from Tinto Fino, Albillo, and Garnacha, is one of the best and freshest from the region, and there are good Señorío de Nava *crianzas* and *reservas*.

Serrada

Another of the winemaking villages of the small DO RUEDA. Much of the house wine in the bars and restaurants of VALLADOLID is sold as "Serrada".

Telmo Rodríguez, Compañia de Vinos

DO r ✩✩✩ *99 00 01 02*

DO Toro. One of a number of ventures of gifted oenologist Telmo Rodríguez, formerly of the GRANJA REMELLURI in Rioja, this young firm is already producing some of the best Toro wine from 100 per cent Tinta de Toro, labelled as Gago or Pago de Jara.

Tierra de Medina

Traditional name for what is now the DO RUEDA. Before the phylloxera epidemic of 1909 there were 90,000 hectares under vines, but this is now reduced to 24,000 hectares, of which the DO Rueda occupies 7,000 hectares.

Tionio
r ☆☆☆

Promising red wines from Ribera del Duero made by a young offshoot of the Alella firm of Parxet (*see* "Cataluña", page 70).

Toro
DO r ☆☆→☆☆☆☆

This demarcated region to the east of Zamora, with 15,000 hectares under vines, of which 5,329 qualify for DO, is one of the most parched in Spain, having an annual rainfall of only 300 millimetres. In strength and body its red wines are rivalled only by those from Priorato (*see* "Cataluña", page 71), Jumilla, and Yecla (*see* "Valencia and Murcia", pages 170 and 174) and were formerly among the most prized in Spain, being much drunk by the students and academics of Salamanca University. The principal vine varieties are the Tinta de Toro and Tinto de Madrid, together with some Garnacha. Not so long ago, winemaking methods were primitive and the wines overstrong. But a technological revolution is now under way, initiated by Bodegas FARIÑA and spearheaded by new concerns such as MAURODOS, NUMANCIA TERMES, Dos Victori, and Vega Sanco, whose complex and concentrated wines can hold their own with all-comers.

Torremilanos
DO r ★★→★★★ *95 96 98 99 00*

Name of the light, well-made red wines from Bodegas PEÑALBA LOPEZ in the RIBERA DEL DUERO.

Valbuena
DO r ☆☆☆ *89 90 91 92 93 95 97 99*

Made by the prestigious VEGA SICILIA with the same grape varieties, but sold when five years old. It is best drunk at about ten years and some prefer it to its elder brother.

Valdevimbre
VdT r ☆→☆☆

This is the largest of the Comarca de LEÓN sub-districts, and with the neighbouring LOS OTEROS there are 3,900 hectares under vine. Its light-red wines, known as *claretes*, can be aromatic, light, and fruity. They are traditionally made by adding bunches of Prieto Picudo to the must during secondary fermentation, so prolonging it and giving the wine a refreshing prickle. In some of the more primitive bodegas, the proprietors try for the same result by adding fizzy lemonade! Some of the best wine is bottled by the Cooperativa Vinícola Comarcal under the label of Señorío de Valdes Artesanal. *See also* VINOS DE LEÓN.

Valduero, Bodegas
DO r res (w) ★★→★★★ *90 91 95 96 98*

Gumiel del Mercado (Burgos). DO Ribera del Duero. Founded in 1984, the bodega has a reputation for good and good-value *reservas*.

Valladolid

Home to a famous university and once the capital of Spain, Valladolid is a good base for visiting the RIBERA DEL DUERO, RUEDA, TORO, BIERZO, and CIGALES. The superb fifteenth-century Colegio de San Gregorio houses the National Museum of Polychrome Sculpture, with its outstanding collections of sculptures and paintings.

Vega de la Reina, Bodegas

w dr ll DYA

Formerly famous for its rich and oaky reds, the bodega now makes only white wines from Verdejo, Sauvignon Blanc, and Viura.

Vega Sicilia, Bodegas

DO r ☆☆☆→☆☆☆☆ *53 60 64 66 68 70 73 75 76 80 81 82 83 85 86 89 90 91 Reserva Especial*

Valbuena de Duero (Valladolid). DO Ribera del Duero. Vega Sicilia is a name to conjure with in Spain, where its wines, all red, are strictly rationed and supplied only for state functions and to the best hotels and restaurants. The estate of some 900 hectares, with 240 under vines, borders the river in the RIBERA DEL DUERO, east of VALLADOLID, at a height of 765 metres. As far back as 1864 select French vines were acquired from Bordeaux and acclimatized in its chalky, pine-fringed vineyards. They have subsequently been replanted with the same three varieties, Cabernet Sauvignon, Merlot, and Malbec, whose musts are blended with those of the native Tinto Aragonés and white Albillo. The bodega believes in vinifying and maturing its wines very slowly; only the must which separates naturally after light crushing is used, and after vinification the Vega Sicilia is matured for not less than four years in oak (and often much longer) with three more in bottle. The bodega also makes a five-year-old red VALBUENA. The wines, of 13.5 per cent alcohol or more, are full-bodied, deep in colour, complex, and intensely fruity, with a fragrant nose, compounded of oak and fruit, and a long finish. Some experts have criticized Vega Sicilia for the degree of volatile acidity, preferring the VALBUENA, with its shorter period in cask. *See* also Bodegas y Viñedos ALION.

Viña Pedrosa

r ☆☆☆ *94·95 96 97 98 99 01*

Fruity red RIBERA DEL DUERO from Bodega Hermanos PEREZ PASCUAS.

Viñedos de Nieva

DO w dr ★★★ *DYA*

Nieva (Segovia). DO Rueda. Beautifully fresh and fragrant Blanco Nieva wines made from Verdejo and Sauvignon Blanc, some fermented in barrel.

Vinos del Bierzo, Sociedad Cooperativa

DO r res (p w) ★★

Cacabelos (León). DO Bierzo. The traditional red Guerra *reservas* from this large co-op, made with 100 per cent Mencía and aged in oak, are soft and well-balanced with hints of coffee and spices.

Vinos Blancos de Castilla

DO w dr ★★★ *DYA*

Rueda (Valladolid). DO Rueda. The bodega was constructed – with advice from Professor Peynaud of Bordeaux University – by the Rioja firm of MARQUÉS DE RISCAL, which did not, at the time, market a white wine. Its capacity is 4.8 million litres: the wines are cold-fermented in stainless-steel tanks and made with ninety per cent Verdejo, but Peynaud found that they improved through blending with a little Viura and by maturing for a few months in oak casks. Fresh and fruity, they are sold under the label of the Marqués de Riscal, most of the output going for export. More recently the bodega has introduced a fresh and outstanding young 100 per cent Sauvignon Blanc, and a first-rate, characterful Marqués de Riscal Reserva Limousin, which is matured in oak.

Vinos de León-VILE, Bodegas

VdT r p w dr ★→★★ *92 94 95 96 98*

Armunia (León). Long known as VILE, a somewhat unfortunate abbreviation, this large private consortium owns a modern winery with a capacity of twelve million litres and 2,000 casks for maturing the wines. The group has vineyards of its own, but buys most of the grapes – mainly Prieto Picudo, Tempranillo, Mencía, Tinto del País, and Garnacha for the red and rosé wines, and Verdejo and Palomino for the white – from independent proprietors in VALDEVIMBRE and LOS OTEROS. Its crisp, young red and white wines have proved very popular in the UK. Among its more select and older wines are the red Catedral de León and good, full-bodied Don Suero and Palacio de los Guzmanes *reservas*.

WINE AND FOOD

If one had to name the type of dish most typical of Castilla-León it would be the roasts; of lamb, suckling pig, and kid, and the baby milk-fed lamb, or *lechazo*, is at its best around Valladolid. However, the region has much else to offer: partridge from the mountains, trout from the cold streams, and the rib-warming *cocidos* made from chickpeas and local varieties of pork sausage.

Arroz con cordero Rice combined with tomato sauce and stewed lamb, finished in the oven to crisp the top. The dish matches a light red or rosé with a little residual acidity, such as Vinos de León's Castillo de Coyanza, or Calderona from Bodegas Frutos Villar.

Besugo al ajoarriero Sea bream in a sauce made with olive oil, garlic, onions, parsley, and vinegar. A fresh, young Rueda: for example, Verdejo Pálido.

Cabrito asado Roast kid.

Cachelada leonesa Potatoes boiled with seasoning and *chorizo* sausage, from which they take the cheerful orange colour and spicy flavour.

Cochinillo asado Roast milk-fed suckling pig of a tenderness and succulence rarely found in Britain or the US, where the piglets are killed when they are older. A fine red *reserva* such as Valbuena, Pesquera, or Vega Sicilia – if you can find it.

Cocido castellano A substantial stew made of chickpeas, brisket, marrow bones, ham bones, black pudding, chorizo, pork, potatoes, and green vegetables. Go the whole hog and wash it down with a sturdy Cebreros!

Cordero asado/lechazo Roast lamb/milk-fed baby lamb, often cooked in a baker's oven. A good red, such as Torremilanos.

Jamón de Guijuelo Cured *páta negra* ham, from semi-wild pigs.

Judías blancas a la castellana Stew of haricot beans, tomatoes, onions, garlic, and seasoning. Try the local red house wine.

Leche frita Squares of a stiff custard, dredged in beaten egg and breadcrumbs and fried crisp in hot olive oil.

Lentejas zamoranas Lentils stewed with black pudding, onions, paprika, garlic, parsley, and seasoning.

Liebre en su salsa Hare, marinated in white wine and garlic, cooked in an earthenware dish with onions, carrots, turnips, nutmeg, and red wine. The sauce is thickened with the liver. A full-bodied red, such as Gran Colegiata from Bodegas Fariña.

Mantecadas Small cakes made with butter, flour, and eggs and baked in paper cups.

Pantortillas de Reinosa Fluffy pancakes made from puff pastry flavoured with *anís* and eaten cold.

Pisto castellano A vegetable dish resembling ratatouille, with potatoes, bacon, and often with eggs.

Rebozos zamoranos Small cakes made with flour, eggs, and lemon.

Ropa vieja Meat from a *cocido* served with a sauce made of fresh peppers, aubergines, and tomatoes.

Tomates rellenos Tomatoes stuffed with olives, anchovies, rice, and peppers.

Truchas a la montañesa Trout cooked in white wine, bay leaves and onions. A white wine with a hint of oak, such as Marqués de Riscal Limousin.

HOTELS

Aranda de Duero *Bodegas Peñalba López* operates a twenty-room hotel and visitors' centre in the vineyards.

Fermoselle *Hacienda Durius,* a hotel and visitors' centre attached to the bodega.

León You need stir no further than the memorable *Parador San Marcos*, housed in a splendid sixteenth-century monastery, to sample a good range of wines from the Comarca de León and Bierzo in its sophisticated restaurant.

Quintanilla de Onésimo (Valladolid) *Bodegas Arzagua Navarro* runs a sizeable twenty-four-room hotel.

Sierra de Gredos The *Parador de Gredos* is a former hunting lodge of King Alfonso XIII, set high in the mountains among pine forests, and a delightful place to stay.

Valladolid The best hotels are the four-star *Meliá Olid, NH Ciudad de Valladolid*, and the somewhat old-fashioned, but recently renovated *Felipe IV*.

Zamora A pleasant stopping place in this historic old town, especially if you are en route for Galicia, is the *Parador de Turismo de Benavente Fernando II de León*, with its magnificent Renaissance courtyard. Also *Convento I*, hotel-restaurant in converted religious house; *Meliá Horus Zamora* with restaurant.

RESTAURANTS

Aranda de Duero *Mesón de la Villa* serves good charcuterie and regional dishes.

Burgos *El Asador de Aranda "Papamoscas"* is the best place to eat lamb.

León *Independencia; Parador San Marcos* serves regional dishes and a selection of local wines; *Regia* provides local fare and Bierzo wines in a thirteenth-century house near the cathedral.

Palencia *Lorenzo* and *Casa Damián* are both run by the same family, and are worth the stop when approaching Valladolid from Burgos or Santander.

Peñafiel *Asador Mauro* for roast suckling pig and baby lamb, and regional wines; *El Molino de Palacios* is housed in an old mill, and is especially good for roasts.

Valladolid *Mesón Panero, La Criolla, La Parrilla de San Lorenzo, La Perla de Castilla, and La Coya* all offer well-cooked Castilian dishes and a selection of regional wines.

Cataluña

The resourceful and industrious Catalans claim that they make wines in
a greater variety of styles than any other region of Spain, pointing to the
fine table wines from the Penedès; the sparkling wines (described under
"Sparkling Wines", page 176), which account for ninety per cent of Spanish
production; the maderized *rancio*; and the old *solera*-made dessert wines
of Tarragona, which so resemble málaga or sweet oloroso sherry. All these,
plus some of the best brandy in the country and a gamut of vermouths
and liqueurs, both indigenous varieties and foreign brands made under
licence, give substance to that claim.

Comprising as it does the provinces of Gerona (Girona), Barcelona,
Lérida (Lleida), and Tarragona, with an area about the size of the

DO Zones

① Ampurdán-Costa Brava
② Pla de Bages
③ Alella
④ Penedès
⑤ Tarragona
⑥ Priorato
⑦ Terra Alta
⑧ Conca de Barberà
⑨ Costers del Segre

Netherlands or Belgium, Cataluña's landscape is rugged and broken – it has been described as a flight of stairs rising from the coastal plains of the Mediterranean towards the peaks of the Pyrenees and its associated spurs to the south. In the more mountainous areas the slopes must be terraced to allow a foothold for the vines, a system still employed in upland areas such as Priorato, and you need not leave the *autopista* from Barcelona through Penedès to see disued terraces. Many of these were constructed during the late nineteenth century, when every available patch of ground was pressed into service to supply wine to a France desolated by phylloxera – at that time the epidemic had not yet reached Spain.

Patterns of agriculture date from the times of the Kingdom of Aragón, which was among the most powerful medieval states of the Mediterranean, when James the Conqueror (1213–76) turned over the territories recaptured from the Moors to working farmers, instead of handing over large estates to the nobility, as happened in Castile. The tradition of the small peasant farmer was reinforced by the institution of the *Rebassa Morta*, which provided for a landowner to lease part of his land to smallholders for the plantation of vineyards in exchange for half of the produce. To this day, the great bulk of the wine is made in cooperatives from fruit supplied to them by small farmers, and even the large and well-known private firms buy more grapes than they grow in their own vineyards, and purchase large amounts of cooperative-made wine for further elaboration in their bodegas.

Until recent decades the emphasis was on bulk rather than quality, and the emergence of wines rivalling those of Rioja in quality is a comparatively new phenomenon. This has largely been a matter of climate. Vineyards are thickest on the ground in the coastal regions of Penedès and Tarragona, with their Mediterranean climate and hot summers. When the grapes were fermented by traditional means, temperatures often rose to 30°C or more, and much of the fruity nose and flavour were lost during a fast and furiously tumultuous fermentation. The first stainless-steel vats with provision for cooling were introduced about 1960, and they are now extensively used.

This has revolutionized the Catalan wine industry. Given suitable soils and the excellent quality of the fruit, there is now nothing to prevent the production of wines as good as those from more northerly European regions; indeed, Cataluña has one advantage over the traditional producers of fine wines such as Bordeaux, Burgundy, and the Rhine, namely the reliability of its weather conditions. In Cataluña the winters are not too severe and the summers uniformly sunny and hot, though still tempered by breezes from the Mediterranean. Harvests are good in ninety per cent of the years.

Grape Varieties

Although Torres and increasing numbers of other bodegas have successfully acclimatized noble vines from France and Germany, most of the wine is made from native grapes. The most important varieties are as follows.

WHITE

Macabeo Known as Viura in Rioja and widely grown in Spain, Macabeo produces pale-coloured, fruity, well-balanced wines, resistant to oxidation and well suited to cold fermentation.

Xarel-lo A native of Cataluña, known in Alella as Pansà Blanca, its wines are of medium alcoholic strength, though over-acidic in the relatively rare years when it does not fully ripen. It is one of the grapes much used for making sparkling wines in Penedès.

Parellada (or **Montonec**) Grown exclusively in the higher areas of Penedès Superior and Conca de Barberà, its musts are low in alcohol (nine to eleven per cent) and high in acidity. Again much used for making sparkling wines, it is the Parellada which gives the exceptionally fresh and fruity bouquet to still wines such as the Torres Viña Sol.

Garnacha Blanca Also grown in Rioja, it is extensively cultivated in Terra Alta and the Campo de Tarragona, yielding wines high in alcohol with little acid.

Malvasía This is the well-known Malmsey, of Greek origin but grown for centuries in Spain. Its musts are fruity and medium strength and (as also in Madeira, where malmsey is the name given to the sweetest wine) when fortified and aged gives rise to dessert wines like those of Sitges.

Pansé Grown in the Campo de Tarragona, Conca de Barberà, and the Ribera d'Ebre, it matures late and prolifically, but the wines are coarse and high in alcohol.

Pedro Ximénez Much grown in Andalucía, where it is used for sweet wines, and in Montilla, where it makes dry, Pedro Ximénez is grown in small amounts in Priorato and Terra Alta, where its musts are mixed with those from other varieties.

BLACK

Cariñena Originally a native of Aragón, Cariñena produces wines of eleven to twelve per cent strength, robust, rich in colour and extract, but without a very distinctive nose.

Garnacha Peluda A mutant of the Garnacha Tinta, cropping more regularly but otherwise with similar characteristics.

Garnacha Tinta Another native Spanish grape, very widely grown in Rioja and other parts of Spain. Its wines are high in alcohol (eleven to fourteen per cent), full-bodied, fruity, and deep in colour, but oxidize rapidly, turning a brick-red when aged in wood.

Garrut A noble black grape indigenous to Cataluña and recently revived by TORRES for its Grans Muralles.

Monastrell A native grape, also widely grown in the central regions of Spain. The yield is small, but its wines are deep in colour, of considerable elegance, and mature well.

Ull de Llebre (Ojo de Liebre) The well-known Tempranillo of Rioja or Cencibel of Valdepeñas, which produces wines of eleven to thirteen per cent strength, with good acid balance, a distinctive fruity nose, and good ageing properties.

Sumoll Once widely cultivated in Penedès, it produces aromatic but very tart wines and is now being phased out.

In addition to these native grapes, foreign grapes are increasingly grown in the area, and the following varieties have been authorized by various *consejos reguladores*. Red: Cabernet Sauvignon, Cabernet Franc, Merlot, Pinot Noir; white: Chardonnay, Chenin Blanc, Sauvignon, Gewürztraminer, Riesling, Muscat d'Alsace.

Cataluña now possesses nine *denominaciónes de origen*, of which control has passed from the Instituto Nacional de Denominacines de Origen (INDO) to the Institut Català de Vì (INCAVI), an agency of the Generalitat, the autonomous governing body of Cataluña. The areas, together with production figures for 2002, are: Penedès (27,692 hectares, thirty-eight million litres); Alella (560 hectares, 850,000 litres); Tarragona (7,280 hectares, twenty-four million litres); Priorato (1,600 hectares, 1.9 million litres); Ampurdán-Costa Brava (2,033 hectares, 6.5 million litres); Conca de Barberà (6,000 hectares, 24.5 million litres); Terra Alta (9.200 hectares, 20.2 million litres); Costers del Segre (4,165 hectares, 8.7 million litres); Pla de Bages (600 hectares, 1.2 million litres); and the new Montsant (2,020 hectares, 6.6 million litres). In addition, a new DO Cataluña was instituted in November 1999 which embraces all the above *denominaciónes*; but producers must choose between registering for one of the smaller, more specific DOs or the general one, which permits them to make wine with grapes – or a combination of grapes – from any of the DOs already in place.

Vintages

Vintages, as has been explained, are remarkably consistent, and the only really poor one in recent decades was in 72. The following chart for the Penedès gives some idea of the variation.

Year	Red Wines	White Wines
79	*fair to good*	*good*
80	*good*	*good*
81	*excellent*	*very good*
82	*very good*	*very good*
83	*good*	*good*
84	*excellent*	*good*
85	*good*	*good*
86	*fair*	*good*
87	*excellent*	*good*
88	*very good*	*excellent*
89	*good*	*fair*
90	*very good*	*very good*
91	*excellent*	*excellent*
92	*good*	*good*
93	*very good*	*excellent*
94	*good*	*very good*
95	*excellent*	*excellent*
96	*very good*	*very good*
97	*very good*	*very good*
98	*very good*	*excellent*
99	*very good*	*very good*
00	*very good*	*very good*
01	*very good*	*very good*

With a car, it is not difficult to plan a visit to the Catalan winemaking areas, since four of them (Ampurdán-Costa Brava, Alella, Penedès, and Tarragona) lie along the axis of the A17 *autopista* from the French border to Barcelona, and its southward extension (the A7) to Tarragona and Valencia. Costers del Segre is near Lérida (Lleida). Conca de Barberà, Priorato, Montsant, and Terra Alta, in the hills of the hinterland, are less easy to reach and require fairly time-consuming side trips, but there are notable consolations in the rugged and well-wooded countryside, the hill-top castles, and in the great monasteries of Montserrat and Poblet, which are so closely associated with the development of viticulture in the region. Cataluña also boasts the pleasant coastal resorts and the splendid cliff scenery of the Costa Brava; and it would be a single-minded devotee of wines who did not pause in Barcelona to visit Gaudí's astonishing cathedral of La Sagrada Familia or its magnificent museums and galleries, or in Tarragona to see the remarkable Roman remains.

Large bodegas, such as Miguel Torres, with its elaborate visitors' centre, are happy to welcome visitors without an appointment, arranging guided tours and instructive tastings. Even in the smallest co-op you will be able to taste and buy the wine, and will receive a friendly welcome – if you can muster enough Spanish to communicate. If in doubt about your reception, ask the porter at the hotel to telephone beforehand. Catalan food, meanwhile, is interesting and varied, though sometimes more than substantial in country hotels and restaurants.

The Catalans take their regained autonomy seriously. Under Franco it was forbidden to speak in Catalan; now it is a point of pride to do so. Most signs and place-names are now in Catalan, which is a separate language and not a dialect, although the Castilian equivalent is generally added. This also applies to menus, although these sometimes appear exclusively in Catalan in smaller restaurants. The waiter or proprietor will, however, always explain in Castilian.

Albet i Noya
DO w dr (p) r res ☆☆→☆☆☆☆ *93 94 95 96 97 98 99 00 01*
Sant Pau d'Ordal (Barcelona). DO Penedès. Best-known Spanish producer of organic wines, growing a range of grapes in its fifty-hectare vineyard. The best wines are labelled Collecció and made from 100 per cent Chardonnay, Xarel-lo, Syrah, Tempranillo, and Cabernet Sauvignon.

Alella
DO (r p am) w dr sw II'III
The tradition of winemaking in this small region dates from Roman times, but it is now threatened by urban expansion from Barcelona towards the south. Despite a surprising extension of the DO zone in 1989, of the 1,400 hectares that were under vine in 1967 only 560 survive, producing mostly white wine. The grape varieties approved by the *consejo regulador* are: for white wines, Xarel-lo (or Pansà Blanca), Pansà Rosada, Garnacha Blanca, Parellada, Chardonnay, Sauvignon Blanc, and Chenin Blanc; and for the reds, Tempranillo (Ull de Llebre), Garnacha Tinta, Garnacha Peluda, Cabernet Sauvignon, Merlot, Syrah, and Pinot Noir. Many of the vineyards, all of them small and few exceeding 1.5 hectares, are owned by professionals dedicated to preserving the wine industry. The vines are planted on granitic slopes sheltered from the prevailing east wind, one of

which – with a northerly aspect – produces wine of high acidity. The wine from the other, southerly, slope is rather sweeter and lower in acidity.

Altar wine

Altar wine, made without chemical additives especially for the celebration of Holy Communion, is a speciality of Tarragona – particularly of DE MULLER, supplier to popes Pius X, Benedict XV, Pius XI, Pius XII, and John XXIII. It is often made with Macabeo from the CAMPO DE TARRAGONA, alcohol being added to the musts to make a sweet white *generoso* of fifteen per cent strength. Recently De Muller has been making drier wines to suit a younger generation of priests. It is exported all over the world in resin-coated steel drums.

Alvaro Palacios

DO r ☆☆☆ 93 94 95 96 97 98 99 01

Gratallops (Tarragona). DO Priorato. For fifteen years this gifted emigré from the Rioja has been making some of the most fashionable and expensive red wines in Spain, with grapes from his tiny twenty-five-hectare vineyard. They include Finca Dofí, L'Ermita, and Les Terrases.

Amadis

r res ☆☆☆ 95 96 97 98 99 00

Much sought-after red PRIORATO from small and sophisticated Rotllan Torra.

Ampurdán, Cavas del

DO r p w sp ★→★★

Perelada (Girona). DO Ampurdán-Costa Brava. Situated in the village of Perelada near Figueres, on the verges of the Pyrenees, this is the sister ship of the well-known cava concern of the Castillo de Perelada. The white and rosé Cresta Azul are made in *cuves closes* pressurized to only a quarter of the normal extent. It was this concern that produced a *cuve close* sparkler, the subject in 1960 of the celebrated "Spanish Champagne" case, brought by the French Champagne companies in England and known in France at the time as "the Second Battle of the Marne".

Ampurdán-Empordà-Costa Brava

DO r p w dr ☆→☆☆

Known as "Empordà-Costa Brava" in Catalan, this is a fairly recently demarcated region, abutting the Pyrenees in the province of Girona and inland from the holiday coast. A problem for the growers here is the prevailing north wind, the *tramontana*, which blows 100 days in the year, at velocities of up to hurricane force. For this reason the vines are staked. The area under vine is 2,033 hectares, with thirty bodegas, and the main vine varieties are the black Garnacha Tinta and Cariñena, and the white Macabeo and Xarel-lo. Seventy per cent of the wine, made mostly in co-ops, is rosé, but the region is now producing a fresh young *vi novell* in the manner of Beaujolais Nouveau.

Anoia, Comarca de

VdC r (p)

Winemaking area bordering PENEDÈS to the west.

Bach, Masía

DO r p w dr sw res ☆☆

Sant Esteve Sesrovires (Barcelona). DO Penedès. Shortly after World War I some elderly bachelor brothers from Barcelona built a flamboyant, Florentine-style mansion in PENEDÈS and started a small winery. It grew, like Topsy, and when it was taken over by the great cava firm of Codorníu, it embraced vast cellars and 9,042 oak casks with a total capacity of 7.8 million litres. Once gloriously independent and renowned for its sensational sweet, oaky Extrísimo, it is now just another large Penedès producer.

Baix Ebre-Montsià, Comarca de

VdC (r) w dr

Winemaking area lying in the extreme south of the province of Tarragona, bordering the Ebro delta.

Barcelona

Barcelona, the capital of Cataluña and second city of Spain, takes its name from the Carthaginian general Hamilcar Barca, but was founded long before his time, probably by the Phoenicians. Apart from being an excellent base for visits to the wine areas of Cataluña, it is a metropolis of outstanding interest. Do not miss the old city, with its Roman remains, its Gothic cathedral, the Palace of the Generalitat (the governing body of Cataluña), and the flower-decked Ramblas; or again, the many buildings by that master of Art Nouveau, Antonio Gaudí, foremost among them the extraordinary unfinished cathedral of La Sagrada Familia. There are many museums and galleries, including those devoted to primitive art, Picasso, and Miró. Once every two years, in mid-March, Barcelona is of special interest to gastronomes, when it mounts the Salón Internacional de la Alimentaria, one of the largest international wine and food fairs, with exhibits from every Spanish wine firm of consequence. It is a city long famous for its high culinary standards, and in recent years especially its restaurateurs have been among the most innovative in Spain.

Bombonas

These large, loosely stoppered pear-shaped glass carboys were used for making the traditional, sherry-like Catalan RANCIO (*rancí*) wine in an open-air *campo de añejamiento*.

Campo de Tarragona

DO r w dr sw l

Large sub-denomination of the DO TARRAGONA occupying much of the centre of the province and embracing the towns of REUS, Valls, and TARRAGONA itself. Its vineyards are the most extensive of the Tarragona region, but in recent years farmers have found that hazelnuts are a more profitable crop, and the plantations, which amount to some seventy per cent of arable land in certain areas, have been making severe inroads. Most of the wines are sturdy whites made from the Macabeo (Viura) and Xarel-lo, known locally as the Cartuxà, but the Cooperativa de Valls makes small quantities of a smooth, ruby-coloured wine from the Ull de Llebre (Tempranillo) and Trepat – however, the whole production is pre-empted by the Mossos d'Esquadra, the security force of the Catalan Generalitat.

Campo de añejamiento

Name given to the open-air plots where the maderized RANCIO, known in Catalan as *vi rancí*, is made in BOMBONAS by a method corresponding to that of a rough-and-ready *solera* (*see* "Sherry", page 161). *Campos de añejamiento* are occasionally to be found in other parts of Spain, as in La Seca near Valladolid (*see* "Castilla-León", page 53).

Can Ràfols dels Caus

DO r w dr ☆☆☆ *89 90 91 94 96 97 98 99 00 01 02*

Avinyonet del Penedès (Barcelona). DO Penedès. This small firm, established in 1980, makes first-rate wines from Cabernet Sauvignon, Cabernet Franc, and Merlot. Its Gran Caus spends seven months in cask and twenty in bottle, and is a big, fruity wine with masses of extract. The Gran Caus Blanco, a blend of Chardonnay, Chenin Blanc, and Xarel-lo, is clean and buttery, and there is a first-rate rosé (01) made from 100 per cent Merlot. Also less expensive Petit Caus Blanco and Tinto, and a good Extra Brut Reserva cava containing forty per cent Chardonnay and sixty per cent Xarel-lo. Best is Caus Lubis (98) 100 per cent Merlot.

Castillo de Perelada, Cavas del
DO r p w dr res ✩✩→✩✩✩✩ *94 96 98 99 00*

Perelada (Girona). DO Ampurdánu-Costa Brava. Better known for its cavas (*see* "Sparkling Wines", page 183), the Castillo also makes some worthwhile red, rosé, and white wines. Best are the red Gran Claustro Reserva (00), Finca Malaveína (99), and Castillo de Perelada Ex-Ex3 (99) made from Cabernet Sauvignon, Garnacha, Cariñena, and Merlot.

Castell del Remei
DO r p w dr res ✩✩→✩✩✩✩ *95 96 97 98 99 00 01*

Penelles (Lleida). DO Costers del Segre. Old-established firm with its own vineyards in the extreme west of Cataluña, near Lleida. It was taken over by the Cusiné family in 1982, who embarked on extensive replanting of the vineyards with Sauvignon Blanc, Chardonnay, Cabernet Sauvignon, and Merlot, and also modernized the bodega, replacing most of the old oak casks. The wines include good Chardonnay blends, good Gotim Bru and Oda made from Tempranillo, Merlot, and Cabernet Sauvignon, and Premium 1780, for which the Merlot is replaced by Garnacha.

Celler Bàrbara Forés
DO w dr p r ✩✩→✩✩✩✩

Gandesa (Tarragona). DO Terra Alta. Worthwhile wines from one of the best bodegas in Terra Alta. Best is the red Coma d'en Pou (99 01).

Celler de Capçanes
DO p r ✩✩ *99 00 01*

Celler de Capçanes (Tarragona). DO Montsant. Large ex-cooperative, makes some of the best new-wave wines from Tarragona. Typical is the Cabrida (99), meaty, concentrated, and somewhat tannic, repaying time in bottle.

Cims de Porrera
DO r res ✩✩ *96 97 98 99 01*

Porrera (Tarragona). DO Priorato. One of the best known of PRIORATOS, fruity, complex, concentrated, and long. The second label is Solanes.

Clos de l'Obac
r res ✩✩✩✩ *95 99 01*

Prestigious red PRIORATO from COSTERS DEL SIURANA.

Clos Mogador
DO r res ✩✩✩→✩✩✩✩✩ *94 95 96 97 98 99 00 01*

Gratallops (Tarragona). DO Priorato. All the wine from this tiny bodega owned by René Barbier (no connection with Freixenet) is made from grapes grown on its twenty hectares of vineyard. The *reserva*, containing forty per cent Garnacha, forty per cent Cabernet Sauvignon, and twenty per cent Syrah, is deep, complex, and elegant, and made to last for decades.

Comercial Vinícola del Nordeste (COVINDOSA)
DO w dr sw p r ✩→✩✩✩

Mollet de Perelada (Girona). DO Ampurdán-Costa Brava. The bodega belongs to the same group as the CASTILO DE PERELADA and CAVAS DEL

AMPURDAN. It makes drinkable white, rosé, and red wines, but the most noteworthy is the sweet Garnatxa de L'Emporda of 14.5° strength made from a blend of red and white Garnacha.

Conca de Barberà
DO (r p) w dr

This hilly region, bordering PENEDÈS to the west, was demarcated in 1989 and in 2002 its 6,000 hectares of vineyards produced 2.4 million litres of wine, most of it white and for everyday drinking – though standards are improving with the construction of hi-tech wineries – made from Parellada and Macabeo (Viura) grapes. Its Parellada grapes are also much in demand for making the cavas of SANT SADURNI D'ANOIA. A little red and rosé is also made from the Ull de Llebre, Sumoll, and Trepat, but until recently the only concern to bottle any wine (in REUS, outside the region) was the great co-op combine, the UNION AGRARIA COOPERATIVA. *See also* Bodegas CONCAVINS.

An interesting development in the region has been the purchase by Miguel TORRES of the twelfth-century castle of Milmanda and its surrounding vineyards, after investigation had shown that the soils were exceptionally well-suited for growing Cabernet Sauvignon and Pinot Noir. It is here that the grapes for the exciting new Grans Muralles (*see* TORRES) are grown; the plantations also supply Chardonnay for the exceptional MILMANDA, vinified and matured in cask.

Conca de Tremp, Comarca de la
VdC r w dr (p)

Area to the far northwest of Cataluña in the province of Lleida, better known for its hydroelectric schemes than its wine. The better wines are made by Bodegas Valeri Vila, which produces red, white, and rosé Castell d'Orcau. A major development in the area has been the plantation of large vineyards by Miguel TORRES.

Concavins, Bodegas
DO w dr (p) r ☆☆

Conca de Barberà (Tarragona). DO Conca de Barberà. This former co-op sells its well-made wines as Castillo de Montblanc and is best known abroad for its red and white Santara.

Conde de Caralt
DO r p w dr sw res ☆☆→☆☆☆

Sant Sadurní d'Anoia (Barcelona). DO Penedès. Long known for its sparkling wines made by the Champagne method, this old family firm is now part of the Freixenet group, sharing premises with Segura Viudas (*see* "Sparkling Wines", page 176) and RENÉ BARBIER. Apart from sparkling wine it now produces a range of sound still wines: Conde de Caralt Tinto, Rosado, Blanco Seco, Blanco Suave. The light, soft red *reservas*, containing a proportion of Cabernet Sauvignon and a hint of cedarwood at the end, are wines of considerable sophistication. *See also* "Sparkling Wines".

Conti, Celler Oliver
DO r ☆☆→☆☆☆

Capmany (Girona). DO Ampurdán-Costa Brava. New estate in the Ampurdán producing a single, high-quality Bordeaux blend (Cabernet Sauvignon/Cabernet Franc/Merlot) in soft Graves style.

Cooperativa Agrícola de la Germandat
DO w dr r g ☆☆☆ *00*

Villalba dels Arcs (Tarragona). DO Terra Alta. Large co-op with 750 hectares of vineyard and 500 oak *barricas*, making some of the best wine from

Terra Alta, including a barrel-fermented white and a good red called
Vall de Berrvs.

Costers del Segre
DO r p w dr res sp ☆☆→☆☆☆

Demarcated in 1986, the region comprises four small separate sub-zones
around the city of Lleida: Artesa to the northeast, Valls de Riu Corb and
Les Garrigues to the southeast, and Raimat to the west. It was undoubtedly
because of the successful development of the 3,000-hectare estate of
RAIMAT by the Raventós family of Codorníu and the growing prestige of
its wines, inside and outside Spain, that the region was demarcated. The
total area under vine is 4,165 hectares and production of wine in 2003
was 8.7 million litres. A large quantity of the grapes goes to RAIMAT and to
SANT SADURNI D'ANOIA for making cava; the other two wineries of note in
the region are CASTELL DEL REMEI and the small co-op of L'Olivera.

Costers del Siurana
DO r (w dr sw) res ☆☆☆☆ *94 95 96 97 98 99 01*

Gratallops (Tarragona). Carles Pastrana was one of the originators of a
new generation of handcrafted Priorato wines made in tiny dedicated
bodegas. His Clos de l'Obac and Miserere, made from a blend of
Garnacha, Cabernet Sauvignon, Merlot, Cariñena, and other grapes,
remain among the most sought after. There is also an intriguing sweet
Dolç de l'Obac containing Garnacha, Cabernet Sauvignon, and Syrah.

COVIDES
DO r w p sp res ★★→★★★

Sant Sadurní d'Anoia (Barcelona). DO Penedès. Large former co-op
making good Duc de Foix white and equally attractive Cabernet
Sauvignon, Cabernet/Tempranillo, as well as first-rate Duc de Foix cava.

Dalmau Hermanos
DO r w dr sw am gen ☆→☆☆

Tarragona. DO Tarragona. The firm began blending and exporting wines
as long ago as 1830, and, like many of the large houses in Tarragona, it is
mainly concerned with bulk shipments abroad. It does, however, bottle
some of its better wines exclusively for the home market.

De Muller, SA
DO r p r g sp ★→★★★

Reus (Tarragona). DOs Tarragona, Terra Alta, Priorato, Cava. Famous old
Tarragona firm and long-term supplier of altar wines to the Vatican, has
recently moved its headquarters and bodegas to REUS. If its Solimar table
wines are not up to Penedès standards, it makes a good Chardonnay
fermented in barrel (02), while its fortified and *solera*-made wines –
reminiscent of old and round olorosos and málagas – are outstanding. They
include Priorat Dom Joan Fort tinto, Solera 1865; Priorat Dom Berenguer
Tinto, Solera 1918; and Aureo Semidulce, Solera 1954. *See also* ALTAR WINES.

Europvin Falset SA
DO r ☆☆→☆☆☆ *99 00 01*

Falset (Tarragona). DO Montsant. A new bodega linked to Bordeaux-based
Christopher Canan, whose red wines are made by RENÉ BARBIER of
CLOS MOGADOR. They are an elegant Laurona and Vinyes de Laurona.

Falset, Comarca de
DO r w dr ★→★★★

Up-and-coming sub-denomination of the DO TARRAGONA to the southwest
of the region.

Fransola

w dr ★★★ 02

Marvellously fresh and fruity white wine from Miguel TORRES, containing ninety per cent Sauvignon Blanc and ten per cent Parellada.

Gran Coronas Mas La Plana

DO res ☆☆☆☆ 93 94 95 99

The famous varietal from Miguel TORRES, which in its 1970 vintage was declared the best Cabernet Sauvignon in the world at the 1979 *Gault-Millau* "Olympiad".

Hill, Cavas

DO r p w dr s/sw sw res sp ★★→★★★ 94 95 96 97 98 99 00 02

Moja-Vilafranca del Penedès (Barcelona). DO Penedès. The Hill family emigrated from England in 1660, planting a vineyard and establishing a bodega which was much expanded by Don José Hill Rose in 1884. The firm now makes wines by the Champagne process and a range of still wines, including good whites Blanc Bru and Chardonnay, also excellent red Gran Civet and Gran Toc *reservas*. Masía Hill is one of Penedès' best young Tempranillos. *See also* "Sparkling Wines", page 181.

INCAVI

Following the death of General Franco and the restoration of local autonomy to the four provinces of Cataluña between 1978 and 1980, the Instituto Nacional de Denominaciónes de Origen (INDO) transferred control of the demarcated regions and oenological stations in Cataluña to an agency of the revived Generalitat, the Institut Català de Vi. Under the energetic direction of the late Jaume Ciurana, it demarcated the new regions of CONCA DE BARBERA, TERRA ALTA, COSTERS DEL SEGRE, and PLA DE BAGES, and more recently MONTSANT.

Josep Anguera Beyme

DO r ☆☆☆ 97 98 99 00 01

Darmos (Tarragona). DO Montsant. The wines from this bodega, labelled Joan d'Anguera, show steady improvement. The 97 El Bugader, made from a blend of Syrah, Garnacha, and Cabernet Sauvignon, meaty and well-structured, is very nice indeed.

León, Jean

DO r w dr res ☆☆☆ 91 93 94 95 96 97 98 99

Plà del Penedès (Barcelona). Founded in 1962 by a Los Angeles restaurateur of Spanish descent and bought by Miguel TORRES in 1995, this small bodega was the first to plant foreign vines in Penedès and, unusually for Spain, grows all its own grapes. The vineyards extend to sixty hectares, planted mainly with Chardonnay and Cabernet Sauvignon. The annual production amounts to 10,000 bottles of Chardonnay, 200,000 of Cabernet Sauvignon, and a little Merlot, much of it exported to the USA. All are excellent wines. The Chardonnay (00), fermented in cask, is round and buttery. To begin with the reds were huge, fruity, and tannic, but have become lighter in style.

Marqués de Alella

DO ★★→★★★ DYA

Fresh cava and elegant white Alella wines from PARXET.

Marqués de Monistrol

DO r p w pt dr res ★★→★★★ 96 98 99

Sant Sadurní d'Anoia (Barcelona). DO Penedès. Old family concern now belonging to Arco Bodegas Unidas (Berberana, *see* "Rioja" page 125). Excellent sparkling wine since 1882 and still wines since 1974. Best are refreshing and incipiently *pétillant* young Blanc de Blancs (forty per cent Parellada, forty per cent Macabeo, twenty per cent Xarel-lo), bottled only two months after the grapes are picked; a fruity rosé; a good Cabernet Sauvignon/ Tempranillo and a premium Reserva de l'Hereu made from Cabernet Sauvignon, Merlot, and Tempranillo. *See also* "Sparkling Wines", page 181.

Mas Martinet Viticultors

DO r res ☆☆☆☆ *94 95 96 97 98 00 01*

Falset (Tarragona). DO Priorato. The Pérez Ovejero family has been in the vanguard of making high-quality, estate-grown PRIORATOS. Here, Garnacha is enhanced with Cabernet Sauvignon, Merlot, and other grapes, of which the intense, juicy, and well-structured Clos Martinet is a leading example.

Masies d'Avinyo

DO w dr p r ☆☆ *98 99 00 01*

Santa María d'Horta d'Avinyo (Barcelona). DO Pla de Bages. Well-made Abadal wines: barrel-fermented Chardonnay (01), *rosado* (01), Merlot (00), and Cabernet Sauvignon (99). The second-label Ramón Roqueta is to be avoided.

Mascaró, Cavas

DO r p w dr ☆☆→☆☆☆ *92 93 94 96 97*

Vilafranca del Penedès (Barcelona). DO Penedès. Makers of a lemony, fresh Viña Franca white as well as an excellent Anima Cabernet Sauvignon (96). *See also* "Sparkling Wines", page 182 and "Spirits, Aromatic Wines, and Liqueurs", page 191.

Milmanda

DO w dr ☆☆☆☆ *98 99 00*

This beautiful Chardonnay from Miguel TORRES takes its name from the castle of Milmanda below the monastery of POBLET, where the grapes are grown. Vinified and matured in small oak casks, it is one of Spain's best white wines.

Mollet de Perelada, Cooperativa de

DO r p w dr gen ★→★★

Perelada (Girona). DO Ampurdán-Costa Brava. Simón Serra, the French-trained oenologist of this sizeable co-op with a storage capacity of some 2.8 million litres, is making very fresh red, white, and rosé *vi novell* after the style of Beaujolais Nouveau, of which the most attractive is perhaps the red. It also makes a very full and fruity dessert wine from Garnacha Blanca grapes, fermented with their skins for a few days before the addition of grape spirit, and small quantities of a good sparkling wine. *See also* COMERCIAL VINICOLA DEL NORDESTE.

Montsant

DO w dr ☆☆→☆☆☆

Tiny DO of 2,020 hectares formed in 2001. An enclave within PRIORATO sharing much in common with its wines and now fashionable with well-heeled entrepreneurs from further afield. *See* CELLERS DE CAPÇANES.

Montserrat, Monastery of

On the northwest fringe of PENEDÈS, the imposing monastery of Montserrat is an essential stop for any visitor to the area. The precipitous hill to which it clings, with its massive outcrops of rounded, weather-worn rock, is extraordinary enough to have inspired Wagner's *Parsifal*, and appropriately enough the splendid boys' choir is the oldest musical conservatory in Europe. In medieval times its vineyards, along with those of POBLET, were among the most important in Cataluña. The Virgin of Montserrat, whose blackened wooden image is preserved in the monastery, is the patron saint of Cataluña, and the monastery, which was founded in the eleventh century, is the object of mass pilgrimages. Its huge restaurants have panoramic views across PENEDÈS.

Olivella Sadurní

DO w dr p r ★★

Subirats (Barcelona). DO Penedès. Old family firm housed in new bodega. Wines include a Prima Lux made with Xarel-lo and Chardonnay, and Prima Nox and Prima Vesper reds, the first a 100 per cent Cabernet, the second a Cabernet/Merlot blend.

Parxet

DO w dr ★★→★★★ DYA

Santa María de Martorelles (Barcelona). DO Alella. Founded in 1920 as a cava producer, Parxet began making still wines in 1981. It owns 200 hectares of vineyards, mostly Pansà, and makes its new-style white wines by cold fermentation in stainless steel without ageing in oak. Its MARQUES DE ALELLA Clásico, 100 per cent Pansà Blanca, is light and clean with delicate fruit. The Marqués de Alella Seco, made with additional Macabeo and Chenin Blanc, is aromatic and lively, and there is a light and delicious Marqués de Alella Chardonnay. *See also* "Sparkling Wines", page 183.

Penedès

DO r p w dr s/sw sw am g res ★→★★★★

Penedès, with its 27,692 hectares of vineyards and 189 bodegas, is a limestone region southwest of Barcelona best known for its sparkling wines. But the best of its still wines rival those of Rioja. The region slopes upwards from the Mediterranean coast to a height of 700 metres in the hills of the interior. The temperate climate and adequate rainfall are ideal for growing grapes. There are three sub-regions: the hotter Bajo Penedès near the coast is best suited for black grapes; the Medio Penedès, at an average altitude of 200 metres, produces some sixty per cent of the wine from the area as a whole, much of it made from the white Xarel-lo and Macabeo and used for sparkling wines; and the typical grape of the cooler and hillier Penedès Superior is the white Parellada, used both for the dry, fragrant, and refreshing white wines and also for sparkling cavas, which are widely produced in the area.

The *consejo regulador*, whose standards are rigorous, approves the following native varieties: the white Macabeo (or Viura), Xarel-lo, Parellada (or Montonec), and Subirat-Parent; and the black Cariñena, Monastrell, Garnacha Tinta, Samsó, and Ull de Llebre (or Tempranillo). Cabernet Sauvignon, Chardonnay, and a variety of other foreign noble grapes, first acclimatized by Miguel TORRES, are also permitted. Owing to the favourable climate, vintages are remarkably consistent, the best of the last two decades are: 91, 93, 94, 95, 96, 97 98, 99, 00, and 01. The only really disastrous year in the last three decades was 1972.

The best base for visiting Penedès is VILAFRANCA DEL PENEDÈS where there is one of the best wine museums in the world. Many visitors prefer to stay in one of the comfortable hotels of the pleasant, relatively unspoilt coastal resorts of SITGES, which is just half-an-hour's drive from Vilafranca, or in BARCELONA, an hour away by the *autopista*.

Pere Guadiola
DO w dr p r l'll

Capmany (Girona). DO Ampurdán-Costa Brava. The bodega produces a
range of wines under the label of Floresta. Preferred are the young white
and rosé, but the *crianza* improves considerably with airing in the glass.

Piñol, Vinos
DO w dr sw r ☆☆→☆☆☆

Batea (Tarragona). DO Terra Alta. Small firm, one of the few in Terra Alta,
making worthwhile white and red wines under the labels of L' Avi Arrufi
and Nuestra Señora del Portal. Best is the red Mather Teresina Selección.

Pla de Bages
DO ☆→☆☆

New Catalan DO centred on Manresa, northwest of Barcelona. Best of its
bodegas is MASIES D'AVINYO, maker of good Abadal. There is also a large
co-op, Cellers Cooperativa d'Artés, making drinkable Artium table wines.

Poblet, Monastery of

Famous Cistercian monastery dating from the twelfth century in the hills
of CONCA DE BARBERA, and the burial place of the kings of Aragón and
Cataluña. During the Middle Ages it was the abbeys and monasteries that
fostered viticulture and, along with those of the monastery of MONTSERRAT,
the vineyards of Poblet were important in keeping winemaking traditions
alive in Cataluña. It has magnificent arched wine cellars.

Pontons

Superior vineyard area at a height of 700 metres in the PENEDÈS, developed
by Miguel TORRES for growing the native Parellada and the Riesling,
Gewürztraminer, and Chardonnay from the cooler climes of northern
Europe. Hailstorms are dispersed by rockets charged with silver iodide.
The results are so promising that other producers are moving into the
area.

Porrón (*Catalan* Porró)

This conical-shaped glass drinking vessel with a spout and handle, which
is now sold in debased form in souvenir shops, has been used for centuries
in Cataluña. When in use, the spout does not touch the lips, so that the
porrón enables a party of drinkers to enjoy their wine without the need for
glasses.

Priorato (*Catalan* Priorat)
DO r (w dr) am ☆→☆☆☆

A small, mountainous enclave, with 1,600 hectares of vines and forty-seven
bodegas, within the much larger DO TARRAGONA. The name, "priory",
derives from that of the ruined monastery of SCALA DEI. The grapes are
grown in small plots or on terraces in the volcanic soils of the steep
hillsides: decayed lava with a high silica content which, in combination
with the hot summer sun, produces good, very full-bodied wines with high
alcohol content. Authorized grapes for the red wines are the traditional
Garnacha Tinta, Garnacha Peluda, and Cariñena, as well as the more
recently introduced Cabernet Sauvignon, Merlot, and Syrah; and for the
whites, the Garnacha Blanca, Macabeo (Viura), and Pedro Ximénez. The
traditional wine is red, almost black in colour, with a huge amount of
extract, containing up to eighteen per cent alcohol. It was formerly much
in demand for blending. Another speciality was a golden-yellow RANCIO.
With modern methods of fermentation in stainless steel, the wines, while

still preserving their rich, brambly taste, have been lightened and now average around 13.5 degrees of alcohol.

A decade or so ago only three firms bottled and labelled their wines, but with the spread of small boutique bodegas such as COSTERS DE SIURANA, CLOS MOGADOR, and ALVARO PALACIOS with expert and dedicated winemakers at the helm, the region has become the most fashionable and fastest growing in Spain, producing some of the country's choicest and costliest wines. Currently some sixty new producers, including TORRES, Freixenet, and the Rovira family are about to release their wines. But has the hype from the likes of Robert Parker been overdone? Sober voices in the trade have their reservations and predict that, despite "the fantastic black colours and bewitchingly aromatic surface aromas", the promise of structural immortality is illusory and that after a certain (and not necessarily unduly long) time in bottle the wines will inevitably "reduce down to the intrinsic elements of terroir and defy the prognostications of gurus who should have done a little more homework".

Puig y Roca, Cellers
DO w dr r ☆☆☆ 94 96 97 98 00
El Vendrell (Tarragona). DO Penedès. New firm with growing reputation and international grapes, making estate-grown wines: most noteworthy are a barrel-fermented Augustus Chardonnay; a good Cabernet Sauvignon, and an intense and fruity Augustus Merlot.

Rabassa Morta
The historic form of land tenure in Cataluña was that a proprietor leased land to a farmer on condition he planted it with vines, and that the former should share the produce with the farmer, whose right to cultivate the land expired only with the death of the first-planted vines. After phylloxera (from 1876) and replanting with grafts, the life of the vines became much shorter, and the institution fell into disuse. It is now usual for small farmers to own their land.

Raimat
DO w dr r res ★★★ 94 95 96 97 98 99 00
Raimat (Lleida). DO Costers del Segre. Winemaking in the area had declined until the sparkling wine company of Codorníu (*see* "Sparkling Wines", page 178) bought the castle of Raïmat and its 3,000-hectare estate. With advice from Davis University in California, 2,245 hectares have been irrigated and planted with selected native vines, together with Cabernet Sauvignon, Chardonnay, Merlot, and Pinot Noir. A brand-new winery has been built into the side of a hill, and as a result Raïmat is now making some of the most attractive wines from Spain. They include first-class Raimat Chardonnay (01 02); a red Abadía made from a blend of Cabernet Sauvignon, Tempranillo, and Merlot; wines made with 100 per cent Merlot and 100 per cent Tempranillo; and a "4 Varietales" containing Cabernet Sauvignon, Merlot, Tempranillo, and Pinot Noir. Perhaps most attractive of all is a Raïmat Cabernet Sauvignon made with eighty-five per cent Cabernet and fifteen per cent Merlot, aged in oak and bottle, with strong varietal characteristics and overtones of coffee and tobacco.

Rancio (*Catalan* **Ranci**)
A maderized or oxidized white wine, popular in various parts of Spain, but particularly so in Cataluña. *Rancios* vary enormously in character and quality, from the tart and sour product of a peasant bodega or local co-op,

where the wine is left to oxidize without sufficient hygiene, to the perfected wines of DE MULLER. These are sweetened with *mistela* (a must in which fermentation has been checked by the addition of alcohol) or *arrope* (boiled-down must), and aged in *solera* (*see* "Sherry and Manzanilla", page 161). They can be magnificent, resembling in their different styles very round and old oloroso sherries. Another type is made in large glass carboys, known as *bombonas*, and left partially unstoppered and open to the sun and wind. What all *rancios* have in common is a deep golden-yellow colour, a sherry-like nose, more or less marked, and a high degree of alcohol.

Raventós i Blanc, Josep María
DO w dr ☆☆→☆☆☆
Sant Sadurní d'Anoia (Barcelona). DO Penedès. Producer of a good 100 per cent Chardonnay and El Preludi Macabeo/Xarello/Parellada/Chardonnay. *See also* "Sparkling Wines", page 184.

René Barbier
DO r p w dr sw res ★★ *96 97*
Sant Sadurní d'Anoia (Barcelona). DO Penedès. This company, like CONDE DE CARALT, with which it shares cellars at the *cavas* of sparkling wine firm Segura Viudas near Sant Sadurní d'Anoia in PENEDÈS, is part of the Freixenet group (*see* "Sparkling Wines", page 179). It makes a first-rate100 per cent Chardonnay Selección fermented in barrel; and there are good reds made with a blend of Cabernet, Tempranillo, and Garnacha. The bodega, which has invested heavily in new oak, also makes a 100 per cent Cabernet Sauvignon.

Reus
Important wine town with 80,000 inhabitants, west of TARRAGONA. It is here that the great cooperative combine, the UNION AGRARIA COOPERATIVA, has its central site for blending, maturing, and bottling wines from outlying co-ops. There are also many private firms engaged in elaborating both wines and vermouth.

Ribera d'Ebre
r w dr ☆
Sub-denomination of the DO TARRAGONA, adjoining the DO TERRA ALTA in the far southwest of the province of Tarragona. The wines are like those of FALSET but rather more acidic.

Rotllán i Torra
DO r w sw ☆☆☆ *95 96 97 98 99 00*
Torroja del Priorat (Tarragona). DO Priorato. Small family winery with twenty-four hectares of vineyard and 300 oak *barricas*. Their Reserva and Balandra are dark and traditional; Amadis and Tirant, aged in French oak and incorporating small amounts of Merlot, Syrah, and Cabernet Sauvignon are more spectacular. Also a sweet Blanqueria containing Moscatel/Pedro Ximénez/Macabeo/Garnacha Blanca.

Roura
DO w dr p r ☆☆→☆☆☆ *97 98 99 02*
Alella (Barcelona). DO Alella. This bodega makes good 100 per cent Chardonnay and Sauvignon Blanc, 100 per cent Merlot, and Cabernet Sauvignon/Tempranillo.

San Miguel de las Viñas, Cofradía de
Catalan order of *tastevins*, celebrating its functions at the historic old castle of San Martí, near Vilafranca del Penedès. Its light-hearted inauguration

ceremony, which is conducted to the strains of a band in traditional costume, includes drinking from a PORRON and distinguishing blindfold between a white and a rosé wine – which is much more difficult than it sounds – on pain of continuing the tasting indefinitely.

San Sadurní de Noya (Catalan Sant Sadurní d'Anoia)

Township in the east of PENEDÈS towards Montserrat, where most of the *cavas* making sparkling wines are situated. Now that firms such as MARQUÉS DE MONISTROL, CONDE DE CARALT, RENÉ BARBIER, and Freixenet are diversifying, it has also become a centre for making still wines. *See also* "Sparkling Wines", page 184.

Sangre de Toro

r ★★

Sound and big-selling Garnacha/Cariñena from Miguel TORRES.

Sant Cugat del Vallés, Monastery of

Located between BARCELONA and MONTSERRAT, Sant Cugat, with its beautiful Romanesque cloisters, was one of the great religious houses that did so much to foster viticulture. Among its monuments is a deed recording the gift of a vineyard to the monastery in 927.

Santamaría, Cellers

DO r (p) res ★★→★★★

Capmany (Girona). DO Ampurdán-Costa Brava. Small family concern with a history of winemaking going back to 1767. Made with a Cariñena and Garnacha blend, its Gran Recosind is ruby in colour, full-bodied, soft, fruity, and long on the finish.

Scala Dei, Cellers de

DO r res (w dr p) ☆☆ *96 97 98 99 00*

Scala Dei (Tarragona). DO Priorato. Housed in an ancient stone building near the ruined monastery, founded in 1974, and recently taken over by Codorníu, the Cellers are equipped with stainless-steel fermentation vats, underground *depósitos* coated with epoxy resin and oak *barricas*. The bodega makes a young red Novell, now called Negre Scala Dei and containing 100 per cent Garnacha, and a good Cartoixa Scala Dei aged in oak and bottle, which is deep and complex in flavour, and has 13.8 per cent alcohol. Recently it has been rather eclipsed by the newer boutique wineries.

Scala Dei, Monastery of

When visiting the bodega it is worth walking the ten minutes to the great roofless monastery, choked with trees and aromatic vegetation, a victim of Mendizábal's anti-clerical reforms of around 1830. According to legend, it was founded when angels were seen ascending and descending a ladder into the heavens, and the theme of the ladder is embodied in the seal of the *consejo regulador* for PRIORATO. There are now plans to restore the ruin.

Serra, Jaume

DO r w dr (p) res ☆☆

Vilanova i la Geltrú (Barcelona). DO Penedès. Formerly one of the only three producers in ALELLA. Has transferred to PENEDÈS. Good barrel-fremented Chardonnay and reliable Tempranillo, Cabernet Sauvignon, and Merlot.

Sitges

The *Subur* of the Romans, Sitges, on the coast south of BARCELONA, is now a pleasant and relatively unspoiled seaside resort with a palm-fringed promenade, though bursting at the seams in summer. Its famous dessert wine, made by allowing Malvasía and Moscatel grapes to wrinkle on the branch before picking, with the addition of grape spirit to the must and long maturation in oak, is now made only in minuscule amounts. Sitges celebrates a harvest festival in early September, with a harvest queen, decorated floats, the solemn pressing and blessing of the first fruits, and a fountain flowing with free wine.

Tarragona

The imperial *Tarraco* of the Romans, Tarragona is a city rich in historic remains, including massive walls built by the Romans on a much earlier foundation of monolithic blocks, an aqueduct and forum, and a fine Gothic cathedral. It is an important wine city specializing in the blending of wines, both from the surrounding region and other parts of Spain, and their bulk export. It is most reputed for the Tarragona *clásicos*, sweet dessert wines, both red and white, containing up to twenty-three per cent alcohol. A cheap *clásico*, sold as "Tarragona" and also known by the less complimentary names of "poor man's port" and "red biddy", was once popular in English pubs. Another important activity in the town is the production of vermouths and liqueurs.

Tarragona

DO r w dr dr am ☆→☆☆☆

Tarragona (7,280 hectares under vines; an output in 2002 of 2.4 million litres) is divided into the sub-regions of CAMPO DE TARRAGONA, FALSET, and RIBERA D'EBRE. Its beverage wines, made mainly in co-ops, were traditionally sturdy and high in alcohol, and lacked the delicacy of those from PENEDÈS to the north. But there has been a great improvement in quality, and the wines, from the DO MONTSANT, recently split off from the DO Tarragona, rival those of PRIORATO in quality.

Terra Alta

DO r w dr ☆→☆☆☆☆

Terra Alta, with 9,200 hectares under vine and forty-six bodegas, lies in mountainous country in the extreme southwest of Cataluña, bordering the province of Teruel. It makes robust but characterful wines, white, and red, the best from the Celler Cooperativa Gandesa VINOS PIÑOL and CELLER BARBARA FORES. Now that modern equipment has been installed, the wines are becoming lighter.

Torres, Miguel

DO r p w dr s/sw sw g res ★★→★★★★ 92 93 94 95 96 97 98 99

Vilafranca del Penedès (Barcelona). DO Penedès. The Torres family has been making and selling wine in PENEDÈS since the seventeenth century. It is now the most reputed firm in Cataluña to make still wines, exporting all over the world – exports to the USA alone top two million bottles annually – and still very much a family concern.

Miguel Torres Riera, with a French degree in oenology, has been responsible for introducing a variety of foreign vines to PENEDÈS, grown in addition to native vines on the firm's 1,852 hectares, where the quality of the fruit has been improved by clonal selection of the vines and careful evaluation of the soils for the most suitable varieties. In common with almost all Spanish bodegas, the firm also buys grapes from independent farmers. Foreign varieties include the white Chardonnay, Gewürztraminer, Riesling, and Sauvignon Blanc; and the red Cabernet Sauvignon, Cabernet Franc, Petit Syrah, and Pinot Noir. Those vines that are accustomed to a cooler habitat are grown on sites in the hills of the hinterland.

Torres has been responsible for many technical innovations and was the first winery in Spain to introduce temperature-controlled fermentation in stainless steel. Typical of the cold-fermented whites are the dry, fresh, and fruity Viña Sol (100 per cent Parellada); Gran Viña Sol (ninety per cent Chardonnay, ten per cent Parellada); the marvellously fruity single-vineyard Fransola made from eighty-five per cent Sauvignon Blanc and fifteen per cent Parellada; the Waltraud Riesling; and luscious semi-dry Esmeralda, made with Gewürztraminer and Moscatel d'Alsace. MILMANDA, a Chardonnay of exceptional quality, is fermented and aged in traditional fashion in small French-oak casks.

The red wines spend less time in oak casks – usually one to two years – and correspondingly more time in bottle than most traditional Riojas, and are therefore less oaky in nose and flavour. Both the fruity and full-bodied Sangre de Toro and Gran Sangre de Toro are made with native grapes; Coronas contains eighty-six per cent Tempranillo and fourteen per cent Cabernet Sauvignon, and Gran Coronas eighty-five per cent Cabernet Sauvignon and fifteen per cent Tempranillo. Viña Magdala contains seventy per cent Pinot Noir, and the award-winning Gran Magdala and single-estate MAS BORRAS are made with 100 per cent Pinot Noir.

More recent introductions are the light and fruity Atrium Merlot for summer drinking, and the superb Grans Muralles, a full-bodied red made from a blend of the native Monastrell, Garnacha Tinta, Garró, and Samsó. Pride of the Torres stable are the newly introduced Reserva Real, velvety, smooth, intensely fruity, and long in finish and GRAN CORONAS MAS LA PLANA Black Label, made with selected Cabernet Sauvignon. It is now history that at the Gault-Millau "Olympiad" in Paris in 1979, the 70 vintage was judged by a short head to be better than the less fully developed 70 Château Latour.

The institution of the DO Cataluña has enabled Torres to source some of its wines, like the white and red Nerola, from different DOs in the region. The first-rate Praedium, made entirely from grapes grown in the firm's new Priorato vineyard, is also labelled as DO Cataluña, since it is vinified at the main winery in the DO Penedès.

Torres also makes excellent brandies (see "Spirits, Aromatic Wines, and Liqueurs", page 193) and an orange liqueur; owns vineyards and a winery in Chile; and makes wine in California and China.

Trobat, Bodegas
DO w dr r p g ★★

Garriguella (Girona). DO Ampurdán-Costa Brava. This small firm makes the fresh, delicious rosé served by the Hotel-Restaurant Ampurdán in Figueres, and also produces a Blanc de Blancs, a trio of red wines, and a good 100 per cent Garnacha dessert wine.

Unión Agraria Cooperativa
DO r p w dr sw res ☆→☆☆

Reus (Tarragona). This vast combine, founded in 1962, handles wines from all the co-ops in the province. It sells large quantities of wine to private firms for further elaboration and bottling. More select growths are matured in the central cellars at REUS, and then bottled and sold under their own label. Among its many labels are the red and white Tarragona Unión; red, white, and rosé Yelmo; the dry, semi-dry, and rosé Collar Perla, Collar Zafiro, and Collar Rubí; and also *reservas*.

Vallformosa, Masía
DO r p w dr g res ☆☆→☆☆☆ *96 97 98 99 00*
Vilobí del Penedès (Barcelona). DO Penedès. A family firm producing fresh white and rosé wines, and good red *crianzas* and *reservas*, made with native grapes and Cabernet Sauvignon. *See also* "Sparkling Wines", page 185.

Ventura, Jané
DO w dr p ☆☆☆ *94 95 96 97 98 99 00 01*
El Vendrell (Tarragona). DO Penedès. Small family firm making a fresh, flowery, well-structured white wine from Xarel-lo and Parellada; a distinguished rosé from Tempranillo and Garnacha; a really first-rate red ('94) from ninety per cent Cabernet Sauvignon and ten per cent Tempranillo; and sparkling wines (*see* "Sparkling Wines", page 185).

Vilafranca del Penedès
Vilafranca, a small town off the *autopista* between BARCELONA and TARRAGONA, is the centre of the still wine industry in PENEDÈS and the home of many of its best-known bodegas. It also makes sparkling wine by the Champagne process and is the headquarters of the Spanish offshoot of Cinzano. Apart from the bodegas, the great point of interest is the wine museum, installed in a thirteenth-century palace of the kings of Aragón, and one of the best in the world. The exhibits begin with tableaux illustrating winemaking from ancient times onwards. There are numerous examples of Greek, Carthaginian, and Roman amphorae. The main hall houses every type of agricultural implement, press, and barrel, many originating from old bodegas in the region; there are also pictures and drawings, drinking glasses, and PORRONES. The visit ends in a small bar, where local wines may be sampled. The museum is the headquarters of the old-established Academía de Tastavins de Sant Humbert, a wine fraternity devoted to maintaining traditions and quality of Penedès wines. Closed Monday.

Vinícola del Priorat
DO r w dr p ☆☆ *99 00 01 02*
Gratallops (Tarragona). DO Priorato. The Catalan Government closed the seven small village co-ops in PRIORATO in 1990 and constructed this brand-new plant with stainless-steel vats and up-to-date facilities, with a capacity of 750,000 litres. It numbers some 400 members with 480 hectares of vineyards, makes good white Mas de L'Alba and rosé Clos Gebrat, together with an excellent L'Arc Cabernet blend, and a fruity and full-bodied Onix, made from Garnacha and Cariñena.

Vins Valdosera
DO w dr sw (r) ☆☆→☆☆☆
Olèrdola (Barcelona). DO Penedès. This bodega has taken on a new lease of life since Agusti Torello, famous for his cava, took a hand in it. It offers a range of stylish white wines, most intriguing of which is the sweet Parent V. Tardia made from Subirat Parent, and a single, well-structured red Gravels d'en Cayo (00) which will improve with bottle age.

WINE AND FOOD

Cataluña has a long-established tradition of gastronomy. The raw materials, especially fish, shellfish, and fresh vegetables, are first rate. There are five famous sauces: *alioli* (the aïoli of Provence), and the piquant *picada, chanfaina, sofrito*, and *romesco*. Appetites are hearty, and in the smaller regional restaurants even the soups and starters are meals in themselves. Some of the restaurants found in places such as BARCELONA and the province of GIRONA are among the most sophisticated in Spain.

Anec amb figues Duck with figs.

Bolets Field mushrooms, often cooked on a charcoal grill with garlic and parsley. Torres Viña Sol, or other dry white.

Botifarra catalana A white sausage, resembling *boudin blanc*, which is eaten raw, cooked on its own, or used in other dishes.

Brandada de bacalla Creamed salted cod.

Calçotada Made only in the spring, this is spring onions sliced in half and grilled over a wood fire. They are served with a sauce resembling *romesco*. Marqués de Monistrol Vin Natur Blanc de Blancs or other light dry white.

Conill con cargols Young rabbits stewed with snails, herbs, cinnamon, almonds, and biscuit crumbs. One of the lighter reds from René Barbier, Hill, Conde de Caralt, Torres.

Costellas amb alioli Grilled ribs of lamb served with *alioli*. A medium-bodied red such as Raimat Tempranillo.

Crema catalana The local variation on cream caramel or "flan", made with egg yolks, milk, and cinnamon and topped with a brittle layer of caramel. Bach Viña Extrísimo.

Eriços de mar gratinados al cava Sea urchins *au gratin* with cava.

Escudella i carn d'olla This most typical of Catalan dishes is served in two parts: first the *escudella*, a meaty soup with pasta; and then the *carn d'olla*, a rich stew containing veal, chicken, pork, blood sausage, egg, breadcrumbs, and vegetables. A full-bodied red, such as Cartoixa Scala Dei, or the less potent red Bach Viña Extrísima.

Espinacs a la catalana Boiled spinach with pine kernels and raisins. Try one of the lighter *rancios*.

Fabes a la catalana Vegetable dish containing fresh broad beans, *botifarra negra* (Catalan black sausage), and belly of pork, together with spring onions, fresh mint, bay leaf, and parsley. Marqués de Monistrol rosé or Trobat Rosado.

Llagosta a la catalana Stewed lobster with onions, carrots, garlic, herbs, parsley, saffron, pepper, sweet paprika, also with chocolate, nutmeg, and brandy. Obviously calls for a wine of character such as the Torres Milmanda Chardonnay.

Mel i mató Fresh cream cheese with honey. Torres San Valentín or other sweet or semi-sweet wine.

Menja blanc A dessert of ground almonds, cream, kirsch, and lemon. Ideally, De Muller Moscatel Oro.

Oca amb peres Roast goose with pears.

Pa amb tomàquet Catalan country-style bread rubbed with fresh tomatoes, oil, and salt. It appears at the beginning of the meal and is sometimes served with slices of cured ham. Any full-bodied Mediterranean-type dry white.

Panellets A dessert made either with almonds, sugar, and eggs, or with pine kernels in the form of a marzipan.

Parrillada de prix amb salsa romesco Mixed grill of fish served with the typical Catalan *romesco* sauce and mayonnaise.

Perdiu a la catalana Partridge with herbs and lemon. Marqués de Monistrol Gran Reserva or Raimat Cabernet Sauvignon.

Pollastre amb chanfaina Chicken stewed with aubergines, green peppers, tomatoes, wine, and herbs, and served with croûtons. Cavas Hill Castell Roc or other light red.

Postre de músico Mixed plate of almonds, raisins, hazelnuts, walnuts, figs, or other dried fruit.

Rap a la Costa Brava Anglerfish cooked with fresh peas, red pimientos, mussels, saffron, garlic, parsley, and white wine, with a little lemon. Cavas del Ampurdán Pescador.

Salchichón de Vic A salami, for which the mountain town of Vic, in the Pyrenees near the French frontier, is famous.

Sarsuela de mariscs Literally a "variety show", this famous dish is a mixture of shellfish and firm white fish in a sauce of saffron, garlic, white wine, and parsley. With such seafood, Spaniards often drink red wine. The choice is between a good medium-bodied red, such as a Conde de Caralt or René Barbier Tinto, or a dry white like the Jean León Chardonnay with sufficient character to stand up to the rich flavours.

Sopa de musclos catalana A soup made with mussels and flavoured with tomatoes, *aguardiente*, garlic, parsley, and cinnamon. Torres Dry Solera, a dry sherry or montilla, or a spicy white from Valencia, Jumilla, or Alicante.

Sopa de pilotes Chicken broth containing small meatballs and flavoured with cinnamon, garlic, and chervil. Dry sherry.

Suquet Catalan fish and potato soup.

Truita de botifarra i mongetes A hearty omelet of Catalan sausage served with haricot beans, first boiled and then fried. Perelada Tinto Cazador or other honest-to-goodness red.

HOTELS

Barcelona Of its many hotels, the best are *Arts* and *Ritz*; reasonably priced establishments with high standards are the *Colón*, near the cathedral; the *Regente*; the traditional, but renovated *Oriente*; and new *Rivoli* in the Ramblas.

Sant Sadurní d'Anoia A new two-star hotel, the *Sol*, is four kilometres out on the Vilafranca road, with a good restaurant.

Sitges A good base for visiting Penedès, the best hotels are the four-star *Subur Maritim*, the three-star *Calípolis*, and the *Antemare*.

Tarragona A good base for visits to the outlying regions; the most comfortable hotels are the four-star *Ciutat de Tarragona*, *Husa Imperial Tarraco*, and three-star *Lauria*.

Vilafranca Two modern four-star hotels are the *Domo* and *Alta Penedès* with the restaurant offering good Mediterranean dishes.

RESTAURANTS

Barcelona is full of good restaurants. *El Racó d'en Freixa* is one of the best and most innovative restaurants in Spain. *Jaume de Provença* is especially good for Catalan and *cuisine naturelle* dishes. Neichel is the leading, most sophisticated Barcelona exponent of *cuisine naturelle*.

Reno was recently taken over, but remains is a classical Barcelona establishment with high standards. *Vía Veneto* offers excellent cooking and service with stylish surroundings in belle époque style. *Botafumeiro* and *Els Pescadors* both serve good fish and seafood.

Cambrils (near Tarragona) *Can Bosch* and *Joan Gatell-Casa Gatell,* both specialize in fish and seafood.

Espluga de Francoli *Hostal del Senglar* near the Monastery of Poblet is especially good for wild boar and game in general. With rooms.

Figueres *Empordà,* located in the Hotel Empordà outside Figueres, is a highly sophisticated restaurant started by Josep Mercader, founder of the new Catalan cuisine). *Hotel Durán* serves good Catalan food and a long list of Ampurdán wines.

Lleida *Forn del Nastasi, Sheyton, and Xalet Suis.*

Platja d'Aro *Big Rock,* a first-rate restaurant and hotel in a splendid fifteenth-century house, is run by one of Cataluña's leading chefs, Carles Carmós. A speciality of *Torre del Remei* is a dish of beef cooked with mangos, pepper, and chocolate.

Rosas/Roses *El Bulli* rated the best restaurant in Spain, is closed from 1 October to 1 April, while chef Ferrán Adriá experiments with new flavours and dishes. *Almadabra Park* is an outpost of the Subirós family, with cooking to match that of the *Empordà* in Figueres.

S'Agaro *La Gavina:* sophisticated international cooking in this most elegant and expensive of Costa Brava hotels.

Sitges Try the *menu de degustación* at *Maricel. Picnic* offers good fish, especially *sopa de pescadores.*

Tarragona *Merlot, Barquet,* and *Les Coques.*

Vilafranca del Penedès *Cal Ton* has good seafood and a worthwhile wine list. *Casa Joan* next to headquarters of Torres, is known for solid traditional fare.

Extremadura and the Southwest

Extremadura lies between the two Castiles and Portugal in the southwest of Spain. It suffered from mass depopulation after the expulsion of the Moors in the thirteenth century, and again in the sixteenth, when the Extremeños joined in the conquest of the New World.

It remains an empty and sparsely populated area, and in its high *sierras*, clothed with cork-oak, beech, and chestnut, sheep are more numerous than humans. Cultivation of vines is somewhat sporadic, the most densely planted area being the new DO of the Ribera del Guadiana in the province of Badajoz, comprising the sub-zones of Ribera Baja, Ribera Alta, Tierra de

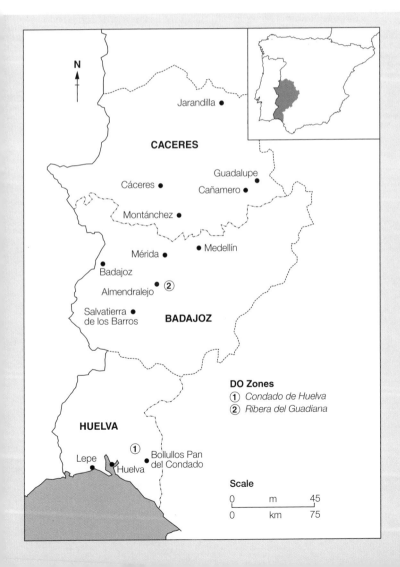

Barros, Matanegra, Cañamero, and Montánchez. Here, summers are hot and rainfall low, with an annual average of only 411 millimetres. The principal grape is Cayetana Blanca, with an astonishingly high yield – thirty-six hectolitres per hectare – of a neutral white wine of low acidity.

Of the annual output of some seven million litres, much goes to Jerez, Asturias, and Galicia for blending; the remainder is consumed locally or distilled. Not so long ago, only a handful of bodegas bottled their wines, but since the demarcation of Ribera del Guadiana the number of officially registered bodegas – some making much-improved wines – has risen to 106.

There are two small areas in Extremadura – Cañamero and Montánchez – that produce *flor*-growing wines of marked individuality; but to taste them you will have to visit the region. Although often ignored by foreign tourists, it is of great scenic and historical interest, with its forgotten towns of Medellín and Trujillo, the birthplaces of Cortés and Pizarro, the splendid monastery of Guadalupe, and, above all, Mérida, with its little-known and marvellous Roman monuments.

The other vine-growing area in the far southwest is the demarcated region of Condado de Huelva, again with nostalgic associations, since it was from Palos, near the city of Huelva, that Columbus first sailed for the Americas. It is known for decent white table wines but more for *generosos* in various sherry styles, which would be more familiar if they had not for many years been sent to Jerez de la Frontera for blending.

Almendralejo

The main wine town of the demarcated region of Ribera del Guadiana in the province of BADAJOZ. Its main street is crowded with bodegas and distilleries.

Badajoz

A province of Extremadura which flanks the Portuguese frontier and lies between the provinces of CÁCERES to the north and CONDADO DE HUELVA to the south. The principal vine-growing area is TIERRA DE BARROS.

Bollullos par del Condado

The most important wine town in the DO CONDADO DE HUELVA, with numerous bodegas making white table wine as well as sherry-like *generosos*. It is also a centre for distilling the *holandas* used for making brandy (*see* "Spirits, Aromatic Wines, and Liqueurs", page 190).

Cáceres

r w dr

Province of Extremadura bordering Portugal and to the north of BADAJOZ, whose most characterful wines are CAÑAMERO and MONTANCHEZ. The other winemaking areas are those of Miajados, west of GUADALUPE, and Jerte, Hervás, Cilleros, and Ceclavin, which are scattered around the historic old towns of JARANDILLA and Plasencia in the north of the province. In the main, their wines are *tintos* and *claretes*, but Cilleros on the Portuguese border makes a sturdy white, characteristically turbid and of around fifteen per cent strength.

Cañamero

DO w dr ☆☆

This small hill town in the Ribera del Guadiana, situated a few miles southwest of GUADALUPE, is famous for a *flor*-growing white wine much sought after by Spanish aficionados. The soils consist of clays layered with slate and quartzite and the vineyards extend to 1,200 hectares.

Eighty per cent of the grapes are made up of the white Alarije, Bomita, Airén, and Marfíl; red varieties are Garnacha Tinta, Morisca, Palomino Negro, and Tinto Fino. The wines are made in the cement vats of small bodegas and develop a film of yeasts on the surface in the manner of sherry. They are aged in oak casks and become turbid after fourteen to eighteen months, but subsequently clear. The wines are a yellow colour, becoming paler with age; round and smooth on the palate with a fragrant, sherry-like nose, and fifteen per cent alcoholic strength.

Condado, Vinícola del
DO w dr g ★
Bollullos par del Condado (Huelva). DO Condado de Huelva. The best of the co-ops in the DO CONDADO DE HUELVA, making white table wines and *generosos* in the style of sherry. Best of the whites is the refreshing Privilegeo del Condado, made from 100 per cent Zalema. Its sherry-style *generosos* include a *fino*, *oloroso*, and sweet.

Condado de Huelva
DO w dr g ☆
The province of Huelva lies in the southwest corner of Spain, between the Portuguese frontier and the Atlantic. The demarcated region covers 6,000 hectares and in 2002 produced 3.9 million litres of wine, which comprised white table wine, *generosos* of the sherry type, and other wine used for distillation. The region has always been overshadowed by its more famous neighbours, Jerez and Montilla, and the best of its *generosos* were sent to Jerez for blending. However, when the region was demarcated in 1964 this practice was outlawed. The soils are chalky and of the same general type as those of Jerez, though they are darker in colour. In the past, ninety per cent of the vineyards were planted with the white Zalema, but this is being replaced by Palomino, Mantúa, Garrido Fino, Pedro Luís, and Pedro Ximénez. The *solera*-made *generosos* are of the same general types as those of Jerez – fino, amontillado, oloroso – but lack the finesse of the best sherry. The white table wines, now being cold-fermented, are acceptable enough for holiday drinking but have no great distinction.

Condado de Niebla
Ancient domain of the Guzmán Counts, who occupied it after its reconquest from the Moors, and now the heart of the vine-growing area of the province of Huelva.

Guadalupe
High in the mountains northeast of Mérida, the little town of Guadalupe clusters around a monastery founded by Alfonso XI in 1340, in thanksgiving for his victory over the Moors at Salado. It later became the shrine of the Conquistadores and was enriched by generations of princes and grandees; among its many treasures is a magnificent series of paintings by Zurbarán. The bars of Guadalupe are the best place to sample the *flor*-growing CAÑAMERO; it is also the house wine at the comfortable *parador*.

Huelva *See* CONDADO DE HUELVA.

INVIOSA, Bodegas *See* LAR DE BARROS-INVIOSA

Jarandilla
r ☆
The *claretes* from Jarandilla, in the north of the province of Cáceres, were once rated among the best in Spain, and were the prime favourites of the Emperor Charles V during his last years at the nearby monastery of Yuste.

Lar de Barros-Inviosa

DO w dr r res ☆→☆☆ *98 99 01 02*

Almendralejo (Badajoz). DO Ribera del Guadiana. Established in 1980, this concern makes the best-known wine from the TIERRA DE BARROS, but not from native grapes. The cold-fermented white Lar de Barros is made from Macabeo, and both the red Lar de Barros and the full-bodied and spicy Lar de Lares *reserva* are made from a Riojan blend of Tempranillo, Garnacha, and Graciano. Inviosa also makes a good Bonaval cava from Macabeo and is one of the few concerns in the Extremadura to export its wines, but is not what it was when it first put Extremaduran wines on the map.

Lepe

Small town west of HUELVA near the Portuguese frontier. Its wines, the precursors of sherry, were mentioned by Chaucer.

Martínez Payva, Bodegas SAT

DO w dr r ☆

Almendralejo (Badajoz). DO Ribera del Guadiana. One of the few concerns in Extremadura to achieve national distribution for its wines. The range includes a 100 per cent Cayetana white, a 100 per cent Chardonnay, and a drinkable red Payva made from a blend of Tempranillo, Mazuelo, and Graciano.

Medina, Bodegas

DO r p w dr ☆→☆☆☆

Puebla de Sancho Pérez (Badajoz). DO Ribera de Guadiana. Family firm founded in1931 with sixty-six hectares of vineyards. It makes a large range of wines, red, white, and rosé. Best are the red Jaloco and Marqués de Badajoz, both made from Cabernet Sauvignon, Tempranillo, and Garnacha.

Mérida

Once the tenth city of the Roman Empire, Mérida, in the north of BADAJOZ, is the best placed and most interesting town from which to visit the winemaking areas of Extremadura. Its Roman remains, including a theatre, a circus, an amphitheatre, and a triumphal arch, as well as bridges, aqueducts, and tessellated pavements, are among the most impressive in Europe.

Montánchez

DO Ribera del Guadiana r w dr ☆

This small village, high in the hills above MÉRIDA, is remarkable for making a red wine which grows a *flor* in the manner of sherry.

Ruíz Torres, Bodegas

w dr ★→★★

Cañamero (Cáceres). The only bodega of any size to make and bottle the individual *flor*-growing white wine of CAÑAMERO. Non-DO, it may be sampled at the *parador* or in the bars of nearby GUADALUPE. It also makes red *crianzas* and *reservas* from Cabernet Sauvignon, Cencibel, and Monastrell.

Ribera del Guadiana

DO w dr r ☆→☆☆

Newly demarcated DO with headquarters at Almendralejo, comprising the sub-zones of Ribera Baja, Ribera Alta, TIERRA DE BARROS, Matanegra, CAÑAMERO, and MONTANCHEZ. It currently covers 19,099 hectares of vineyard and 106 bodegas, the best of which are LAR DE BARROS-INVIOSA, VIÑA EXTREMEÑA, Marcelino Diaz (with a good red El Campillo), Sociedada Cooperativa San Marcos Almendralejo (Campobarro wines), and Casimero Torrinio Boraita (good red and white Viña Puebla).

Salas, Bodegas
DO g ☆☆

Bollullos par del Condado (Huelva). DO Condado de Huelva. Bodegas Salas is a family concern which makes some of the best of the sherry-like wines of the region.

SOVICOSA
DO w dr p ☆→☆☆ *DYA*

Bollullos par del Condado (Huelva). DO Condado de Huelva. This bodega, belonging to the Sanlúcar firm of José Medina y Cía (*see* "Sherry and Manzanilla", page 157), makes fresh young Viña Odiel from 100 per cent Zalema, the traditional and predominant grape of the region, which is among the best of its type.

Tierra de Barros
DO Ribera del Guadiana r w dr ☆→☆☆

The Tierra de Barros, centring on ALMENDRALEJO in the province of BADAJOZ, has the somewhat dubious distinction of making the cheapest wine in Spain, even "exporting" some of it to La Mancha! The village of Salvatierra de los Barros on the verge of Portugal does, however, make small amounts of an aromatic and intensely coloured red wine, highly prized by Spanish connoisseurs.

Viña Extremeña
DO w dr p r ☆→☆☆

Almendralejo (Badajoz). DO Ribera del Guadiana. Founded in 1970 this family firm owns 1,000 hectares of organically cultivated vineyard. Standards are high and it exports its wines on some scale. Among the labels are Palacio de Monsalud, Monasterio de Tentudia, Viña Extremeña, and Corte Real.

WINE AND FOOD

When General Junot sacked the monastery of Alcántara in 1807 and ordered its medieval manuscripts to be used for making cartridges, one was salvaged and sent to the famous chef Escoffier, who commented that "it was the only positive advantage which France reaped from the [Peninsular] War". It contained the first directions for the use of truffles, still abundant in the region, and for making *pâté de foie gras*. Its pheasant, Alcántara style remains a classic recipe, but today the region is perhaps best known for its remarkable *charcuterie – chorizo* (pepper sausage), *jamón serrano* (cured ham), and the rest. As regards the wines, the difficulty is to find the local growths in the better hotels and *paradors*, which offer the standard list of Riojas. Nevertheless, the house wine at the *parador* in Guadalupe is a thoroughly typical white Cañamero; in hotels and restaurants generally, the carafe wine (when available) will probably be a sturdy red or white from Almendralejo

Boquerones en adobo Fresh anchovies, marinated in olive oil, vinegar, garlic, parsley, and seasoning and eaten raw.

Cochifrito Lamb cooked and served in an earthenware dish with onions, garlic, paprika, freshly ground pepper, parsley, and lemon juice.

Coliflor al estilo de Badajoz Cauliflower, boiled and divided into florets, dredged in egg and breadcrumbs and then fried crisp in olive oil.

Frito típico extremeño Kid fried with garlic, parsley, black pepper, and bay leaves.

Huevos a la extremeña A sauce is first prepared with olive oil, onions, and fresh tomatoes, then boiled potatoes, *chorizo*, ham, and seasoning are added. Eggs are then broken on the top and the dish finished in the oven.

Huevos serranos Large tomatoes, halved, scooped out and stuffed with chopped ham, topped with fried eggs, and sprinkled with grated cheese, before being browned to perfection in the oven.

Riñonada A dish made with a mixture of lambs' kidneys and sweetbreads.

Solomillo de cordero Lamb marinated with salt, pepper, olive oil, and red wine, and cooked slowly with the marinade in a casserole.

HOTELS

Guadalupe The comfortable *Parador de Guadalupe* faces the monastery and is housed in a fifteenth-century hospice for pilgrims.

Mérida The four-star *Parador de Mérida* is housed in an historical convent and provides good regional wines and cooking.

RESTAURANTS

Badajoz *Aldebarán* with sophisticated cooking and an elegant ambience. *La Toja* serves Galician cuisine and seafood.

Cáceres *Atrio* is on the up and up and now one of Spain's best restaurants with spectacular food, wine, and cigars.

Guadalupe *Hospedería del Real Monasterio* serves typical dishes at moderate prices; *Mesón el Cordero* offers family cooking with local ingredients.

Huelva *Las Candelas* has good fish and seafood, as well as an extensive wine list; *Las Meigas* is known for good Galician cooking.

Jarandilla de la Vera *Parador de Turismo*; *Carlos V* at Losar de la Vera, eight kilometres from Jarandilla, provides good cooking and reasonable prices.

Mérida The *Parador de Turismo* has won various gastronomic awards for its cooking; *Altair* serves regional food, original and of high quality; and *El Caballo* offers good, simple dishes.

Puebla de la Reina (south of Mérida) It is worth the detour to visit *Mesón de la Jara Casa Andrés*, a small restaurant with atmospheric ambience and typical Extremeñian fare.

Galicia

Galicia, in the far northwest of Spain, bounded to the south by Portugal
and to the west and north by the Atlantic, comprises the provinces
of La Coruña, Lugo, Pontevedra, and Orense, of which the two last
produce significant amounts of wine. With its green hills, its chestnut
forests, its unspoiled sandy coves and wide *rías* (deep salt-water inlets
like fjords), it is a romantic part of Spain. Its wines, too, will appeal to
wine romantics.

The granitic soils and wet climate are similar to those of northern
Portugal, and traditional methods of viticulture, especially in the more

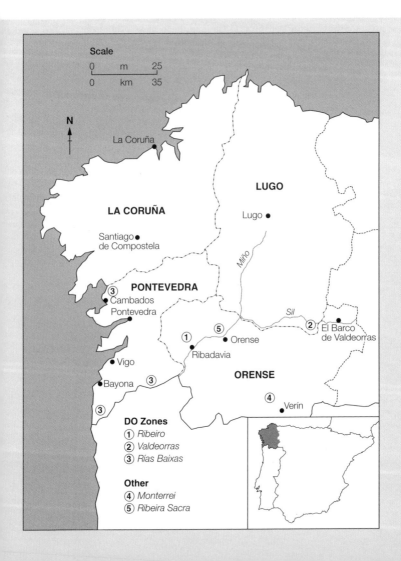

Scale

0   m   25
0   km   35

N

La Coruña

LUGO

LA CORUÑA

Lugo

Santiago
de Compostela

Miño

③ **PONTEVEDRA**

Cambados
Pontevedra

Sil

① ⑤

② El Barco
de Valdeorras

Orense

Ribadavia

Vigo

Bayona ③

ORENSE

④

Verín

③

DO Zones
① *Ribeiro*
② *Valdeorras*
③ *Rías Baixas*

Other
④ *Monterrei*
⑤ *Ribeira Sacra*

westerly coastal districts, are strikingly similar, with high-climbing vines being trained away from the damp ground on chestnut stakes, or grown in the form of a *pergola* along wires stretched from granite pillars. The traditional wines often undergo a prolonged secondary or malolactic fermentation, which leaves them with a subdued and refreshing *pétillance*. Since many of the grape varieties are the same or akin to those of the Vinho Verde area of Portugal, there is a strong family resemblance between the wines from both sides of the River Miño (or Minho).

On balance, Galicia consumes more wine than it produces and what has added to the natural difficulties of cultivating vines on the steep, terraced hill slopes is a persistent emigration from the region, especially to South America. There were until fairly recently only a handful of large cooperatives in the whole of Galicia, and it was common practice for the larger private firms to "stretch" the local wine, often flowery and fruity in flavour, but distinctly acidic, with neutral white wine from La Mancha.

The whole picture and perception of Galician wines has changed during the past decade. The reasons for this are twofold. First, there has been the rediscovery of the excellence of the indigenous grapes. The Albariño has long been famed, but grapes like the white Treixadura and red Mencía have been undervalued and neglected, and, one of the best, the white Godello (or Verdello) was approaching extinction until new plantations were undertaken. The second important change is associated with the *welcome* introduction of modern technology and cold fermentation in stainless-steel tanks. Hand in hand with this, a new generation of small boutique bodegas, often financed by entrepreneurs from outside the region and equipped with the very latest in hi-tech equipment, has sprung up in the Rías Baixas region. Their luscious and fragrant wines have little in common with those of the traditional Vinho Verde type, and are establishing themselves as among the best white wines from Spain – and they command correspondingly high prices.

In his definitive study of the wines, *Os Viños de Galicia*, Xosé Posada has listed and described no less than 136 grape varieties grown in the area. The more important of them are mentioned in the following A–Z listing, in connection with the different regions. Of these, five have been demarcated: Ribeiro, Valdeorras, and Monterrei in the province of Orense to the south; Rías Baixas, comprising three separate areas in the province of Pontevedra; and the newly demarcated Ribeira Sacra, north of the town of Orense and partly in the province of Lugo.

The best and most characterful wines are made with the white Albariño, sometimes with the addition of a smaller proportion of Treixadura or Loureira, from the zones of the Val do Salnés, O Rosal, and the Condado de Tea. In Monterrei, the most easterly region, the vines are grown low, *a la castellana*, as in most other parts of Spain, and are pruned and trained by the method of *poda en vaso* ("goblet-shape"). Its wines, mostly red and of some fourteen per cent strength, resemble those of León more closely than those from the more westerly regions of Valdeorras and Ribeiro, where the vines are grown higher and the wines are lower in strength and often *pétillant*.

Adega Condes de Albarei
DO w dr ☆☆→☆☆☆ *DYA*

Cambados (Pontevedra). DO Rías Baixas. Reliable wines made with 100 per cent ALBARIÑO and labelled as Condes de Albarei. Best is the barrel-fermented Carballo Galego.

Agro de Bazán
DO w dr ☆☆☆

Villanueva de Arosa (Pontevedra). DO Rías Baixas. Small but select winery, with thirteen hectares of vineyard planted exclusively with ALBARIÑO. The wines are sold as Granbazán, a regular Verde in a green bottle, and an Ambar made from free-run juice, which gives it exceptional fragrance. There is also a Limousin, one of the few from the region matured for a year in oak – but *see* Bodegas Del Palacio de FEFIÑANES.

Albariño
Most famous of Galician grapes, sometimes said to have been introduced to the region from the Rhine by the Benedictine monks from Cluny, similar to the Portuguese Alvarinho. Such is the quality of its white wines, crisp and flowery, with overtones of apple, pear, or peach, that in the first place (in 1980) a *reglamento* was promulgated covering wines made from the grape, irrespective of their origin. This was replaced in August 1988 by the DO RÍAS BAIXAS, covering the three areas where the Albariño is most prevalent.

Alanis
DO w dr ☆☆ *DYA*

Barbantes-Estación (Orense). DO Ribeiro. This Galician outpost of Allied Domecq's Bodegas y Bebidas makes a good white San Trocado from Treixadura and Torrontés.

Amandi
DO r ☆

According to tradition, the *claretes*, made exclusively from the Mencía grape and produced by winemakers in this small village in the new DO Ribeira Sacra, were once favourites with Caesar Augustus, who drank them with his spiced lamprey.

Cambados
Small seaside town to the northwest of Pontevedra, and the only place of any size in the VAL DO SALNES. Cambados celebrates an annual *Fiesta del Albariño* on the first Sunday of August, at which the wines are judged by expert tasters and are also available to the public.

Chaves, Bodegas
DO w dr pt ☆☆→☆☆☆*DYA*

Barrantes-Cambados (Pontevedra). DO Rías Baixas. A small family operation with its own vineyards and a bodega equipped with modern stainless-steel fermentation and storage tanks, as well as refrigeration equipment for precipitating tartrates. Most of the bodega's annual 50,000 bottles of good *pétillant* ALBARIÑO are only available in local hotels and restaurants, but its Castel de Fornos was one of the very first Albariño wines available in the UK.

Condado de Salvatierra
An alernative name for the CONDADO DE TEA.

Condado de Tea
DO w dr r ☆→☆☆☆ *DYA*

Also known as the Condado de Salvatierra, this small sub-zone of the DO RÍAS BAIXAS lies in the south of the province of Pontevedra, flanking the

River Miño. Principal grape varieties are the black Caíño, Brancellao, Espadeiro, and Alicante; and white Treixadura and ALBARIÑO. The predominant wines are traditionally red and claret-like, but the new hi-tech bodegas make fresh and characterful Condado de Tea white from at least seventy per cent Albariño or seventy per cent Treixadura (or a blend of both).

Condes de Albarei
DO w dr ✩✩✩ *DYA*

Cambados (Pontevedra). DO Rías Baixas. Flowery, 100 per cent ALBARIÑO from the VAL DO SALNES, made by Bodegas SALNESUR.

Cooperativa Vitivinícola do Ribeiro
DO r p w pt ★→★★

Ribadavia (Orense). DO Ribeiro. Situated in Ribadavia at the confluence of the Miño and Sil rivers, this is by far the largest co-op in Galicia, with some 800 members. It has modern equipment for vinifying, refrigerating, and bottling the wine, and produces some six million litres annually with storage capacity for another four million. The wines are sold under the PAZO label (meaning a baronial house). The white is flowery, dry, and not too acidic, without much sparkle, and has won prizes in international exhibitions. The red, *pétillant*, dry, and astringent to a degree, resembles the red Vinhos Verdes from over the border. The co-op also bottles superior white Amadeus, made with eighty-five per cent Treixadura and fifteen per cent Torrontés, and Viña Costeira with sixty per cent Palomino, thirty per cent Torrontés, and ten per cent Treixadura.

Cosecheros del Vino del Ribeiro
DO r w dr ✩

Ribadavia (Orense). DO Ribeiro. Bottlers of representative RIBEIRO wines under the labels of Ouro, Agarimo, and Campo Hermoso.

Fefiñanes, Bodegas del Palacio de
DO w dr ✩✩✩

Fefiñanes (Pontevedra). DO Rías Baixas. For decades before the present vogue for young, cold-fermented wines emerged, the most famous of ALBARIÑOS – now labelled as Fefiñanes – was produced by the Marqués de Figueroa, in a tiny bodega occupying a wing of the historic palace of Fefiñanes, on the outskirts of CAMBADOS. They were aged in oak casks for several years. The bodega now makes fragrant, peach- and citrus-flavoured, young, modern-style Albariño wines.

Fillaboa, Granxa
DO w dr ✩✩✩ *DYA*

Salvaterra de Miño (Pontevedra). DO Rías Baixas. This is one of the newer, small Galician bodegas (established in 1986). Its modern equipment helps in making one of the very best of the ALBARIÑO wines: the Fillaboa is fermented in small casks and the Selección de Familia in stainless steel.

Gallegas, Adegas
DO w dr ✩✩→✩✩✩ *98 99 00*

Salvaterra do Miño (Pontevedra). DO Rías Baixas. Its wines are of consistently high standard. Best is the complex, peachy Veigadares, fermented and aged for six months in barrel and made from eighty-five per cent ALBARIÑO, ten per cent Treixadura, and five per cent Loureiro.

Gallega, Bodegas

r w dr ☆

Los Peares (Lugo). Emigration and the tricky terrain of the steep valleys of the Miño and Sil mean wine production in this area of Lugo has greatly declined. This bodega's Tres Ríos, once produced locally, is now a blend of wines from León and La Mancha.

Gargalo SL

DO w dr r ☆☆→☆☆☆ *01 02*

Verín (Ourense). DO Monterrei. A good red wine, but the best from this bodega, founded in 1997, is the fresh and lemony white Terra de Gargalo with its herbal overtones made from a blend of Godello, Treixadura, and Doña Blanca.

Godeval SAT

DO w dr ★★

El Barco de Valdeorras (Orense). DO Valdeorras. A small bodega, sited in the ancient monastery of Xagoaza, was founded in 1986 by a group devoted to the revival of the traditional white Godello grape. It makes wine only from the Godello, the best being the clean and extremely fresh Viña Godeval.

Guitián Godello

DO w dr ☆☆☆ *00 01 02*

Rubiá de Valdeorras (Orense). DO Valdeorras. Made by Bodegas Tapada, these splendidly fruity, fragrant, and complex 100 per cent Godello wines, rated among the very best whites in Spain, typify the renaissance of native grapes in Galicia. The barrel-fermented type has the slight edge and improves with bottle age.

Joaquín Rebolledo SA

DO w dr r res ☆☆→☆☆☆ *94 96*

A Rua de Valdeorras (Ourense). DO Valdeorras. Small firm making a fresh and fragrant 100 per cent Godello (02), a good red Mencía, and a highly idiosyncratic *reserva* made from eighty-five per cent Merlot and fifteen per cent Cabernet Sauvignon, aged in local oak.

Jesús Nazareno, Bodega Cooperativa

DO r w dr ★→★★

El Barco (Orense). DO Valdeorras. Aside from bulk wine, this co-op bottles large amounts of very drinkable dry reds and whites, without *pétillance*, and sold as Valdeorras Tinto, Valdeorras Blanco, and Moza Fresca. It also makes a superior Aurensis Godello, fermented in barrel.

Lagar de Cervera

w dr ☆☆☆

See LAGAR DE FORNELOS.

Lagar de Fornelos

DO w dr ☆☆☆ *DYA*

O Rosal (Pontevedra). DO Rías Baixas. A subsidiary of La Rioja Alta (*see* "Rioja", page 138), this small firm makes a first-rate, 100 per cent Lagar de Cervera ALBARIÑO, pale -straw in colour, light, refreshingly acidic, and highly aromatic.

Lapatena, Bodegas

Non-DO w dr r (sp) ★→★★

Santa Cruz de Arrobaldo (Orense). Built in glass and marble, this huge, innovative bodega opened in 1990. It buys from local farmers and makes fresh, juicy white wines (best is the Fin de Siglo, a Palomino, Torrontés, and Treixadura blend), characterful reds, sparkling wine, and *aguardiente*.

Martín Codax

DO w dr ☆☆☆ DYA

One of the best of ALBARIÑOS from an innovative co-op, Bodegas de VILARIÑO-CAMBADOS.

Miño, Condado de

See CONDADO DE TEA.

Miño, River

The Miño, rising in the centre of Lugo province, is the principal river of Galicia, flowing south through Orense and finally forming the northern border of Portugal, where it is known as the Minho.

Monterrei

DO r p w dr ☆→☆☆

Small wine area and recently restored DO in the south of Orense, centred on the River Támega valley, bordered by Portugal, and subdivided into the VERIN, Monterrei, Castrelo, and Oimbra districts. Sheltered by the Sierra de Larouco, vines grown low *a la castellana* produce the strongest of Galician wines, of up to fourteen per cent strength. About seventy per cent of the wine is red from the Alicante Negro, Garnacha, Tintorera (Mencía), Tinta Fina, Tinta de Toro, and Monstelo. The main white grapes are Godello, Doña Blanca, and "Xerez" (Palomino). The largest producer is the Cooperativa de MONTERREI. The young GARGALO also makes first-rate whites and reds.

Monterrei, Cooperativa de

DO r p w dr ☆

Verín (Orense). DO Monterrei. Founded in 1963 and, until recently, the only concern in the region of Monterrei in the south of Galicia near the Portuguese border to bottle its wines. It makes fresh young red, rosé, and white wines labelled Monterrei, and a two-year-old Castillo de Monterrei.

Morgadío, Bodega

DO w dr ☆☆☆ DYA

Creciente (Pontevedra). DO Rías Baixas. Outstanding 100 per cent ALBARIÑO Morgadío: it is clean, flowery, and intense, with a long finish.

Moure, Adegas

DO w dr r ☆☆→☆☆☆ 99 00 01 02

Escairón (Lugo). DO Ribeira Sacra. This bodega is the flagship of the new DO. It makes an excellent white Abadía da Cova (02) ALBARIÑO, with eighty-five per cent Albariño and fifteen per cent Godello, and a 100 per cent red Mencía, clean, fruity, and well balanced.

Orense

Orense is the most southerly of the provinces of Galicia, bounded by Pontevedra to the west and Portugal to the south. It embraces the demarcated regions of RIBEIRO and VALDEORRAS, as well as MONTERREI and some smaller areas. Orense itself is not the most attractive of Galician towns, and it is more pleasant to stay in VERIN or on the coast.

Pazo

(r p) w dr ★ DYA

One of the biggest-selling and most frequently encountered branded Galician wines; made by COOPERATIVA VITIVINICOLA DO RIBEIRO.

Pazo de Barrantes, Bodegas
DO w dr ☆☆→☆☆☆ DYA

Ribadumia (Pontevedra). DO Rías Baixas. First-rate ALBARIÑO from the late Conde de Creixell of the Riojan Marqués de Murrieta.

Pazo de Señorans
DO w dr ☆☆☆ DYA

Meis (Pontevedra). DO Rías Baixas. New small bodega (founded in 1980) producing a fresh and fruity estate-grown ALBARIÑO. Made by the president of the *consejo regulador*, it is now one of the most consistent of all Albariños.

Pontevedra
Province in the southwest of Galicia, bordered by the River Miño and Portugal to the south, and by the Atlantic to the west. Its green and hilly coastline is deeply penetrated by the picturesque *rías*, on one of which stands the port of Vigo. It is in this region that the famous ALBARIÑO grape and the high-climbing vines, trained on wires stretched between granite pillars, come into their own. All three sub-zones of the DO RÍAS BAIXAS lie within this province.

Queimada
See "Spirits, Aromatic Wines, and Liqueurs", page 192.

Rías Baixas
DO w dr (r) ☆☆→☆☆☆

Instituted in 1988, the DO replaces a provisional measure of 1980 applying to the ALBARIÑO grape rather than the area of production. It covers the five sub-zones of the VAL DO SALNES, focusing on the town of CAMBADOS, O ROSAL, the CONDADO DE TEA lying back from the coast along the River Miño on the Portuguese frontier, and with the recent additions of Soutomaior and Ribera do Ulla. Their combined area is 10,197 hectares, of which 2,100 are demarcated, with 178 bodegas. Production in 2002 totalled 9.1 million litres.

Ribeira Sacra DO
DO 99 00 01 02

A new DO in the north of Galicia, lying between the Rivers Sil and Miño. At present it comprises some 1,200 hectares of vineyard of very varied soil types. The permitted grape varieties are: the white Godello, ALBARIÑO, Treixadura, Torrontés, Doña Blanca, and Loureiro; and the red Mencía, Brancellao, and Merenzao. The leading bodega is Adegas MOURE.

Ribeiro
DO r p w dr pt ☆→☆☆

The most productive vine-growing area in Galicia, situated in the west of the province of ORENSE in the basin of the River Avia. At a height of 100 to 300 metres and with 3,000 hectares under vines and ninety-six bodegas, it produced nine million litres of wine in 1997–8 (recent figures not available). It is subdivided into three districts: Ribeiro de Avia, the oldest and most traditional area, making excellent white wines from Gomariz and reds from Beade, Regada, and Costeira; Ribeiro del Miño, also producing good red and white wines; and Ribeiro de Arnoia, with its light and fragrant growths. The best of the white grapes are the Treixadura, Torrontés, Godello, Macabeo, Albilla, and Loureiro, the Godello in particular giving the wines a fresh and fragrant nose. The best and most perfumed of the red wines are made from the Sousón. By far the largest producer in the region is the

Bodega Cooperativa del RIBEIRO. Of other concerns bottling their wines, the newest and most spectacular is Bodegas LAPATENA, opened in 1990 but non-DO, because it draws on fruit from outside the region, *e.g.* Ribeira Sacra. *See also* VIÑA MEIN.

Rodrigón

A post, usually of chestnut, used for training the vines clear of the damp ground, especially in the more westerly districts of Galicia.

Rosal, O

DO (r) w dr pt ☆☆→☆☆☆ DYA

Small sub-zone of the DO RÍAS BAIXAS to the extreme southwest of the province of Pontevedra, near the mouth of the River Miño. The main grapes are ALBARIÑO, Treixadura, and Loureira Blanca. In the past the wines, made unscientifically by a host of small proprietors, have been variable in quality. New regulations require DO wines to be made from at least seventy per cent Albariño or seventy per cent Loureira (or a blend of both), and a new generation of small, modern bodegas is producing fresh, soft wines, often with a peachy flavour.

Santa María de los Remedios, Cooperativa

DO r w dr ★→★★

Larouco (Orense). DO Valdeorras. The co-op bottles limited amounts of dry red and white VALDEORRAS, without *pétillance* and also a clean, fresh, and fragrant 100 per cent Godello.

Santiago de Compostela

Santiago lies northeast of the VAL DO SALNES, less than an hour's drive from CAMBADOS. It is the only city in Galicia with direct flights from Madrid, Barcelona, and abroad. It possesses an old university, but most importantly it is the shrine of St James the Apostle, the patron saint of Spain, whose remains are buried there, and from the eleventh century onwards it has been the destination of pilgrims from all over Europe. Its cathedral is one of the most impressive in Spain.

Santiago Ruíz

DO w dr ★★★ DYA

San Miguel de Tabagón (Pontevedra). DO Rías Baixas. This bodega, which pioneered new techniques in O ROSAL, is still one of the best. It makes and bottles a first-rate 100 per cent ALBARIÑO, also a blended Albariño with twenty per cent Loureiro, and ten per cent Treixadura.

Señorío de Sobral

DO w dr ☆☆→☆☆☆

Salvaterra do Miño (Pontevedra). DO Rías Baixas. Good 100 per cent ALBARIÑO wines. The intense and aromatic 00 won first prize at the annual Fiesta del Albariño in CAMBADOS.

Socalco

Name given to the steep hillside terraces in Galicia, sometimes so difficult to access that the peasants set up simple presses to vinify the wine *in situ*.

Terras Gauda, Bodegas

DO w dr ☆☆☆ DYA

O Rosal (Pontevedra). DO Rías Baixas. The winery, renowned for the fragrance and elegance of its wines, has two large vineyards in the very south of the region, near the Miño, growing ALBARIÑO, Loureiro, and Caiño. It makes three types of wine: Abadía de San Campio from 100 per cent

Albariño; Terras Gauda from a blend of Albariño, Loureiro, and Caiño; and Etiqueta Negra from a similar blend, but fermented in barrel.

Tutor

Another name for the RODRIGON.

Val do Salnés

DO w dr ☆☆→☆☆☆

Now a sub-zone of the DO RÍAS BAIXAS, the Val do Salnés, lying along the coast and *rías* north of Pontevedra, has always been the heartland of the famous ALBARIÑO grape. According to the new regulations, its DO wines must contain at least seventy-five per cent Albariño and are frequently made with 100 per cent. At their best, they are marvellously fresh and crisp with a long finish. When in CAMBADOS, it is well worth visiting the historic bodega of the Marqués de Figueroa in the palace of Fefiñanes, but keep an eye on its opening hours.

Valdeorras

DO r w dr ☆→☆☆☆

The most easterly of the winemaking areas of ORENSE, Valdeorras lies in the mountainous valley of the River Sil and comprises three sub-regions, those of Rúa-Petín, Larouco, and El Barco de Valdeorras, each of which possesses its own co-op. About ninety per cent of the white wine is made from the "Xerez" (a variety of the Palomino) and eighty per cent of the red from the Garnacha de Alicante. The white wine is of eleven to twelve per cent alcohol, clean and a little drier than that from RIBEIRO; the red is cherry-coloured, fragrant, and of eleven to twelve per cent.

By far the largest producer of bottled wine is the Bodega Cooperativa JESUS NAZARENO. There are a number of smaller concerns which are, however, producing interesting wines from the traditional white Godello, whose popularity is now being revived, and red Mencía. At their best, the Godellos are now rated among the top white wines from Spain. *See* JOAQUÍN REBOLLEDO, GODEVAL, SANTA MARÍA DE LOS REMEDIOS, and especially GUITIAN GODELLO.

Verín

Wine town in the southeast of the province of ORENSE.

Vilariño-Cambados, Bodegas de

DO w dr ☆☆☆ *DYA*

Cambados (Pontevedra). DO Rías Baixas. A co-op bodega with stainless steel and the latest equipment, founded in 1986. Its MARTÍN CODAX is an excellent example of the new generation of clean, fruity, and flowery ALBARIÑOS.

Viña Mein

DO w dr ☆☆☆ *01 02*

Leiro (Ourense). DO Ribeiro. Small, individual bodega with twelve hectares of vineyard, making perhaps the most sophisticated wine in Ribeiro, from a blend of white native grapes: Treixadura, Godello, Loureiro, ALBARIÑO, Torrontés, and Albillo. *See also* "Hotels".

Vino de aguja

Term used to describe wines, like many from Galicia, with a slight *pétillance* derived from a secondary malolactic fermentation. These are also known in Spain as *vinos verdes* – to the annoyance of the Portuguese, who have registered the description Vinho Verde or "green wine" with the OIV (Office International du Vin).

Virgen de las Viñas, Bodega Cooperativa
DO r w dr ☆
La Rua (Orense). DO Valdeorras. The co-op sells most of its output in bulk, but bottles some red and white wine under the labels of Rua Pingadelo, Brisel, and Marquesíno.

WINE AND FOOD

Galicia is famous for its *mariscos* or shellfish – mussels, lobsters, scallops, prawns, scampi, clams, cockles, oysters, *percebes* (an edible barnacle), and *nécoras* (a species of spider crab). In seaside places you'll often find *marisquerías* which serve nothing else, pricing the portions by weight. There are strong affinities with the cooking of northern Portugal; in the soups, rich fish stews, and highly spiced tripe – hearty fare suitable for the long, wet winters. As regards wine to go with this rich and nourishing assortment of dishes, the Galicians by preference drink a white ALBARIÑO with shellfish, which is perfectly matched by the acidity of the wine. The astringency of the red wines is a good counter to the richness and full flavour of the more substantial dishes.

Caldeirada gallega Akin to the French *bouillabaisse*, this is served in two parts: first the broth, accompanied by slices of toast, and then the fish.

Caldo gallego A nourishing thick soup with shank or hock of ham and haricot beans.

Callos a la gallega Tripe with chickpeas, pigs' trotters, paprika, *chorizo*, and hot seasoning.

Centollo relleno/Changurro relleno The spider crab is boiled and the meat removed, then added to a mixture of cooked hake, onion, parsley, garlic, and lemon juice. This is filled back into the shell, topped with breadcrumbs and grated cheese and browned in the oven.

Empanada gallega Savoury tart containing a variety of meat or fish with tomatoes, onions, and *chorizo*. *Xouba*, for example, is filled with small sardine-like fish, and *raxo* with loin of pork.

Filloas Thick, fluffy pancakes, usually rolled and filled with jam.

Lacón con grelos Smoked shank of ham cooked with *chorizo* and sprouting turnip tops.

Lamprea a la gallega Lamprey prepared with shallots, garlic, olive oil, vinegar, sweet paprika, cinnamon, and white wine.

Merluza al hinojo Hake cooked with fennel.

Pato al estilo de Ribadeo Duck cooked with turnips, orange segments, carrots, boiled chestnuts, pork, white wine, *anís*, and a *bouquet garni*.

Pulpo a feira Stewed octopus with a sauce of olive oil, garlic, and sweet red peppers.

Rape al queso Anglerfish baked with grated cheese.

Salsa salpicada Sauce made with hard-boiled eggs, onion, garlic, vinegar, olive oil, and seasoning; served with fish and shellfish.

Santiaguiños Large crayfish appropriately marked with the cross of Santiago (Saint James).

Tarta de almendras Almond tart.

Tarta de Puentedeume A tart made with almonds, sugar, and egg yolks.

Vieiras al Albariño Scallops marinated in Albariño, seasoned with parsley, garlic, and nutmeg, sprinkled with breadcrumbs then browned in the oven or under the grill.

HOTELS

Bayona *Parador de Bayona* on the coast south of Vigo, a luxurious *parador* with beaches and yacht basin, is conveniently situated for visits to winemaking areas.

Cambados *Parador de Cambados* is the pleasantest of places to sample the Albariño wines and local shellfish.

Leiro (Ourense) *Viña Mein* bodega runs a small six-room hotel for visitors.

Pontevedra *Parador de Pontevedra* is housed in an old baronial mansion.

Santiago de Compostela *Parador de Santiago,* a sixteenth-century palace in the magnificent cathedral square, is among the most memorable hotels in the country.

Tuy *Parador de Tuy* is located on the Portuguese frontier and adjacent to O Rosal and the Condado de Tea.

Verín *Parador de Monterrei* offers local wines and food.

RESTAURANTS

Cambados *Maria José* for razor shells *a la plancha* and monkfish with clams.

La Coruña *Casa Pardo* serves good seafood and lobster salad, but is specially known for monkfish; *A Penela* for local dishes, good wines, and most reasonable prices.

Orense *San Miguel* serves regional food, as well as Ribeiro and Condado de Tea wines.

Pontevedra *Baden Baden* for regional dishes, especially hake stuffed with shellfish; choose your shellfish live from the *vivarium* in *Casa Román*.

Santiago de Compostela *Toñi Vicente,* try the scallop salad with truffles or braised sea bass; *Roberto* at San Xulián, seven kilometres from Santiago, has few, but select dishes, especially scallops Albariño style. Good wine list.

Vigo *La Oca* is inventive and sophisticated; *Puesto Piloto Alcabre,* a beach restaurant, serving fish and regional dishes, and Albariño and Condado de Tea wines; or *El Mosquito* especially for fish and shellfish.

Villagarcía de Arosa *Lolíña* superb cooking of local ingredients famous for its in a former customs house; *Chocolate,* is located in a celebrated Galician restaurant, specializes in grills – and the famous chocolate ice cream; *O Paspallás* serves fresh, home-grown vegetables – try the vegetable pie – sardine pâté, and raspberries with blackberry sauce.

Montilla-Moriles and Málaga

Montilla-Moriles, one of the hottest and sunniest parts of Spain, lies in hilly country south of Córdoba. It makes wines of the sherry type matured in *solera* and, until it was demarcated in 1945, much of its wine was shipped to Jerez for blending. Sweet Pedro Ximénez (PX) wines are still, by special dispensation, supplied to sherry bodegas for making sweet olorosos and cream sherries.

The best of its soils is the chalky white *albero*, resembling the *albariza* of Jerez; but by far the most predominant grape is not Palomino, but Pedro Ximénez, picked here when fully ripe but still waxy white, and fermented to completion without sunning. Other grapes are the white Airén, Baladí,

and Moscatel, and the yield from the low-pruned vines is small. The area under cultivation has declined sharply in recent years, with vineyards being grubbed up to plant olive trees, and now stands at 9,500 hectares. There has been a corresponding reduction in the number of bodegas making the wine.

The main difference between the making of sherry and montilla was that, in Montilla-Moriles, the must was traditionally fermented in the pear-shaped earthenware *tinajas*, also typical of Málaga and La Mancha (*see* "Castilla-La Mancha", page 40); but as elsewhere, these have largely been replaced by temperature-controlled stainless-steel tanks. The *tinajas* are now mainly employed for holding the wine while it undergoes secondary fermentation and clears. Once the wine "falls bright", some months after completion of its secondary fermentation, it is transferred to a *solera*, operated in almost exactly the same way as those in Jerez, except that the musts are so rich in sugar that they produce wines a little higher in alcohol and are not fortified.

As in Jerez, the musts are classified by the cellar master and emerge as one or other of the styles familiar in Jerez: fino, amontillado, palo cortado, oloroso (*see* A–Z listing for details). The style for which the region is best known is the light, aromatic, and very dry fino, which is made from the first pressing of the grapes and develops a vigorous *flor*. The olorosos are made from a must obtained by a second and firmer pressing.

Some years ago the sherry shippers brought a legal action in England, contesting the use of the terms fino and amontillado as descriptions of montilla – ironically, as it happens, since in the first place the Jerezanos borrowed the name "amontillado" from montilla. For this reason, montilla on sale in the UK is often labelled "Fine Dry", "Medium", and "Cream". It contains between thirteen and fifteen per cent alcohol. Until 1980 exports of montilla were slow and some firms struggled to survive, but thanks to excellent quality and competitive prices there was a marked revival, especially in Britain. The largest of the firms, Alvear, exports some twenty-five per cent of its production, and Compañía Vinícola del Sur some fifty per cent. The most important foreign markets are Britain and the Netherlands. However, montilla, in common with fortified wines, has suffered a decline in sales. To combat this, some of the producers have turned to making *joven afrutado* (young and fruity) beverage wines. Whether these can compete with the white wines from the regions of the north remains to be seen.

Sweet wines from Málaga were famous in Roman times and reached their zenith during the nineteenth century, with the largest exports to North America. Like other sweet dessert wines their popularity has declined, and the tourist boom along the Costa del Sol has taken its toll of vineyards (now 1,114 hectares) and bodegas (now only sixteen). In 1829 production was 17.5 million litres, whereas in 2002 it had fallen to only 2.6 million litres. With the closure of the famous Scholtz Hermanos, only two large firms remain: López Hermanos and Larios. Nevertheless, málaga at its best remains a glorious wine, and not all of it is sweet.

The grapes are grown in two areas of the surrounding hills, one to the north of the city and neighbouring the DO Montilla-Moriles, and the other to the east. In days past there was a profusion of vine varieties, but the *consejo regulador* now authorizes only the Pedro Ximénez and Moscatel for new plantations. Some of the different styles of málaga are separately described in the A–Z listing. The most common is the *dulce color*, dark amber in colour, full-bodied, and sweet (sometimes cloyingly so) through to the end; but there are others, more resembling tawny port, with a bitter-sweet flavour and dryish finish.

Albero

The best of the soils, containing thirty to sixty per cent chalk. It is most widespread in the *sierras* of MONTILLA and Alto Moriles, where most of the large bodegas have vineyard holdings. Production is higher in the lower-lying areas, but the wines are not of the same alcoholic degree or quality.

Alvear

Montilla (Córdoba). DO Montilla-Moriles. The largest firm in the region was founded by the Alvear family, which settled in MONTILLA in 1729, planting vineyards and establishing the original bodega. It was much expanded by Don Francisco de Alvear y Gómez de la Cortina, Conde de la Cortina, during the early years of the last century and now possesses 20,000 American-oak casks in its SOLERAS and has a storage capacity of ten million litres. Alvear makes montilla in a dozen styles, including two excellent dry finos, the soft and delicate Fino Capatáz and Fino CB, named after a former head cellarman, Carlos Billanueva; Amontillado Carlos VII, fruity, fragrant, and bone dry, more resembling a fino than an amontillado; Oloroso Asunción; the bitter-sweet Oloroso Asman Abocado; a sweet Festival Cream; and a remarkable trio of PX wines: 1927, 1999, and Solera 1910. Alvear also produces a light wine, the Marqués de la Sierra, and large amounts of brandy made from *holandas* (*see* "Spirits, Aromatic Wines, and Liqueurs", page 190).

Amontillado

The original style of MONTILLA, first made by a Conde de la Cortina in the eighteenth century, but without maturation in SOLERA. The Jerezanos later produced a wine with similar characteristics, but aged it in *solera*; and the *bodegueros* from Montilla followed suit. Amontillados from Montilla are sixteen to eighteen per cent strength, amber-coloured, full on the palate, and with a pungent, nutty nose.

Antequera

The old town of Antequera lies north of MÁLAGA on the winding uphill road to CÓRDOBA and Sevilla, and on the southern fringe of one of the two main vineyard areas of the DO Málaga. This northern area (500 metres high) is a limestone region, and the predominant grape is PEDRO XIMÉNEZ.

Aragón y Cía

Lucena (Córdoba). DO Montilla-Moriles. This is a well-known firm whose wines include the fino Moriles 47; amontillado Pacorrito and Boabdil Viejisimo (with twenty degrees alcoholic strength); Moriles Palo Cortado; and the sweet Araceli and Pilycrim PX.

Axarquia

The second and larger of the vineyard areas of the DO MÁLAGA, to the east of the city and stretching back from Vélez-Málaga and Torrox near the coast into the mountains, which rise sharply to a height of 2,000 metres. The soils are a mixture of decomposed slate and a limestone clay, and its vineyards are planted with ninety per cent MOSCATEL.

Benavides

The vineyards here are among the best in the MORILES area; they supply wine only to TORO ALBALA.

Compañía de Vinos Telmo Rodríguez

DO Málaga. With bodegas regularly closing in MÁLAGA, it is encouraging that the innovative Telmo Rodríguez, formerly of Remelluri in Rioja, is now making a luscious 100 per cent MOSCATEL málaga.

Compañía Vinícola del Sur

Montilla (Córdoba). DO Montilla-Moriles. A large company, the Compañía Vinícola del Sur was formerly a part of the Rumasa group (*see* "Sherry and Manzanilla", page 160), whose Monte Cristo wines are well known in the UK. Dry, Medium, Pale Cream, and Cream are also exported to the USA.

Conde de la Cortina

Montilla (Córdoba). DO Montilla-Moriles. The company is controlled by ALVEAR, with which it shares premises. Its best-known brands are the well-made Cortina Pale Dry, Medium, Cream, and Pale Cream.

Córdoba

A little to the north of the DO Montilla-Moriles, Córdoba was formerly the headquarters of a number of firms which maintained bodegas and SOLERAS in the city for maturing their wines. For 300 years, until the Caliphate disintegrated in 1031, Córdoba was the capital of Moorish Spain; and the Great Mosque, now the cathedral, resembling nothing so much as a cool grove of palm trees with its myriad arches and columns, was the most important in western Islam and second only in size to that of Mecca. Other Moorish survivals are the fourteenth-century Alcázar or fortified palace, with its mosaics and gardens, and the Judería, or ancient Jewish quarter, a maze of narrow alleys, criss-crossing at random and providing shelter from the sun. About half-an-hour's drive from MONTILLA, Córdoba, with its historic interest and restaurants, is the obvious base for a visit to the region.

Crismona, SA

Doña Mencia (Córdoba). DO Montilla-Moriles. Maker of the good Los Cobales fino, Crismona Vieja oloroso, and a sweet PX.

Cruz Conde, Bodegas

Montilla (Córdoba). DO Montilla-Moriles. Well known for attractive Cruz Conde fino and PX; also makes a light white wine.

Delgado SL

Puente Geníl (Córdoba). DO Montilla-Moriles. Old-established bodega making good Segunda Bota fino, Faraon amontillado, and PX. The young white wines are fruity and refreshing, but of less interest.

Doña Mencía

Village to the southeast of MONTILLA with three concerns making DO wines: Bodegas CRISMONA, Bodegas (Miguel Fernández Gan) Lama, and Bodegas Luque.

Dulce color

The most familiar style of MÁLAGA wine, sweetened with *arrope* – to which it owes its dark amber colour, as well as the hint of treacle in the nose and the high eight to twelve degrees *baumé*. The alcohol content ranges from fourteen to twenty-three per cent.

El Naranjo

Another favoured vineyard area near MORILES.

Fino

Pale, dry with a greenish tint, slightly bitter, and light and fragrant on the palate, the unfortified fino, containing fifteen to seventeen per cent alcohol, is the best known of the various styles of MONTILLA.

Gracia Hermanos

Montilla (Córdoba). DO Montilla-Moriles. Firm within the same group as PÉREZ BARQUERO and COMPAÑIA VINÍCOLA DEL SUR making traditional, good-quality MONTILLAS. Labels include María del Valle fino, Tauromaquin amontillado, cream, oloroso, and PX.

Jesús Nazareno

Baena (Córdoba). DO Montilla-Moriles. Large co-op making light white Don Bueno; Baena and Cancionero finos; Minguillar cream oloroso.

Lágrima

The word means "tear" and is used to describe the choicest and most luscious of the MÁLAGA wines, made with the juice which emerges from the grapes without the use of mechanical means and simply as a result of the pressure from the grapes at the top of the load. It therefore comes from the pulp nearest the skins of the ripest grapes, and is vinified separately from the *yema* (or "yolk") which is obtained by further light pressing. The wine is old-gold in colour, very full bodied, with an aromatic oloroso nose and long sweet finish. It has six to ten degrees *baumé* and fourteen to twenty-three per cent alcohol.

Larios

Málaga. DO Málaga. Known for its gin, Larios also makes good MÁLAGAS, especially the *dulce* (sweet) Málaga Larios. *See also* "Spirits, Aromatic Wines, and Liqueurs", page 191.

López Hermanos

Málaga. DO Málaga. Founded in 1885 and run by the third generation of the López family, the bodega owns 500 hectares of vineyards in the MOLLINA area and makes some of the most popular MÁLAGAS in Spain, including the dry Trajinero, made from ninety-five per cent PEDRO XIMÉNEZ; the sweet dessert Málaga Virgen, containing sixty per cent Pedro Ximénez and forty per cent MOSCATEL; and the luscious Tres Leones Moscatel.

Lucena

Pleasant little town southeast of MONTILLA and halfway between CÓRDOBA and ANTEQUERA. Apart from wine it produces olive oil and is known for its decorative metalwork.

Luque, Bodegas

Doña Mencia (Córdoba). DO Montilla-Moriles. Family firm selling good El Pato fino, El Abuelo Solera 1888 amontillado, and Luque PX.

Málaga

Málaga lies on the coast at some distance from the vineyards in the hills behind it; to qualify for the DO the musts have either to be vinified in one of its bodegas or, as is more usual, brought there for blending and maturation. The inexorable pressure of tourism has ringed it with high-rise apartments but the port remains and, behind it, a network of narrow streets clustering around the market, some of which have restaurant tables on the pavement and cavernous bars where one can settle down to tasting such málagas as remain.

Mollina

The most important of the vineyards in the region's northern zone, beyond ANTEQUERA.

Monte Cristo

Well-known MONTILLAS from COMPAÑIA VINÍCOLA DEL SUR.

Montilla

With the nearby village of MORILES, this quiet hill town, the Munda Betica of the ancients and birthplace of Gonzalo de Córdoba, the Gran Capitán, boasts the early eighteenth-century house of the ALVEAR family, with its splendid arcaded patio. The wine centre of the region, Montilla possesses a number of bodegas making DO wines.

Montisierra

Exporters' association, comprising ALVEAR, COMPAÑIA VINÍCOLA DEL SUR, GRACIA HERMANOS, and PÉREZ BARQUERO.

Montulia, Bodegas

Montilla (Córdoba). DO Montilla-Moriles. Established, well-known firm, now part of the NAVISA group, and maker of some dozen styles of MONTILLA, including JR fino, amontillado, Fabiola, PX, and an excellent palo cortado. Also makes brandy and *anís*.

Moreno SA

Córdoba. DO Montilla-Moriles. Maker of the exceptional 1925 Virgilio PX, as well as an Amontillado Viejo and Fundación oloroso.

Moriles

Although famous for its wines, and lying at the centre of some of the best vineyards in the area, Moriles remains only a tiny village on a by-road twenty kilometres south of MONTILLA.

Moscatel

A style of MÁLAGA made solely with Moscatel grapes, from AXARQUIA, the larger of the vineyard areas of the DO Málaga. The colour varies according to age from golden yellow to light golden brown, and the wine is soft and sweet, with a deep and fruity Moscatel nose. The sugar content varies from six to thirteen degrees *baumé*, with an alcohol content of fifteen to twenty per cent.

"Mountain Wine"

Soubriquet for MÁLAGA in its Victorian heyday. You can still occasionally find silver wine labels with this name in English antique shops.

Navarro, Bodegas

Montilla (Córdoba). DO Montilla-Moriles. A sizeable exporter, established in 1830 and belonging to NAVISA. Its range of wines includes Andalucía MONTILLA, Navarro fino; Solera 1836 Amontillado; and a sweet PX.

Navisa Industrial Vinícola Española

DO Montilla (Córdoba). This group controls Bodegas MONTULIA, Bodegas Velasco Charcón, and Bodegas Cobos. The family-owned Cobos was formerly a household name and one of the largest and most important bodegas in MONTILLA. Navisa makes Cobos and Pompeyo finos and an excellent Tres Pasas Cream, together with a refreshing light wine of eleven degrees strength, made from a blend of PEDRO XIMÉNEZ, Airén, and Baladi.

Oloroso

Style of wine resembling its counterpart from Jerez (*see* "Sherry and Manzanilla", page 157), with sixteen to eighteen per cent alcohol, rising to twenty per cent when very old. Mahogany-coloured, full-bodied, soft, and highly aromatic, it can either be dry or with a hint of sweetness.

Palo cortado

With sixteen to eighteen per cent alcohol, this is a style combining the nutty bouquet of amontillado with the flavour of oloroso.

Pedro Ximénez (PX)

1. The predominant grape variety of Montilla-Moriles, making both dry and sweet wines.

2. A sweet MONTILLA with a high alcoholic degree, which takes its name from the PX grape variety. Made in part with sunned grapes, it is a dark, ruby colour and contains at least a massive 272 grams per litre of sugar.

3. A style of MÁLAGA made solely with Pedro Ximénez grapes from the northern zone. When fully mature it is a dark, treacley colour with a yellow rim and an intense oloroso nose, and is full-bodied and very soft, with a bitter-sweet finish. It varies from six to thirteen degrees *baumé*, with an alcohol content of sixteen to twenty per cent.

Pérez Barquero

Montilla (Córdoba). DO Montilla-Moriles. Another company, formed at the turn of the century, that was formerly part of Rumasa (*see* "Sherry and Manzanilla", page 160), and among the best in the region. Its labels include Viña Amalia light white wines; Gran Barquero fino, amontillado, and oloroso, all of outstanding quality, and La Cañada sweet PX, than which there is no better.

Príncipe Alfonso, Bodegas y Viñedos

Non-DO r res ☆☆→☆☆☆ *99 00*

Ronda (Málaga). Small bodega founded by Prince Hohenlohe, the Marbella property developer, and owned by Bodegas Unidas (*see* "Rioja", page 125). It is best known for its Príncipe Alfonso 100 per cent Petit Verdot and for the Príncipe Alfonso Reserva Privado (95), a red blend including Cabernet Sauvignon, Tempranillo, and Petit Verdot.

Puente-Genil

Small town southwest of MONTILLA. As well as its wines it is famous as the chief producer of *membrillo*, the quince paste so popular in Spain. It is also the headquarters of Cooperativa Vitivinícola de la Purísima and DELGADO HERMANOS.

Raya

A MONTILLA similar to oloroso, but with less flavour and bouquet.

Robles, Bodegas

Montilla (Córdoba). DO Montilla-Moriles. Good Piedra Luenga Ecológico fino and first-rate de Pasa Ecológico PX.

Ruedo

Not a montilla proper, but a dry, pale, light white wine containing about fourteen per cent alcohol and made without any time in SOLERA.

Ruedos de Montilla, Los

The area's grapes are among the best from the Sierra de Montilla.

Scholtz Hermanos

Málaga. DO Málaga. One of the best and most famous bodegas, the firm was founded in 1807, passed into German control in 1885, and reverted back to the Spanish after World War I. Its closure some years ago was a major loss.

Solera

An assembly of 500-litre butts used in Montilla-Moriles for maturing the wine. As in Jerez (*see* "Sherry", page 161), the butts are loosely stoppered and arranged in "scales" containing progressively older wine, and when wine is drawn off for shipment or bottling, the final "scale" is "refreshed" with younger wine. A montilla *solera* usually contains five "scales" for the finos and four for the olorosos. The *soleras* operate almost exactly as those in Jerez, except that the musts are brandied only in occasional years, when they are low in alcohol.

Tercia, La

Well-known vineyard area near MORILES.

Tierras de Mollina SA

DO Málaga. With 775 hectares of vineyard around MOLLINA, the firm makes a range of moderately priced málagas, including the dry white Montelobo and sweet 100 per cent PX Carpe Diem and Carpe Diem Añejo.

Tinajas

Large, pear-shaped earthenware vessels traditionally used for fermenting the wine. The tops are left open during the first stages of fermentation and later covered with wooden lids. Once the wine clears after completion of the secondary fermentation, it is racked and transferred to a SOLERA for maturation. In large modern bodegas *tinajas* have been replaced with stainless-steel tanks, and are used only to allow the wine to settle and clarify. *See also* "Castilla-La Mancha", page 40.

Tomás García

Montilla (Córdoba). DO Montilla-Moriles. Belongs to the same group as Carbonell, one of Spain's largest olive oil producers and, until recently, a maker of MONTILLA which it matured in cellars in CÓRDOBA. Among its many styles are a fresh Verbenera fino; a fragrant, intense Flor de Montilla amontillado; a complex, well-constructed nectar TG oloroso; and a sweet 100 per cent PX TG.

Toro Albalá

Aguilar de la Frontera (Córdoba). DO Montilla-Moriles. One of the oldest and best MONTILLA firms, housed in an old power station – hence the name of its excellent Eléctrico finos. Makes a beautiful, light Amontillado Viejísimo 1922; a delicious Don PX (on sale in the UK); and a superb Bacchus dessert wine (at over £100 a bottle).

Vitivinícola Local SCA, Cooperativa

Aguilar de la Frontera (Córdoba). DO Montilla-Moriles. One of the largest and best-run co-ops in the region, making its own Ipagro *generosos* and selling wine to many of the private firms.

Zona del Albero

Name given to the area around MORILES, where the soils are particularly rich in the chalky *albero*.

WINE AND FOOD

Andalucía is often labelled the *zona de los fritos* or "region of fried food". High on the list of such dishes must come the fries of mixed fish, equally good around Málaga or in Cádiz and the sherry region. The shellfish on offer is varied and abundant; another speciality are the *gazpachos* or cold soups, always containing garlic and a little olive oil and vinegar, but made with a variety of vegetables, chopped or puréed. Málaga is not for drinking with a meal, but afterwards. It is the custom in these parts to begin with a glass of chilled fino montilla, often served with *aceitunas aliñadas* (marinated king-sized olives) and to continue drinking it throughout the meal.

Montilla-Moriles

Brazo de gitano Popular sweet made with eggs, flour, and jam, and resembling a Swiss roll.

Callos a la andaluza Tripe stewed with calves' feet and chickpeas.

Caracoles a la andaluza Snails cooked with garlic and toasted almonds, paprika, tomatoes, onions, white pepper, and lemon.

Huevos a la flamenca Eggs cooked in an earthenware dish with onions, ham, and fresh tomatoes, and decorated with prawns, slices of *chorizo*, asparagus tips, and red pepper.

Membrillo A sweet quince paste, served on its own as a dessert or with cheese.

Perdices a la torera "Bullfighters' partridge", garnished with ham, anchovies, green peppers, and tomatoes.

Polvorones A dry, powdery sweetmeat, a speciality of Estepa, just west of Montilla-Moriles, made with flour, pork fat, sugar, and cinnamon; often served with sherry or montilla.

Rabo de toro Popular Córdoban stew of oxtail with vegetables.

Revuelto de aspárragos trigueros Scrambled eggs with young asparagus.

Salmorejo A thick variation of *gazpacho*, made with garlic, olive oil, and breadcrumbs, but without peppers or tomatoes.

Salsa de patatas A sauce originating from the Sierra Morena, north of Córdoba. Its base is made with fried puréed potatoes, it contains peppers, a bay leaf, cumin, olive oil, and seasoning, and is served with fish.

Ternera con alcachofas a la cordobesa Veal, served with artichokes and cooked with montilla and seasoning.

Tocino de cielo A sweet popular throughout Andalucía, made with egg yolks and sugar flavoured with vanilla.

Málaga

Ajo blanco con uvas de Málaga A cold soup prepared with almonds, garlic, vinegar, and olive oil, together with white grapes, skinned and · without pips.

Chanquetes A minute fish (*aphia minuta*) which is fried crisp like whitebait.

Dulce malagueño A sweet made with semolina, egg yolks, sugar, raisins, and *membrillo* quince paste.

Frito de pescados a la andaluza A mixed fry of small fish, sometimes dipped in seasoned flour or maybe dredged in egg and breadcrumbs, and fried in hot olive oil. Fish such as *chanquetes, boquerones* (fresh anchovies), or squid cut into rings are also fried and served by themselves.

Moraga de sardines Motril Fresh sardines marinated with salt, olive oil, white wine, lemon juice, parsley, and garlic.

Raya en pimentón Skate cooked with sweet paprika.

Salsa andaluza Sauce made with pumpkins, tomatoes, pepper, and garlic.

Sopa al cuarto de hora A soup so called because of the cooking time of fifteen minutes, and containing chopped ham and clams, hard-boiled eggs, onion, parsley, garlic, and bread.

Sopa de almendras de Ronda A sweet soup containing pounded almonds, sugar, a stick of cinnamon, and grated lemon peel, with thin slices of bread.

Tarta helada Sweet made with alternate layers of sponge cake and ice cream.

Tortilla al Sacramonte Omelette originating from the gypsy quarter of Granada and containing lambs' brains, sweetbreads, fresh peppers, potatoes, and toasted breadcrumbs.

HOTELS

Antequera The *Parador de Antequera* is a pleasant place to spend a night in the area, and the cooking in its restaurant, using local ingredients, is inventive.

Córdoba About half-an-hour's drive from Montilla, Córdoba has a number of good hotels: the four-star *NH Amistad Córdoba*, *AC Córdoba*, and *Conquistador* opposite the mosque. Perhaps the quietest, most relaxing place is the spacious, comfortable, modern *Parador de Córdoba*, which looks down on the city from the north.

Málaga The quietest place to stay is at the *Parador de Gibralfaro*, set on a hill above the centre.

RESTAURANTS

Aguilar de la Frontera Eight kilometres from Montilla, *La Casona* offers good food, large helpings, and reasonable prices.

Antequera *Parador Nacional* serves inventive Andalucían food.

Córdoba *Bodegas Campos* is a former winery with very good food, such as lamb stuffed with dates and prune kernels. *Almudaina* offers Córdoban cooking in atmospheric surroundings. *El Churrasco* has a pleasant patio and bar, and serves Córdoban dishes.

Málaga *Café de Paris* provides sophisticated cuisine with local ingredients. *Méson Astorga* has good Málaga cooking: ask for half-portions to sample more of its dishes.

There are also scores of good restaurants – some outstanding, such as *La Meridiana* and *La Hacienda* – in Marbella and in the other Costa del Sol resorts.

Navarra and the Basque Country

Navarra, to the west of Cataluña and extending from the Pyrenees to the Ebro basin, was a kingdom in its own right until it fell to Ferdinand the Catholic in 1512. At one time it extended over the Pyrenees, hence the alternative spelling of "Navarre" for the portion now lying in France. It is an autonomy with wide variations in climate, between the sub-humid conditions of the mountainous north and the dry, Mediterranean-like climate of central and southern Spain which prevails in the Ebro Valley in southern Navarra. The soils are in general chalky, with deposits of silt and gravel along the river valleys, and are well-suited to viticulture.

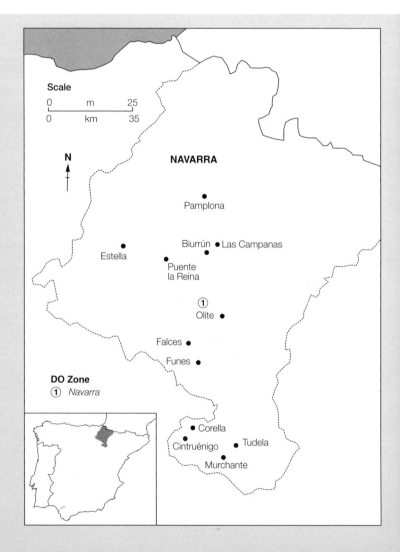

The vine-growing districts extend south from the provincial capital, Pamplona, and were demarcated in 1967. The DO Navarra is further subdivided into the five *comarcas* of Baja Montaña, Valdizarbe, Tierra de Estella, Ribera Alta, and Ribera Baja, with a combined area of 16,244 hectares under vines and an output in 2002 of fifty-five million litres. The small area of Rioja Baja, spilling into the province of Navarra and including the town of San Adrián, is separately described (*see* "Rioja", page 138).

The predominant grape – until recently to the extent of some seventy per cent – is the red Garnacha Tinta, but producers are being encouraged by the government research station EVENA to plant Tempranillo to make longer-lived red wines more suited to oak-ageing. Some twenty-six per cent has been planted; there are smaller plantations of red Graciano and Mazuelo, and of the white Viura, Malvasía, and Garnacha Blanca. Cabernet Sauvignon, Merlot, and Chardonnay are also being grown here in sizeable amounts.

Navarra was once a prolific producer of sturdy red wines and fresh rosés, said to have been a favourite of Catherine the Great of Russia in the early eighteenth century. More recently it has been the rosés – among the best in Spain – that the region has been known for and for which Garnacha is well suited. But now the thrust is towards quality red wines, and thanks to the innovative ideas of EVENA and the re-equipment of the cooperatives, Navarra is making great strides. In general EVENA is working towards red wines made with fifty per cent Tempranillo, thirty per cent Garnacha, and twenty per cent Cabernet Sauvignon. But increasingly, sophisticated producers such as CHIVITE, OCHOA, CASTILLO DE MONJARDIN, and GUELBENZU are making a gamut of wines from Chardonnay, Tempranillo, Cabernet Sauvignon, and Merlot, some of them 100 per cent.

Like Aragón, the district may be visited en route to Rioja from Barcelona via the A2 and A68 *autopistas*; and the A15 to Pamplona. Branching off the road to Logroño beyond Tudela, is the route through the heart of the vine-growing areas. The green and rainy Basque country produces no wine except the *pétillant* CHACOLÍ in miniscule amounts, and Asturias further to the west makes excellent cider and cheeses, but no wine at all.

Vintages

90	*good*	97	*good*
91	*good*	98	*very good*
92	*good*	99	*very good*
93	*good*	00	*very good*
94	*good*	01	*excellent*
95	*excellent*	02	*very good*
96	*very good*		

Agramont
DO r p dr ★→★★
One of the labels used by the large Navarra concern of Bodegas PRINCIPE DE VIANA for its well-made wines.

Ambrosio Velasco

> *See* PALACIO DE LA VEGA.

Aretxondo SAT

> *DO w dr* ☆☆ *DYA*
>
> Munia (Vizcaya). DO Chacolí de Vizcaya. Best of the producers of CHACOLÍ from this DO. Its labels are Bion-Etxea, Luberri Mahastia, Marko, Amunategui, Larrondo, and Nekesola. All are made with a high proportion of Ondarrabi Zuri and are refreshing, lemony, not to say mouth-puckering, white wines.

Baja Montaña

> *DO p* ☆→☆☆
>
> Subdivision of the DO Navarra, to the region's east on the borders of Aragón. It is the highest and wettest of the vine-growing areas and produces some of the best rosés, of twelve to fifteen per cent strength.

Baso

> *DO r* ★★
>
> Brand name of very drinkable red Garnacha made by gifted young oenologist Telmo Rodríguez, formerly of La Granja Remelluri in Rioja.

Camilo Castilla, Bodegas

> *DO w dr sw p r res* ☆☆☆
>
> Corella (Navarra). DO Navarra. An old-established bodega which makes red and dry white wines, but is best known for its excellent sweet Moscatel labelled as Capricho de Goya and Montecristo.

Cantabria

> Autonomy in the north and one of the wettest parts of Spain, bounded by the Bay of Biscay and to the south by the Cantabrian mountains. It produces only the *pétillant* and astringent CHACOLÍ.

Carricas, Bodegas

> *DO r p w dr* ☆☆
>
> Olite (Navarra). DO Navarra. Old-established firm with bodegas in the subterranean passages of the fifteenth-century castle of OLITE. The innovative Carricas brothers label their wines as Mont-Plané: they include a 100 per cent Garnacha rosé and reds made from 100 per cent Garnacha, 100 per cent Tempranillo, or a blend of both.

Castillo de Monjardín

> *DO w dr r (p)* ☆☆→☆☆☆ *94 95 96 97 98 00*
>
> Villamayor (Navarra). DO Navarra. Founded in 1988, this small family concern makes an excellent barrel-fermented Chardonnay (99), a delicious barrel-fermented Merlot rosé, a fruity 100 per cent Pinot Noir, and good reds from Cabernet Sauvignon, Tempranillo, and Merlot. The bodega has recently reverted to oakier wines to the Spanish taste.

Cenalsa, Bodegas

> *See* Bodegas PRINCIPE DE VIANA.

Chacolí (Txacoli)

> *DO (r) w* ☆→☆☆ *DYA*
>
> A "green", *pétillant* wine from the Basque Country (País Vasco), containing only nine to 11.5 per cent alcohol. The vines are ungrafted because the flooding of the vineyards in winter kills the phylloxera bug. There are two types of wine: white Txakoliñ Gorri, from the white Ondarrubi Zuri (akin to the Courbut Blanc), and the red Txakoliñ Zuri from the Ondarrubi Beltza. When the area around Guetería in Guipúzcoa was first demarcated in 1990

it ran to only forty-seven hectares. Currently with 177 hectares and seventeen bodegas this is now known as the DO Chacolí de Guetaría-Getariako Txakolina and still produces the best Chacolí. However, the growers in the neighbouring provinces of Vizcaya have lobbied for their 210 and seventy-seven hectares to be demarcated, with the result that the DOs Chacolí de Vizcaya Bizkaiko Txakolina and Chacolí Arabako Txakolina (with only two bodegas) have recently been established. Neither the white nor red wines undergo malolactic fermentation and are very acidic with a slight prickle, although the nose of the white is fragrant enough. The Basques enjoy them in mouthfuls with the excellent local shellfish.

Chivite, Bodegas Julián

DO r p w dr res ★★→★★★ *94 95 96 98 99 00*

Cintruénigo (Navarra). DO Navarra. Founded in 1860, this family firm is the largest private wine concern in Navarra, with a total capacity of 18.75 million litres, and vineyards and bodegas in other districts of Navarra and in the provinces of La Rioja and Aragón. Its well-made wines range from fresh and fruity young whites, such as the outstanding barrel-fermented Colección 125 Chardonnay (01) and a good GRAN FEUDO (02) rosé, to the attractive young red Viña Marcos, soft and plummy Gran Feudo *crianza*, the rich and oaky Gran Feudo *reservas*, and superb Vendimia Tarde Moscatel, the best from Spain (01).

Cintruénigo

Wine town just to the south of the Ebro in the RIBERA BAJA.

Corella

w sw ☆→☆☆

This village, near CINTRUENIGO, makes a little luscious Moscatel.

Ebro, River

After crossing the Rioja, the Ebro skirts the far south of Navarra, flowing through the RIBERA BAJA. The northerly wine districts lie in the basins of its tributaries, the Ega, Arga, Cidacos, and Aragón.

EVENA

The government-funded Estacíon de Viticultura y Enología de Navarra. Founded in 1981 and formerly headed by Don Javier Ochoa, it is one of the most forward-looking and up-to-date establishments of its kind in the country. The *estación* maintains elaborately equipped laboratories at OLITE and its advice is available not only to the cooperatives and large concerns, but also to the humblest smallholder.

Ezcaba, Chacolí Tinto de

r w dr pt ☆

One of the few wines made in the mountainous north of Navarra; astringent and *pétillant*, the wines resemble better-known CHACOLÍS from Guipúzcoa.

Falces

r p ☆→☆☆

Vine-growing area in the south of RIBERA ALTA, making good red and rosé wines. It also has one of the few monasterial bodegas to survive in Europe, that of Nuestra Señora de la Oliva.

Funes

This village between FALCES and Calahorra has a well-preserved Roman winery from the first century AD. With cement paving and chambers for making and storing the wine, its capacity was of the order of 75,000 litres.

Gran Feudo
DO r p w dr ★★→★★★ *94 95 96 97 98 99 00*
Well-made and affordable range of red, white, and rosé wines from
Bodegas Julián CHIVITE.

Guelbenzu, Bodegas
r res ★★→☆☆☆☆ *97 98 99 00 01 02*
Cascante (Navarra). Non-DO since the family firm has recently acquired
vineyards in Aragón outside the DO Navarra. The Cascante wines are a
blend of Cabernet Sauvignon and Tempranillo, sometimes with a touch
of Merlot and comprise Azul, Evo, and the superb Lautus (99). The wines
are concentrated and meaty, and best opened an hour or two before
drinking.

Gurpegui Muga, Luís
DO w dr p r ☆☆
Vilafranca (Navarra). DO Navarra. Decent Monte Ory wines produced by
the firm that owns Bodegas Berceo in Rioja and is also making wines in
La Mancha.

Innurieta
DO w dr r p ☆☆ *01 02*
Falces (Navarra). DO Navarra. New winery founded in 2003 with excellent
young reds, a Norte made from Merlot and Cabernet, Sur from Garnacha
and Syrah, and a good *crianza* and rosé.

Irache, Bodegas
DO r p w dr res ☆→☆☆ *96 97 98 02*
Estella (Navarra). DO Navarra. Well-known and old-established firm, whose
bodega is next to the beautiful monastery of Irache near Estella. The young
red Irache is plum-coloured and full-bodied. Older wines, matured in its
10,000 French and American-oak *barricas*, include red Castillo Irache, Gran
Irache, and Real Irache, *reserva* Castillo Irache, and *gran reserva* Real Irache
(84); all made with a sizeable proportion of Tempranillo.

Las Campanas
Village south of Pamplona and headquarters of the well-known VINICOLA
NAVARRA, which uses the name for some of its wines.

Magaña, Bodegas Viña
DO r res ☆☆→☆☆☆☆ *85 94 95 97 98 99 00 01*
Barillas (Navarra). DO Navarra. Small bodega, a pioneer grower of French
grape varieties in Navarra. It makes distinguished reds from 100 per cent
Merlot or a blend of Merlot and Cabernet Sauvignon, from its own
120 hectares of vineyards.

Malumbres, Bodegas Vicente
DO r p w dr ★→★★
Corella (Navarra). DO Navarra. A sizeable concern with sixty hectares of
vineyards. The wines are labelled as Malumbres: the best include the fresh
and fruity 02 Garnacha rosé and the meaty 99 red, both from Garnacha
with Tempranillo.

Marco Real, Bodegas
DO w dr p r 98 99 00
Olite (Navarra). DO Navarra. Modern bodega labelling its wine as Homenaje.
Pleasant *crianza* and *reserva* reds, but best is the soft, 100 per cent Garnacha
rosé (02).

Nekeas, Bodegas y Viñedos
DO r p w dr ★★→★★★

Añorbe (Navarra). DO Navarra. This young co-op, with 220 hectares planted with both native and foreign grape varieties, is justly known for the care with which it makes its wines. These include a 100 per cent Chardonnay fermented in barrel (01), a 100 per cent Cabernet Sauvignon rosé, and fruity reds made either from Tempranillo and Merlot or Cabernet Sauvignon and Tempranillo.

Nuestra Señora del Romero, Cooperativa
DO r p w dr res ★★ 95 96 99 02

Cascante (Navarra). DO Navarra. This is one of Spain's largest co-ops, with 1,100 hectares of vines. Although situated in an area best known for its robust Garnacha wine, by modern methods it has succeeded in making wines such as the magnificently light, fresh and fruity Malón de Echaide rosé (02), an attractive young Nuevo Vino in the style of Beaujolais Nouveau, and good Señor de Cascante *gran reservas* which include eighty per cent Tempranillo.

Ochoa, Bodegas
DO r p w dr res ★★→★★★ 97 98 99 00

Olite (Navarra). DO Navarra. This small firm, which owns vineyards near OLITE, has been in family hands since 1845. Its respected oenologist, Don Javier Ochoa, is one of the most expert in the region. All of its wines are well made by modern methods and among the best from Navarra. They include a 100 per cent Viura, a recently introduced and first-rate sweet Moscatel (02), a rosé made from fifty per cent Garnacha and fifty per cent Cabernet Sauvignon, and intensely fruity red *crianzas* and *reservas* made from 100 per cent Merlot and blends of Tempranillo, Cabernet Sauvignon, and Merlot.

Olite

Olite, south of Pamplona in one of the best winemaking areas of RIBERA ALTA, is the site of a fortified palace, once the favourite residence of the Kings of Navarra. Begun by Charles III ("The Noble") in 1403, in its finished form it was the largest palace in Spain.

Palacio de la Vega
DO w dr p r res ☆☆→☆☆☆☆

Dicastillo (Navarra). DO Navarra. Wines from a young (1991) and promising bodega: good, juicy reds, including 100 per cent Tempranillo, Merlot, Cabernet Sauvignon, and Chardonnay.

Pamplona

Pamplona, capital of Navarra, dear to Hemingway and famous for the bull-running through its streets during the Festival of San Fermín in early July, is also a good centre for visiting the more northerly wine areas. An elegant city with a fine cathedral and a spacious central square, it possesses numerous good restaurants.

Piedmonte, Bodegas
DO p r ★★→★★★ 99 00 01

Olite (Navarra). DO Navarra. Produces 100 per cent barrel-fermented Chardonnay, good reds made from 100 per cent Cabernet Sauvignon and 100 per cent Merlot, and blends with Tempranillo, Cabernet Sauvignon, and Merlot. Also an excellent sweet Moscatel.

Príncipe de Viana, Bodegas

DO r p w dr sw ★★→★★★ *01 02*

Murchante (Navarra). DO Navarra. This large firm, founded in 1982 as Cenalsa, has done much to improve winemaking standards in Navarra. It makes reliable wines either by blending and maturing musts bought from the co-ops or by buying in and vinifying grapes. Labels include AGRAMONT and Príncipe de Viana. Red wines are made from Garnacha, 100 per cent Tempranillo, Merlot, and Cabernet Sauvignon; and from blends of these grapes.

Puente la Reina

Small town southwest of PAMPLONA and a few kilometres from one of Navarra's most famous bodegas, the Señorío de SARRIA. Puente la Reina was one of the staging posts on the medieval pilgrim route from France to Santiago de Compostela (*see* "Galicia", page 94), its bridge joining the two main roads over the Pyrenees. Visit the great stone bridge across the River Arga and the honey-coloured churches, especially those of the Crucifix (Crucifijo) and of St James (Santiago), decorated with the scallop shells of the pilgrims.

Ribera Alta

DO r p (w dr) ☆→☆☆☆

Lying centrally between VALDIZARBE and BAJA MONTAÑA to the north and RIBERA BAJA to the south, this is the largest of the sub-regions of Navarra, with thirty per cent of the province's vineyards. Its best wines are the soft, fruity reds and rosés from around OLITE, containing some 11.5 to fifteen per cent alcohol.

Ribera Baja

DO r (w dr) ☆→☆☆

The Ribera Baja centres on the Ebro basin in the extreme south of Navarra. The climate is hot – much drier than in more northerly *comarcas* – and the soils contain large amounts of alluvial silt, conditions producing grapes high in sugar. Cascante and CINTRUENIGO make sturdy, full-bodied wines of up to sixteen per cent strength.

Sanguesa

(r w) p

Area in the hilly BAJA MONTAÑA centred on the basin of the River Aragón. Its soils are a mixture of gravels and chalk, and the best of its wines are the fresh and drinkable rosés.

Sarría, Bodega de

DO r (p w dr) res ☆☆ *96 97 99 00 01*

Puente la Reina (Navarra). DO Navarra. The Señorío de Sarría has made wines since medieval times, and they have been among Navarra's best. The vineyards and winery, owned by a local bank, were the brainchild of a Señor Huarte of the large Spanish construction company, who bought the abandoned estate in 1952. Its 1,200 hectares embrace a large French-style château, orchards, farms, sixty kilometres of cypress-lined private roads, and 160 hectares of vineyards, planted with Tempranillo, Garnacha, Mazuelo, Graciano, Merlot, and Cabernet Sauvignon for red wines, plus Malvasía, Viura, and Garnacha Blanca for whites.

Since the departure of the Huartes and the death of oenologist Francisco Morriones, the model village is deserted, and the estate's international reputation dimmed. Made in Rioja style, the wines mature in the bodega's 6,000 barricas, thirty per cent of Armagnac oak and the rest American or Yugoslavian. All labelled Señorío de Sarría, they include dry and semi-sweet whites; a 100 per cent Garnacha rosé; *crianzas* and *reservas* from 100 per cent Cabernet Sauvignon or 100 per cent Merlot; and blends of Cabernet Sauvignon with Tempranillo, Garnacha, Mazuelo, and Graciano.

Señorío de Andión

DO r ☆☆☆

Olite (Navarra). Founded in 2001 by the Grupo la Navarra, the bodega has made a promising start with a concentrated and fruity Señorío de Andión (01).

Señorío de Otazu, Bodega

DO w dr res ☆☆ *98 99*

Echauri (Navarra). DO Navarra. The wines are labelled Palacio de Otazu and include a barrel-fermented Chardonnay (99) and reds made from Cabernet Sauvignon, Merlot, and Tempranillo.

Tierra de Estella

DO r p ☆☆→☆☆

Subdivision of the DO Navarra, lying to the northeast of Rioja Alavesa and centred on Estella, a town of Romanesque churches and balconied houses, and once the court of the kings of Navarra. Its wines are very similar in character to those of VALDIZARBE further east, some full-bodied and robust reds, and finer *reservas*.

Txomin Etxaniz

DO w dr ☆☆ *DYA*

Guetería (Guipúzcoa). DO Chacolí de Guetería. The largest and best producer of CHACOLÍ; owner Iñaki Chueca has done much to revive interest in the wines. White Txakolí Txomin Etxaniz is freshly floral with a vivid lemon flavour.

Valdizarbe

DO r p ☆→☆☆☆

A subdivision of the DO Navarra, just south of PAMPLONA in the River Arga basin. Because of its chalky soils and more temperate climate it produces perhaps the best wines of the region, including those of the Señorío de SARRIA and the VINICOLA NAVARRA.

Vinícola Navarra

DO r (p w dr) res ★★→★★★ *97 98 99 00*

Campanas (Navarra). DO Navarra. Controlled by Bodegas y Bebidas (formerly Savín and now owned by Allied Domecq), this traditional bodega was built in 1880 against an abbey on the pilgrim route. Until recently it began maturation of some wines in large oak vats inherited from an earlier French firm The red Las Campanas *crianzas* and *reservas* (a blend of Cabernet and native grapes) are full and fruity, and proof of good traditional winemaking. The 100 per cent Garnacha rosé Castillo de Javier (02) is one of the best from Spain.

WINE AND FOOD

Cooking in Navarra has similarities with that of Aragón to the east and the Basque Country to the north. The mountain region in the north is famous for its lamb, served stewed with tomatoes (*espárragos mantañeses*), as a fricassée (*cochifrito*), or in a spicy *chilindrón* sauce. Another speciality is trout, sometimes served with ham. Local wines are varied enough to accompany these dishes. Vegetable dishes and fish call for a white wine; try a rosé with the snails and a good red with the lamb.

Alcachofas con almejas Artichokes with clams.

Caracoles a la corellana Snails cooked with garlic and parsley, cloves, bay leaves, thyme, and lemon juice.

Caracolillas de Navarra Small snails cooked in earthenware dishes with olive oil, tomatoes, green peppers, chillis, breadcrumbs, and seasoning.

Cardo a la Navarra Boiled cardoon (a vegetable that resembles celery) accompanied by a white sauce with ham.

Ensalada de pimientos piquillo Fish salad with piquillo peppers, langoustines, monkfish, fennel, garlic, olive oil, and sherry vinegar.

Huevos revueltos con ajos tiernos Eggs scrambled with young garlic shoots.

Menestra de habas de Tudela Fresh broad beans cooked with garlic, mint, saffron, almonds, artichoke hearts, boiled eggs, white wine, thyme, and seasoning.

Quesos (cheeses)

Cabrales One of the most famous Spanish cheeses, made in the Picos de Europa mountains of the north. Blue-veined and somewhat resembling Roquefort, it is matured in limestone caves for some six months.

Idiazábal A ewe's milk cheese from the Basque country, soft and buttery in consistency with piquant flavour accentuated by smoking over cherry, oak or beech wood.

Roncál A hard ewe's milk cheese with DO made in the Roncál valley in Navarra. Sharp, fully-flavoured, and sometimes smoked, much is exported to France.

Remojón Orange and cod salad.

Ternasco asado Roast leg of lamb basted with lemon juice and white wine.

Tortilla de Tudela Omelet made with the excellent locally grown asparagus.

Truchas a la Navarra The trout is first marinated and then cooked in an earthenware dish with onions, red wine, pepper, mint, thyme, and bay leaves.

Truchas con jamón Fried trout served on top of (or stuffed with) slices of fried ham.

HOTELS

Olite The *Parador de Olite* lies more or less centrally in the wine area – ideal for visiting vineyards and bodegas.

Pamplona Has several extremely comfortable hotels, including: *Iruña Palace Tres Reyes, NH Iruña Park, Blanca de Navarra,* and *AC Ciudad de Pamplona,* with a good restaurant.

RESTAURANTS

Olite *Parador de Olite* has regional dishes and a good list of local wines.

Pamplona *Hartza* serves hake with scallop sauce and *menestra; Josetxo* is particularly recommended for its game and foie gras with grapes, and it also has a good wine list; *Rodero* offers sophisticated French and local cuisine; *Europa* for stewed ox-tongue in Cabernet Sauvignon, salad of prawns, and duck's sweetbreads; *Alhambra* serves good traditional cooking.

Puente la Reina *Mesón del Peregrino* offers food in a pleasant country style.

Tafalla *Tubal* serves crêpes with borage and clam sauce or pheasant breasts with onions.

Tudela *Restaurante 33* for expert cooking with fresh local produce.

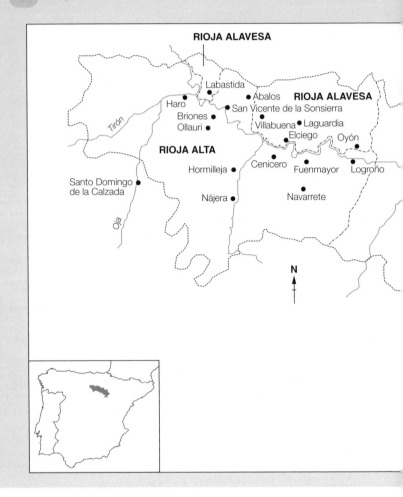

Rioja

Apart from sherry, Rioja is the best known of Spanish wines. Thanks to good quality and reasonable prices, foreign sales have leapfrogged in recent years: in Britain alone, they increased from 180,000 litres in 1970 to some nineteen million litres in 2001, with correspondingly huge increases in sales to Denmark, Germany, Switzerland, and the USA. The bulk of Rioja's wines are red and have traditionally been characterized by the long periods they spend in cask, and by their oaky nose and flavour. In recent years, however, the reds have spent less time in wood and more in bottle, and Rioja has also been making a new style of white wine: light, fresh, and fruity, without age in wood. Rioja was the first Spanish region to be demarcated, when a *consejo regulador* was set up in 1926 to control production and quality, and in 1991 it became the first to achieve the status

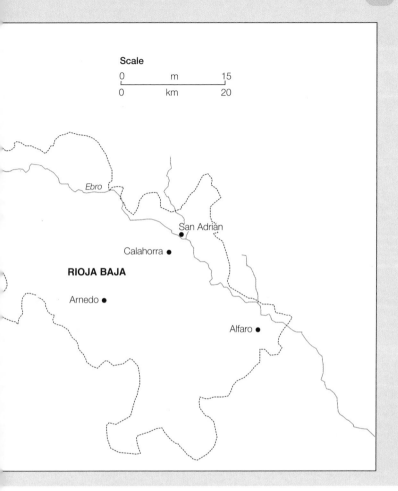

of *denominación de origen calificada,* or DOCa, reserved for wines of the highest quality. It now comprises 62,000 hectares of vineyards within the provinces of La Rioja (formerly known as Logroño), Alava, and Navarra, with production in 2002 of 197 million litres of wine. The vineyards extend for 120 kilometres on both sides of the River Ebro, which flows from the rocky Conchas de Haro in the hilly west of the region to Alfaro in the east.

The valley is bounded by mountains on either side and is a maximum width of forty kilometres. The soils are a mixture of calcareous clay, ferruginous clay, and alluvial silt, with a predominance of calcareous clay in Rioja Alavesa (one of the three sub-regions) to the north of the river. In the west of the area the climate is temperate and fairly predictable, with mild, wet springs, short, hot summers, long, warm autumns, and a little snow and frost in winter. The hotter and more Mediterranean-like Rioja Baja in the east is classified as semi-arid.

The Rioja DOCa is divided into the three sub-regions of Rioja Alta, Rioja Alavesa, and Rioja Baja, of which the first two produce the more delicate wines. (In this chapter the sub-region, not the province or DO zone, is given in parentheses.) Wine was being made in Rioja long before the Roman occupation of the area: the traditional method, which is still practised in the bodegas of smallholders, was to tip the bunches of grapes, stalks and all, into open stone troughs, or *lagos*. Fermentation then proceeded in stages, with progressively firmer crushing of the grapes.

Production of Rioja in its present style began after the double disasters of oidium and phylloxera in France in the late 1800s, when French négociants moved into the district and introduced the methods employed in Bordeaux, notably the destalking of the grapes and the ageing of the wines in 225-litre oak casks. Long after the French reduced the period in wood, the Riojans continued to age the wines, both red and white, for long years in oak – hence the characteristically vanilla-like bouquet and flavour – and it is only in the last decade that more attention has been given to bottle-age. With the widespread production of cold-fermented white wines without maturation in cask, matters have turned full circle, and now a new generation of cask-aged whites has appeared – albeit less fiercely oaky than their predecessors.

The first great Rioja boom took place during the latter decades of the nineteenth century; and the bodegas constructed during that period – Riscal, Murrieta, López de Heredia, CVNE, La Rioja Alta, and the rest – are still among those producing the best wines. Another phase of expansion – financed by banks, sherry firms, Spanish industrialists, and foreign wine concerns – took place in the 1970s. These bodegas are characterized by their size and the modernity of their equipment, but all of them – in conformity with the regulations laid down by the *consejo regulador* – mature their better red wines in the traditional 225-litre oak *barricas*. More recently, a new generation of small bodegas has sprung up, often based in old houses or castles and relying entirely on grapes grown in their own vineyards, of which the region has seen a veritable explosion in recent years, with cash-rich speculators piling in from Madrid and elsewhere. There are now 472 wineries in the region.

Present practice in the newer bodegas is to macerate the red wines, to ferment at controlled temperatures in stainless steel, to avoid prolonged ageing in wood, and to give them more time in bottle. This results in more immediately juicy and fruity wines, which do not always last as long as they used to (*see* "Keeping Riojas"). Although most of the large bodegas own sizeable vineyards of their own, and some of the newer ones have embarked on extensive new plantations, traditional patterns of agriculture persist, with most of the grapes being grown by smallholders on plots interspersed by wheat, potatoes, and other vegetables. All the large concerns buy substantial amounts of fruit from the independent farmers, and some also make use of wine made in the cooperatives, of which there are thirty in the area. In contrast to Bordeaux, the vines are normally grown low, without supporting stakes and wires, and pruned *en vaso* ("goblet-shaped"), with three *brazos* or main stems, each of which bears two *sarmientos* or grafted shoots, bearing two bunches of grapes, so there are twelve bunches in all.

Grape Varieties

Of the many vine varieties formerly grown in Rioja, the *consejo regulador* now approves only the following seven:

BLACK

Tempranillo Also known as the Ull de Llebre, Cencibel, Tinto Fino, or Tinto del País, this is the Rioja grape par excellence, making up fifty per cent or more of the red Rioja Alta wines and eighty per cent or more of those from Rioja Alavesa. Thick-skinned and intensely black, its grapes produce wines of 10.5 to thirteen per cent alcohol, with good acid balance and suitable for ageing, but tending on their own to be short-lived.

Graciano Small, round, and black, the grapes make fresh and aromatic wines, but are too scarce and produce wines too low in alcohol (ten to twelve per cent) to be used on their own.

Mazuelo These large "pointed" grapes yield musts rich in colour, extract, and tannin, and are valuable for wood-aged wines.

Garnacha/Garnacho Medium-sized, thin-skinned, and resistant to oidium, this is the typical grape of Rioja Baja. It is widely grown elsewhere in Spain and, as Grenache, in the Rhône. Its musts contain fifteen to sixteen per cent alcohol and are blended with others to contribute alcoholic degree and body. They are also used on their own for fresh young rosés. Garnacha wines oxidize very easily and it is difficult to judge their age from the colour, since they soon turn a brick red.

In addition to these native varieties, some plantings of **Cabernet Sauvignon** are permitted on an experimental scale.

WHITE

Viura The local name for Macabeo, Viura yields musts with about eleven per cent alcohol and plenty of tartaric acid. Resistant to oxidation, the grapes are particularly suitable for making light and fruity white wines by cold fermentation.

Malvasía Vigorous and large-leaved, but prone to mildew. White-tinted with red when fully mature, these produce fresh wines of about eleven per cent, often made in an admixture with Viura.

Garnacha Blanca Not so much used in the Rioja as the other two varieties, these grapes produce pleasant white wines, but higher in alcohol and with less acidity.

There was a popular superstition that red Riojas are made in *solera*, but this is entirely untrue. They were traditionally made by blending wines from different grape varieties, often grown in separate areas of the region. Varietal wines, often containing one hundred per cent Tempranillo, are now increasingly produced. There is sometimes a limited admixture of wines of different vintage, but the bottle must contain not less than eighty-five per cent of the vintage stated on the label. It was usual in the past – and the custom lingers in other parts of Spain – to label them with a description such as three or five degrees *año*, meaning the wine was bottled during the third or fifth year after harvest. Without knowing how long the wine had been in bottle it was impossible to gauge when it had been made. All exported wines are now labelled with a vintage.

Vintages

Because of the more predictable climate and the former practice of blending a proportion of better wine with the poorer growths, in the past vintage years were not as variable as those in Bordeaux. They are now important – increasingly so as the *consejo regulador* tightens the regulations. Outstanding among earlier years were: 1915, 1920, 1922, 1924, 1925, 1931, 1934, 1942, 1947, 1948, 1949, 1952, 1955, 1958, 1964, 1968, 1970, 1973.

Official ratings for more recent years follow, with a personal assessment (in parentheses) of the current status of the wines since the 1982 vintage. Of course, producers vary, and there are significant exceptions.

Year	Yield (millions of litres)	Rating
81	130	*very good*
82	113	*excellent (although rated above 81, it has not lasted as well)*
83	106	*good (now thin and watery, avoid)*
84	130	*average (as above, avoid)*
85	176	*good (fair intensity, peaked or peaking)*
86	120	*good (good but lean, now drying out)*
87	133	*very good (unduly praised in Spain)*
88	132	*good (thin and mean, avoid)*
89	160	*very good (middle weight, a few hanging on)*
90	166	*very good (light, beyond its best)*
91	146	*very good (medium intensity, drink now, most before their best)*
92	150	*good (soft and immediate, drink now)*
93	175	*good (looking a bit thin and immediate)*
94	169	*excellent (but maturing sooner than expected)*
95	218	*very good (good, and currently drinking well)*
96	244	*very good (lighter, drink now)*
97	253	*good (but lacking structure)*
98	273	*very good (record vintage; rain and lack of sunshine resulted in light, but agreeable wines for earlyish consumption)*
99	216	*good (huge harvest but average wines)*
00	311	*good (huge harvest. Patchy quality; the best are very good indeed)*
01	240	*excellent*
02	197	*good*

Keeping Riojas

An extended range of vintages is printed for a number of Rioja bodegas. However, the quality of the older *reservas* and *gran reservas* is dependent on proper cellarage. Old wines kept for any period in the racks of a warm restaurant will soon deteriorate. My own experience is that red Riojas do not now last as long as their oakier predecessors. For example, some of the 85s, 86s, 87s, 89s, and 90s are already drying out – although, depending on the bodega, an older vintage may well be delightful. Currently, the 95, 98, and 00 vintages are the safest choice.

As when visiting most wine areas, it is a great advantage to have a car, though once in Logroño there is a charming local train which wends its leisurely way by Fuenmayor, Cenicero, and Briones to Haro, depositing you on the doorstep of many of the bodegas and affording better views of the Ebro and the vineyards than those from the main road. The quickest approach to the region is to fly to Bilbao, hire a car, and drive to Haro or Logroño, one and a half to two hours away off the A68 *autopista*. Alternatively, drive from Barcelona by way of Zaragoza and the A2. This route will take you through the heart of the Rioja Baja. It is easy enough to make a leisurely circuit of the Rioja Alta and Rioja Alavesa in a day by driving from Logroño to Haro on the N232 by way of Fuenmayor, Cenicero, and Briones, and returning by the road north of the Ebro, also labelled the N232, through Labastida, Abalos, and Laguardia. It is especially worthwhile to visit Briones and Laguardia, two of the most picturesque hilltop towns of the Rioja. Stay in Logroño, Haro, or Santo Domingo de la Calzada for Rioja Alta and Rioja Alavesa; Calahorra for Rioja Baja. Many restaurants serve good regional food and wine in towns and villages in the region (*see* page 144).

AGE
r (p) w dr res ☆☆
Fuenmayor (Rioja Alta). This large bodega, formed in 1964 by the union of three much older concerns, Azpilicueta, Cruz García, and Entrena, is owned by the BODEGAS Y BEBIDAS group, now controlled by Allied Domecq. Its labels are Azpilicueta, Marqués de Roméral, and Siglo Saco, and the wines are reliable if unspectacular.

Ageing
Riojas, both red and white, have traditionally been aged in cask for much longer than Bordeaux or Burgundy wines, and they have from time to time been criticized for a pronounced oaky nose and flavour (*see* OAK). The present trend is to cut down on the period in cask and to give the better red wines at least a year or two in bottle. *See also* CRIANZA. Significant amounts of wine are also being made by *maceration carbonique* and sold without ageing in wood as *vinos jóvenes*.

Alambrado
A fine wire mesh sometimes used around bottles of *reservas*, now decorative but originally to prevent tampering.

Alavesas, Bodegas
r (p) w dr res ☆☆
Laguardia (Rioja Alavesa). This large concern, with 100 hectares of vineyards, has a capacity of ten million litres and matures its wine in 5,000 OAK BARRICAS. The best known of its wines, made from 100 per cent Tempranillo, are labelled Solar de Samaniego, after a local poet and composer of fables. Once light and thoroughly typical of RIOJA ALAVESA, they are now fuller-bodied in style. To be recommended is the fruity, unoaked Vino Joven.

Aldeanueva, Viñedos de

r w dr ★★ *95 96 98 99 01*

Aldeanueva de Ebro (Rioja Baga). Huge co-op, with 2,700 hectares of vineyard and 8,000 OAK BARRICAS. Good red Azabache wines. The 1996 and 1998 are not up to the standard of earlier vintages.

Alfaro

This small town at the eastern extreme of RIOJA BAJA is the home of several bodegas. Its name is derived from El Faro (meaning "the lighthouse"), and it was the furthest point on the Ebro reached by the Phoenicians in their shallow draught boats. It is an attractive little place with some fine baronial houses and a beautiful seventeenth-century church.

Allende, Finca

r w dr ☆☆☆→☆☆☆☆ *96 97 98 99 00 01*

Briones (Rioja Alta). Miguel Angel Gregorio opened a small bodega in his native Briones in 1994. His wines have been acclaimed by Robert Parker and others as some of the best from Spain. The vastly expensive, dark, concentrated, and intensely fruity Aurus (96, 97) made from eighty-five per cent Tempranillo and fifteen per cent Graciano, has been joined by an equally recondite Calvario (00) containing a little Garnacha.

Amézola de la Mora, Bodegas

r res ☆☆ *94 95 97 98*

Torremontalbo (Rioja Alta). Winemaking at Torremontalbo, an historic castle between Logroño and Haro, was revived in 1986, when the 130-year-old cellars were completely re-equipped. The estate-grown Viña Amézola and Señorío are attractive and well-made reds.

Artadi

w dr p r res ★★ →☆☆☆☆ *94 95 96 98 99 00*

Label used by COSECHEROS ALAVESES for its well-made wines, among the best in Rioja.

Barón de Chirel

res ☆☆☆☆ *88 91 94 95 96 98 99*

Premium wine from MARQUÉS DE RISCAL; concentrated, fruity, and one of the very best from Rioja.

Barón de Ley

r res (w dr) ☆☆☆ *91 94 95 96 97 99 00*

Mendavia (Rioja Baja). The Barón de Ley was established in the late 1980s by the owners of Bodegas EL COTO. Its headquarters are in a meticulously restored hunting lodge, situated in ninety hectares of vineyards. The wines, made from 100 per cent Tempranillo, are savoury and well balanced with overtones of oak. Best is the Finca del Monasterio (00).

Barón de Oña

DO r res ☆☆☆

Excellent red *reserva* from TORRE DE OÑA SA, controlled by La RIOJA ALTA.

Barrica

The 225-litre oak cask in which all the CRIANZA and *reserva* wines must statutorily be matured is a legacy of the *vignerons* from Bordeaux, who settled in Rioja during the phylloxera epidemic of the late nineteenth century.

Berberana, Bodegas

r (w dr) res ★★ *96 98 99 02*

Cenicero (Rioja Alta). The company, now one of the largest in Rioja and part of the BODEGAS UNIDAS group, was founded in 1877 by the Berberana family in OLLAURI, where it still maintains cellars for ageing the wines in bottle. It underwent a major expansion in 1972 and belonged for a period to RUMASA, after which it was temporarily nationalized and then sold to various shareholders in 1985.

The vinification plant in CENICERO incorporates modern stainless-steel fermentation tanks and a huge ageing floor accommodating 60,000 OAK BARRICAS. Berberana embarked on ambitious new plantations at Monte Yerga near Aldeanueva del Ebro in the RIOJA BAJA, growing a high proportion of Tempranillo and Viura in addition to the Garnacha typical of the area, but these are now owned by a separate company. The popular CARTA DE ORO wines (a brand created in 1877) are fruity, well-balanced, and full-bodied, as are the Alarde *reservas*. The big-selling Dragón Tempranillo is not from the Rioja but the VdT Castilla y León; and BODEGAS UNIDAS, of which Berberana is an integral part, is increasingly selling its best wines under the MARQUÉS DE GRIÑON label.

Berceo, Bodegas

r w dr p res ☆☆→☆☆☆ *95 98 99 00*

Haro (Rioja Alta). The sister ship of Bodegas GURPEGUI MUGA, making worthwhile red Viña Berceo and Gonzalo de Berceo.

Beronia, Bodegas

r w dr res ☆☆→☆☆☆ *95 98 00 01*

Ollauri (Rioja Alta). The firm, with ten hectares of vineyards in one of the best areas of the RIOJA ALTA, began operations in 1970, working from a small bodega in the village of Ollauri. Later it moved to an elegant new winery in the midst of the vineyards, and it was the intention of Don Javier Bilbao Iturbe to make wines by traditional methods on a limited scale, but also to take advantage of modern technology. Such was the success among the *cognoscenti* of the dry, fruity, and well-balanced red Berón and the Beronia *reservas* which are made with a high percentage of Tempranillo, that in 1982 the bodega was taken over by the sherry firm of González-Byass, which has since more than tripled production, buying in fruit and sometimes wines to do so. The red wines, including a 100 per cent Mazuelo, maintain high standards and are generally more interesting than the white.

Bilbaínas, Bodegas

r (p) w dr sw sp res ☆☆→☆☆☆ *94 95 96 97 98*

Haro (Rioja Alta). Bilbaínas, founded in 1901, was one of the first firms to build a bodega adjacent to the newly opened railway from Bilbao, and its wines have long been known in the UK, where at one time it maintained its own cellars and office. It owns 260 hectares of vineyards, mostly around Haro, with a smaller holding at Leza in the RIOJA ALAVESA. The bodega's wines include a traditional full-bodied red VIÑA POMAL, made basically with grapes from Leza; and good La Vicalanda *reservas* in a less oaky, more fruity and aromatic modern style. The firm, which has recently been taken over by Codorníu, also makes wines by the Champagne method (*see* "Sparkling Wines", page 178).

Bodegas Unidas

Umbrella organization controlling MARQUÉS DE GRIÑON, MARQUÉS DE MONISTROL, BODEGAS BERBERANA, and Vinícola Mediterránea with its holiday wines. Unidas also owns the winery of the late Prince Hohenlohe in Ronda, famous for its pure Petit Verdot. A new departure are the *haciendas* situated in the vineyards, both making wine and putting up visitors: Hacienda Unamuno (Alto Duero) and Hacienda La Concordia in the hills of RIOJA BAJA.

Bodegas y Bebidas

Formerly called Savín and recently bought by Allied Domecq, this is one of the largest Spanish wine companies, specializing in inexpensive branded wine made to good standards, but also making prestige wines such as the CAMPO VIEJO *reservas*. The company possesses wineries up and down Spain, such as the Casa de la Viña in Valdepeñas and the Vinícola Navarra; in the Rioja it operates a bodega at Aldeanueva del Ebro in the RIOJA BAJA and also controls CAMPO VIEJO in Logroño, Bodegas AGE, and the MARQUÉS DEL PUERTO in FUENMAYOR.

Bordelesa

An alternative name, reflecting its Bordeaux origins, for the 225-litre OAK BARRICA.

Bretón y Cía, Bodegas

w dr p r ☆☆→☆☆☆☆ *95 96 98 00*

Logroño (Rioja Alta). Founded in 1985, the bodega is making a name for itself with its modern-style Loriñon wines, and the 95 Dominio de Conte and Alba de Bretón *reservas* are outstanding.

Briones

A little east of Haro, the small hilltop town of Briones, with its stone-built baronial houses, statuesque church, and long views over the Ebro, is one of the most attractive in RIOJA ALTA and is home to the small but sophisticated bodegas of Finca ALLENDE and MIGUEL MERINO.

Calahorra

The largest town in RIOJA BAJA, birthplace of Quintilian and famous for its protracted siege by Pompey in the first century BC, and a convenient stopping place en route to Logroño from Zaragoza and good base for visiting the sub-region. There is a comfortable *parador*, the Marco Fabio Quintiliano.

Campillo, Bodegas

r res w dr p ☆☆☆ *94 95 96 97 99*

Laguardia (Alava). Opened in 1990 by the group owning FAUSTINO, its first vintages were made with Faustino's grapes. It has an elegant new winery and fifty hectares of vineyards, and makes lightish, high-quality reds from 100 per cent Tempranillo.

Campo Viejo, Bodegas

r (p w dr) res ★→★★★ *94 95 96 97 98 00*

Logroño (Rioja Alta). Owned by the ubiquitous firm of BODEGAS Y BEBIDAS and situated in Logroño itself, Campo Viejo is the largest firm in Rioja, with 70,000 barrels. Its widely advertised San Asensio is among the biggest selling of young *sin crianza* Riojas, and the bodega also produces some big red *reservas*, including the slightly coarse, crowd-pleasing Marqués de Villamagna and reliable 100 per cent Tempranillo Alcorta. The cheap red Albor, made by carbonic maceration, is no longer produced in Rioja. Campo Viejo will soon move to the largest bodega in Spain near Fuenmayor.

Cañas, Bodegas Luís

r res (w dr p) ★★→☆☆☆☆ *89 92 94 95 96*

Villabuena (Rioja Alavesa). This small bodega makes a fresh and fruity Recien (98) with ninety-five per cent Tempranillo and five per cent Viura, and good CRIANZAS and *reservas*. The Reserva Amaren 96, made mainly from Tempranillo, was outstanding.

Carlos Serres, Bodegas

r (p w sw) res ☆→☆☆☆ *94 95 96 98*

Haro (Rioja Alta). Well-known Haro firm, whose younger wines are labelled as Carlos Serres. Its best wines are the red Carlos Serres and Onomástica *reservas* and *gran reservas*.

Carta de Oro

r ★★

Fruity red and white CRIANZA wines from BERBERANA.

Casa del Vino

See LAGUARDIA.

Castillo de Cuzcurrita

r res dr ☆☆

Río Tirón (Rioja Alta). Small bodega in a fourteenth-century castle. It makes good but astringent red wines from grapes grown in its own vineyards, including a reputed Reserva Conde de Alacha.

Castillo Ygay

res ☆☆☆☆ *25 52 64 68 70 75 78 82 85 87 89 94 95 96 97 99*

Gran reserva from the MARQUÉS DE MURRIETA, made only in exceptional years. The 1934 was one of the most complete and beautiful Riojas I have ever tasted. There are also excellent and very expensive white Ygays.

Cenicero

Town on the Ebro west of Logroño in RIOJA ALTA, and the headquarters of important bodegas. It was the burial place of the Roman legions stationed in the area, hence the name, which in Spanish means "ashtray". Cenicero stages an interesting wine festival in September, held in its large, covered *pelota* court.

Compañía de Vinos Telmo Rodríguez

With headquarters in Logroño, the company, founded by Telmo Rodríguez, formerly of REMELLURI, makes excellent wines in various regions other than Rioja, including Málaga, Rueda, and Toro. The best of the Rioja wines is the intense and concentrated Altos de Lanzaga (00) made from Tempranillo, Garnacha, and Mazuelo.

Compañía Vinícola del Norte de España (CVNE)

r (p) w dr sw res ★★→★★★ *94 95 96 97 98 99 01*

Haro (Rioja Alta). CVNE was founded in 1879 in the flush nineteenth-century Rioja boom, and has been making excellent wines ever since. The CRIANZA Cune is a reliable young red Rioja; the Imperial and VIÑA REAL *reservas*, the latter a full-bodied and aromatic Alavesa made in Elciego, are superb, as is the newly introduced Real de Asua (99). CVNE makes a new-style white Rioja without maturation in wood: the oaky Monopole is a traditional white Rioja; and the superior single-vineyard red, CONTINO, made by a subsidiary, is grown in vineyards at La Serna in RIOJA ALAVESA, west of Oyón. These big, mellow, full-bodied wines with blackberry flavour and a long finish are among the best in Rioja.

Conde de Valdemar

res ☆☆☆ *89 90 92 93 94 95 96 97 98 99 00*

Excellent red *reservas* made by MARTÍNEZ BUJANDA.

Contino

res ☆☆☆☆ *94 95 96 97 98 99 00*

Superior single-vineyard red *reserva*, made by Viñedos de Contino in RIOJA ALAVESA, owned by COMPAÑÍA VINÍCOLA DEL NORTE DE ESPAÑA. The first vintage, made in 1974, is fragile but still beautiful, and a newish

introduction, Vinna del Olivio, is outstanding. The bodega also makes a
rare and excellent 100 per cent Graciano.

Corral, Bodegas

r (p w dr) ☆☆

Navarrete (Rioja Alta). The bodega is by the Pilgrim Way to Santiago
and is best known for its Don Jacobo wines. Best is its superior Altos de
Corral (95).

Cosecheros Alaveses

r w dr res ★★→☆☆☆☆☆ *91 92 94 95 96 97 98 99 00 01*

Laguardia (Rioja Alavesa). Innovative firm, formerly a co-op, best known
for its unoaked, well-balanced, and fruity young red Artadi, but now
making excellent 100 per cent Tempranillo Viñas de Gain and Pagos Viejos
reserva wines. Also home to a magnificent Grandes Añadas (00) and an
outstanding Viña el Pisón *reserva* (00) from seventy-year-old single-
vineyard grapes.

Crianza

Literally "nursing"; in terms of wines the word refers to their maturation in
oak cask. The regulations of the *consejo regulador* are strict: to be labelled
con crianza, a Rioja, red or white, must be matured for two years with a
minimum of one in a 225-litre OAK BARRICA and not released before the third
year. (For the *reservas* and *gran reservas, see* "Glossary", pages 14–15.)
Riojas need not, however, be aged in oak to qualify for *denominación de
origen*. There are no rules as regards the ageing of wines *sin crianza*
("without ageing"), which may nevertheless spend a few months in cask.
These are now known as *vinos jóvenes*.

Cumbrero

r w dr ☆☆

Label by Bodegas MONTECILLO for its pleasant, young red and white Riojas.

CVNE

Abbreviation of COMPAÑIA VINICOLA DEL NORTE DE ESPAÑA, whose wines are
known colloquially in Spain as "Cune".

Domecq, Bodegas

r (p) w dr ★★→☆☆☆☆ *94 95 96 97 98*

Elciego (Rioja Alavesa). The origins of the company date from the early
1970s, when the sherry concern of Pedro Domecq and the Canadian firm
of Seagram joined forces to take over Bodegas PALACIO. The partners later
parted ways, and in due course Pedro Domecq constructed its own
bodega, with modern stainless-steel fermentation tanks and a capacity of
some 25,000 OAK BARRICAS for maturing the wines. Bodegas Domecq has
300 hectares of new vineyards in one of the best parts of RIOJA ALAVESA, a
venture notable among other aspects for training the vines in Bordeaux
style, rather than pruning them low in traditional Riojan fashion. The
younger wines, always sound and drinkable, are labelled Viña Eguia. The
MARQUÉS DE ARIENZO *reservas* and *gran reservas* are fruity and complex,
with a long finish. Best is the delicate Marqués de Arienzo Especial (98).

Ebro, River

The Ebro flows through Rioja from west to east, entering through the
rocky gorge of the Conchas de Haro and leaving near Alfaro in RIOJA
BAJA. Vineyards extend upwards from both sides of the river or lie in the
valleys of its seven tributaries, the Tirón, Oja, Najerilla, Iregua, Leza,
Cidacos, and Alama.

El Coto de Rioja

r w dr res ☆☆→☆☆☆ *91 94 95 96 97 98*

Oyón (Rioja Alavesa). Large bodega founded in 1973, later acquired by Alexis Lichine and then by owners of BARON DE LEY, it owns 300 hectares of vineyards, controls 1,200 more, and has 57,000 OAK BARRICAS. Red *reservas* and *gran reservas* (100 per cent Tempranillo from the RIOJA ALAVESA) are labelled Coto de Imaz, El Coto, and Coto Real. Its often delightful wines are somewhat unpredictable – for example the 1998 CRIANZA made in a good year was mediocre, while the dicey harvest of 1997 gave rise to a first-rate Coto Real.

Elciego

Hill village in RIOJA ALAVESA over the EBRO from CENICERO. With steep, narrow streets, and a church dominating the surrounding vineyards, it is famous as the home of the bodegas of the MARQUÉS DE RISCAL.

Estación de Viticultura y Enología

Government laboratory in HARO, working in conjunction with the *consejo regulador*. Its main job is to ensure that wines conform to the standards of the *reglamento*, but it also conducts research into the production of Rioja wines. It has an excellent wine museum.

Faustino, Bodegas

r (p) w dr res ★★→☆☆☆ *91 93 94 95 96 97 99 00*

Oyón (Rioja Alavesa). The Martínez family has been making good wines in Oyón since before 1860, and began bottling them in 1931. Still a family firm, it owns 650 hectares of vineyards in one of the best areas of RIOJA ALAVESA. It does not age its wines overlong in oak, and its excellent *gran reserva*, Faustino I, spends two years there, followed by more in bottle. There is a light, well-balanced, 100 per cent Viura white and the bodega markets a *vino joven* red, made in traditional fashion by carbonic maceration: it is a dark, plum colour, with a yeasty nose and a good blackberry flavour reminiscent of Beaujolais Nouveau. Also good is the premium Faustino de Autor (95). *See also* Bodegas CAMPILLO.

Franco-Españolas, Bodegas

r (p) w dr sw res ☆→☆☆

Logroño (Rioja Alta). Large, established firm with bodegas in the heart of Logroño, just across the bridge over the EBRO. Taken over by RUMASA in 1973 and later resold to entrepreneur Marcos Equizábal, it makes a sweet white Diamante and red Bordón, but its rather old-fashioned wines are not of pre-takeover standards.

Fuenmayor

On the main road from LOGROÑO to HARO and close to the EBRO, Fuenmayor, with CENICERO, is next in importance to Haro among Riojan wine towns.

Gurpegui Muga, Bodegas Luís

r p w dr ★→★★

San Adrián (Rioja Baja). Large family firm founded in 1921 and owning 108 hectares of vineyards in the vicinity of San Adrián. A large supplier of bulk wine, its inexpensive bottled wine is sold under the label Viñadrián and the *crianzas* and *reservas* as Dominio de la Plata. The rosé has always been particularly fresh and good. *See also* Bodegas BERCEO.

Haro

Near the western tip of the region, Haro, a busy little town with a population of 9,500, is the wine capital of RIOJA ALTA and the home of more than a dozen bodegas. Built uphill and downhill above the EBRO, it is a place of narrow streets and stylish old houses, with a wide central square. Points of interest include the wine shops of Juan González Muga, specializing in old and rare vintages and special offers of Riojas from the local bodegas. Haro is the headquarters of a government wine laboratory, the ESTACIÓN DE VITICULTURA Y ENOLOGÍA. At Briñas, on the road north to Vitoria facing the rocky Conchas de Haro, there is a wine museum displaying bottles from most of the bodegas in Rioja, where the wines may also be tasted.

Hormilleja
Village near Nájera in the centre of vineyards producing most of the Garnacha grown in RIOJA ALTA.

Ijalba, Viña
r res w dr p ★★→☆☆☆ *98 99 01 02*

Logroño (Rioja Alta). Founded in 1990, the firm has already established a reputation for the quality of its organically grown young wines, like the 100 per cent Tempranillo Solferino made by carbonic maceration. It makes that rarity, a 100 per cent Graciano, and its attractive CRIANZA is the house wine at the Hotel Los Agustinos in HARO.

Labastida
Village in the RIOJA ALAVESA northeast of HARO, and home of one of the best co-ops in the region.

Labastida, Unión de Cosecheros de
r (p) w dr res ★★→★★★ *97 98 00 02*

Labastida (Rioja Alavesa). The co-op, founded in 1956 and enlarged in 1965, has some 160 *socios* (members) growing grapes in three of the best areas of the region (Labastida, Samaniego, and Villalba). With a total capacity of seven million litres, it is one of the few co-ops in Rioja to possess OAK BARRICAS and to bottle its wines. The CRIANZAS and *reservas* are sold under the labels Solagüen (97) and Manuel Quintana (98) and are very reasonably priced – and of excellent quality. The young Montebuena white is exceptionally fresh, and the red, too, can be delightful but is somewhat variable in quality.

Laguardia
This old walled landmark town crowns a hill in the heart of RIOJA ALAVESA. Its narrow streets and old, dark houses are honeycombed with small peasant bodegas, now mostly disused, and there are large modern wineries on the outskirts. Although it is quiet enough on weekdays, at weekends and on holidays it is a target for visitors from Bilbao and San Sebastián, who come to picnic and to fill their carafes with local wine. The old baronial house of the Fabulista Samaniego, the eighteenth-century author of some rather pointless fables, has been converted into a centre for the study of Alavesa wines: the Casa del Vino. Apart from its interesting exhibits on local history as well as viticulture and oenology, it possesses modern laboratories and advises the smaller producers, or *cosecheros*, of the region.

LAN, Bodegas
r (p) w dr res ☆☆→☆☆☆ *94 95 96 97 98 01*

Fuenmayor (Rioja Alta). Large bodega founded in 1969, taken over by RUMASA and since resold. The wines have been uneven in quality over recent years, but are much improved, thanks to large investment and modernization of the bodega. They include a fresh white Lan not matured in oak, and good red Lan CRIANZAS and *reservas*. Best are the Lanciano *reservas* made from eighty-five per cent Tempranillo and fifteen per cent Mazuelo, and the Premium Mención de Lan (99), and Culmen de Lan (94).

Líbano, Señorío de

r res ☆☆☆ *94 95 96 97 98*

Sajazarra (Rioja Alta). Small bodega making Castillo de Sajazarra *reservas* from grapes grown on its forty-five hectares of vineyards. Very oaky, they contain a proportion of Graciano.

Logroño

Capital of the province of La Rioja, Logroño – with a population of 128,000 – is the only large town in the Rioja and the commercial centre of its wine industry. A handsome city positioned by the EBRO, its spacious tree-lined square, the Espolón, is the focus of the Fiesta de SAN MATEO, which is held from September 21 to mark the beginning of the grape-picking season. Logroño is also the headquarters of the CONSEJO REGULADOR, of the Grupo de Exportadores, and of three of the largest Rioja bodegas, FRANCO-ESPAÑOLAS, CAMPO VIEJO, and OLARRA. It also possesses numerous good restaurants and hotels.

López Agos, Bodegas

See Bodegas MARQUÉS DEL PUERTO.

López de Heredia, R Viña Tondonia

r (p) w dr sw res ☆☆☆→☆☆☆☆ *54 57 61 64 68 70 73 78 81 87 93 94 97*

Haro (Rioja Alta). Founded in 1877 at the height of the phylloxera epidemic in France, López de Heredia is one of the most traditional of bodegas. All its buildings are made from quarried stone, the vessels for making and maturing the wine are mostly of American oak, and the cellars, like the famous El Calado, are tunnelled out of the sandstone seventeen metres below ground, so that the temperature remains an even 12°C with a relative humidity of eighty per cent all year round. The wines, made to last with no concessions to modernity, start rather tannic, but age gloriously after long periods in oak. The old white Tondonias (57, 64, 76), with a subtle blend of oak and fruit, are a revelation to people who think white wines of this age must be flat and oxidized – the 64 is at its peak. The youngest red is the stylish young Cubillo; older reds include Tondonia and Bosconia *reservas*, the latter rather softer and fuller-bodied. Some *reservas* can be described only as classics.

Luberri

r ☆☆→☆☆☆☆ *94 95 96 98 99 00 02*

Elciego (Rioja Alavesa). Small, modern bodega with thirty-two hectares of vineyard, making excellent young reds and CRIANZAS, under the labels of Luberri, Monje Amestoy, and Biga.

Marqués de Arienzo

r res ☆☆→☆☆☆☆ *94 95 96 97 98*

The label used by Bodegas DOMECQ for its excellent wines, both red and white.

Marqués de Cáceres, Union Vitivinícola

r (p) w dr res ★★★ *89 92 94 95 96 97 98*

Cenicero (Rioja Alta). The bodega was founded in 1970 by Don Enríque Forner, who, with his brother, owns châteaux in the Haut-Médoc. Its methods are more similar to those of Bordeaux than to most of the concerns in the Rioja, since it was planned with advice from Professor

Peynaud of Bordeaux University. It describes itself as a *Unión Vitivinícola*, grapes being supplied by a group of substantial local producers.

The wines are fruity, well-balanced, and less oaky than the traditional red Riojas, with a blackberry flavour and long finish. The firm was the first to introduce a new-style white Rioja made by cold fermentation and unaged in cask. Exceptionally light, fresh, and fruity, it is still one of the best wines of its type. The bodega has now added two CRIANZA whites: a semi-sweet Satinela and Antea, which is ninety per cent Viura and ten per cent Malvasía. Both are attractively clean, fresh, and fruity, and have a touch of oak and a long finish. The Gaudium *reserva* (94, 96) and MC (01), made from Garnacha, Tempranillo, and Graciano, are superb wines.

Marqués de Griñón
r res ☆☆ *96 97 98*

Good, fruity wines with vanilla oak. They include a Marqués de Griñón Tempranillo, Collección Personal, and Alea. *See also* BERBERANA and "Castilla-La Mancha", page 38.

Marqués de Murrieta, Bodegas
r (p) w dr ☆☆☆→☆☆☆☆ *25 42 50 52 54 60 68 70 75 78 87 89 94 95 96 97 99*

Ygay (Rioja Alta). Second only in seniority to the MARQUÉS DE RISCAL, the bodega was founded by the Marqués de Murrieta in Ygay, a village just east of Logroño, in 1872. It remained in the family until some years ago when it was bought by the late Vicente Cebrián, Conde de Creixel.

With Riscal, it has been regarded as the aristocrat of Riojas, and the tradition has been to age the red wines for very long periods in oak. Until new regulations came into force, they were kept in BARRICA and bottled only immediately prior to shipment. The bodega's new owner lovingly restored the old buildings, constructing a new fermentation plant as well as extending the vineyards so as to supply not just forty per cent of the grapes, as in the past, but the whole requirement – thus making Murrieta a single-estate wine.

Pride of the *reservas* is the superb CASTILLO YGAY, one of the most sought-after and expensive of Spanish wines. It is made only in exceptional years. The quality of recent vintages has not always matched that of the older, but the ripe and fruity 1989 saw a return to form. There are also round and luscious white and rosé wines.

Marqués de Riscal, Herederos del
r (p) res ☆☆☆→☆☆☆☆ *86 88 90 91 92 93 94 95 96 97 99*

Elciego (Rioja Alavesa). Founded in 1860 by Don Camilo Hurtado de Amézaga, the Marqués de Riscal, the bodega was designed by a *vigneron* from Bordeaux and was the first in Rioja to use French methods for making its wines. Then, as now, a proportion of Cabernet Sauvignon was grown, although as elsewhere in RIOJA ALAVESA the main grape is Tempranillo.

The wines have always been light, stylish, and elegant, and more in the style of claret than most Riojas. They have tended to be a little hard when young, but given time in bottle they age graciously, gaining both in fragrance and intensity of flavour. After some disappointing vintages during the mid-1970s and early-1980s the wines have shown steady improvement and Riscal is again where it belongs – at the top of the ladder. It is difficult to describe vintages such as 1952 and 1938 as anything but perfect. The remarkable 1922, deep in colour, gloriously fragrant and fruity, and long in finish, is reminiscent of one of the best old *crus* from St-Emilion.

Riscal has also introduced an exclusive and very expensive Barón de Chirel, made with fifty per cent Cabernet Sauvignon, which ranks among the very best of all Riojas. The bodega possesses a library of all the vintages from its inception. The best of the older vintages of the present century were: 1910, 1920, 1922, 1925, 1938, 1942, 1943, 1947, 1950, 1964, 1965, 1968, and 1970. Riscal makes a little rosé in the Rioja, but its excellent white wine is from Rueda, near Valladolid (*see* "Castilla-León", p. 50). *See also* "Hotels".

Marqués del Puerto, Bodegas

r (p w dr) res ☆☆→☆☆☆ *94 95 96 97 98 99 00*

Fuenmayor (Rioja Alta). Founded in 1972 as Bodegas López Agos, this is a small concern which makes its wines with some care. The name was changed to Bodegas Marqués del Puerto in 1983 and the firm now belongs to BODEGAS Y BEBIDAS. The red *reservas*, labelled as Marqués del Puerto or Señorío de Agos, have been much praised in Spain.

Marqués de Vargas, Bodegas y Viñedos

r res ☆☆☆ *94 95 96 97 98*

Logroño (Rioja Alta). This small bodega makes only a Marqués de Vargas Reserva and Reserva Privada. Both are wines of high quality, dense and concentrated, and repaying long bottle age.

Martínez Bujanda, Bodegas

r p w dr res ★★→★★★ *90 91 92 93 94 95 96 97 98 00 02*

Oyón (Rioja Alavesa). Founded in 1890, this family concern owns 400 hectares of vineyards and moved into one of the most modern and best-equipped wineries of the region in 1984. It exports a higher proportion of its wines than any other concern in Rioja. One of its most successful wines is a very fruity young (or *joven*) red made in the manner of Beaujolais Nouveau, without time in oak. The bodega also makes a white 100 per cent Viura which is fermented in barrel, an excellent young 100 per cent Garnacha red, and first-rate CONDE DE VALDEMAR *reservas*. *See also* Finca VALPIEDRA.

Martínez Lacuesta, Bodegas

r (p) w dr sw ☆☆

Haro (Rioja Alta). An old-established bodega in the centre of Haro, was founded in 1895 and remains in the family. The bodega has a sizeable capacity of some two million litres, with 7,500 OAK BARRICAS for maturing the wines. It used to own vineyards and make its wine, but this is now bought from local co-ops for maturation and bottling. Its red wines are of two types. The full-bodied Campeador, in Burgundy-type bottles, contains a high proportion of Garnacha, while the lighter Martínez Lacuesta is made with seventy-five per cent Tempranillo. The *reservas* and *gran reservas* of both types are often excellent wines.

Miguel Merino, Bodegas

res ☆☆ *94 95 96 97*

Briones (Rioja Alta). This tiny new bodega has just 352 OAK BARRICAS, but the wines are made with devotion by the owner, Miguel Merino, from grapes bought in from a single vineyard (ninety-four per cent Tempranillo and six per cent others) and have been well received in Spain.

Montecillo, Bodegas

r (p) w dr ☆☆→☆☆☆ *91 94 95 96 98 00*

Navarrete (Rioja Alta). Founded in 1874, Bodegas Montecillo now belongs to the sherry firm of Osborne (*see* "Sherry", page 157). It owns seventy-seven hectares of vineyards and a modern vinification plant near NAVARRETE, and bodegas for maturing its wines in CENICERO. The wines are sold as Montecillo, Cumbrero, and the excellent Viña Monty *reserva*.

Muerza, Bodegas

r (w dr) ☆☆

San Adrián (Rioja Baja). Owned by Bodegas Príncipe de Viana (*see* "Navarra and the Basque Country"), the bodega makes sound and modestly priced RIOJA BAJA reds sold as Rioja Vega.

Muga, Bodegas

r w dr res ★★★→★★★★ *89 90 91 94 95 96 98 99 00*

Haro (Rioja Alta). This small, family firm was founded in 1926, but moved to a new bodega near the station in HARO in 1971. It is entirely unlike the great new bodegas constructed during the Rioja boom of the 1970s in that it started with only 500 BARRICAS – the minimum entitling it to export its wines – but such has been its subsequent success that the number has grown to 15,000. Everything is done in traditional style by a tiny and dedicated workforce, headed by the Muga brothers themselves, and its wines reflect the care that goes into their making – they are currently among the best in Rioja.

Those wines labelled as Muga, made with grapes grown in the firm's own vineyards and others bought from farmers in Abalos, are exceptionally light and fragrant, while the Prado Enea is a deeper-coloured, velvety, and more fully bodied wine, sold in bottles with wax capsules. A new introduction is the superb Torre Muga (94, 95, 98, 00), made with selected grapes (Tempranillo, Mazuelo, Graciano) from its own vineyards. The firm also produces small quantities of a dry white wine and of a light sparkling wine made by the Champagne method (*see* "Sparkling Wines", page 182).

Murua, Bodegas

r res ☆☆→☆☆☆ *94 95 96 98*

Elciego (Rioja Alavesa). Small bodega making worthwhile, Alavesa-type red wines.

Nájera

On the hilly southern fringes of the RIOJA ALTA, west of Logroño, this picturesque little township is the site of a former residence of the Kings of Navarra; and the eleventh-century monastery of Santa María contains the tombs of many of the kings and queens of Navarra, Castile, and León.

Navajas, Bodegas

w dr r res ★★ *95 96 98 99 00 01*

Navarrete (Rioja Alta). One of the best-selling brands in the UK, Navajas is known for its full and fruity red wines with vanilla oak. It also makes a fruity and first-rate white Viura aged in oak, and a cherry-red, vanilla-flavoured CRIANZA *rosado*.

Navarrete

Hill town and winemaking centre southwest of Logroño and the site of the battle in 1367 in which the Black Prince and Peter the Cruel defeated Henry of Trastamara. With a fine sixteenth-century church and baronial houses.

Oak

The pioneer of the oak barrel for maturing wines, now in some ways the "trademark" of Rioja, was Manuel Quintano, who, in 1787, encouraged a group of producers in LABASTIDA to make their wines along French lines. The experiments were short-sightedly discontinued; and it was not until the phylloxera epidemic of the late nineteenth century, followed by an influx of négociants from Bordeaux, that ageing in oak became standard practice.

Because of its dense, even texture, which permits slow transpiration of oxygen, the favourite type of oak is American, though French oak from Nevers and Alliers is increasingly being used. Maturation is much faster in new barrels, and although the casks are systematically scoured, washed, and disinfected after each racking of the wines (decantation from the lees), the pores of the wood gradually become clogged. It is a fact that goes largely unappreciated by visitors to the bodegas, who exclaim at the time the older, more traditional *reservas* spend in wood.

Perhaps it is because the casks in the newer bodegas are so much richer in essential oils and resins, thereby adding an excessively oaky bouquet to the wines, that the canard about oak essence took hold. Such artificial extracts do exist, but no self-respecting bodega uses them; in fact, it would be heavily penalized if caught doing so. The fact that new concerns have invested millions of pounds in oak BARRICAS hardly supports the stories of its widespread employment. The present trend is to reduce the time in oak so as to produce juicer, fruitier wines.

Although maturation in oak – in combination with adequate bottle age – is essential in making the best red wines, its use in making white Riojas has declined, since producers found that it is a great deal less expensive to make the fresh, young white wines (so popular abroad) without maturing them in oak. Fortunately, there has been something of a return to oak-aged whites, and also to fermenting white wines in oak.

Oja, River

Tributary of the EBRO, flowing into it at HARO, which has given its name to the region.

Olarra, Bodegas

r (p) w dr sw res ☆☆

Logroño (Rioja Alta). Founded in 1972 by a group of Spanish industrialists. The bodegas, on the outskirts of Logroño and in the shape of a three-pointed star (symbolizing the three sub-regions), are among the largest in the region, equipped with stainless-steel fermentation tanks and highly sophisticated computerized systems for controlling the flow of the must and other operations. Maturation is, however, carried out by traditional methods in 25,000 OAK BARRICAS. Wines include white, rosé, and red Añares, and a young red Otoñal. Quality is improving, and the Cerro Añon *reserva* (98) is very good.

Ollauri

Small village in the RIOJA ALTA, just south of HARO, and the birthplace of Bodegas PATERNINA and BERBERANA, both of which still maintain their original cellars there for ageing their wines in bottle.

Ondarre, Bodegas

w dr r res ☆☆→☆☆☆ 93 94 95 96 98

Viana (Rioja Baja). Reliable wines, including a 100 per cent barrel-fermented white Viura and a 100 per cent Tempranillo *reserva*.

Ontañón, Bodegas

r res ☆☆ 94 96 97 98

Logroño (Rioja Alta). Like the other wines from Ontañón, the young Linaje de Vetiver makes for easy and pleasant drinking; the Ontañón CRIANZAS and *reservas* have more depth and length.

Oyón

Industrial town in the RIOJA ALAVESA, across the river from LOGROÑO and the home of the Bodegas EL COTO and FAUSTINO.

Paisages y Viñedos SA

DO r ☆☆☆ 00

San Asensio (Rioja Alta). Founded in 1998 by Miguel Angel de Gregorio of FINCA ALLENDE, this small bodega makes high-quality red wines labelled Paisages I, V, VII, and IX, in different styles, all expensive, but with little to choose in quality.

Palacio, Bodegas

r (p) w dr sw ☆☆☆☆ 91 94 95 96 98 99 00 01 02

Laguardia (Rioja Alavesa). Founded in 1894 by Cosme Palacio, the old bodega was bought by Seagram in 1973 and moved to a modern bodega just outside LAGUARDIA. After a management buy-out in 1987, standards have steadily improved and the Glorioso *crianza, reserva,* and *gran reserva* are now excellent wines. The young red Milflores *vino del año* is fresh and attractive and the Cosme Palacio, particularly the Especial (00) is a first-rate wine. *See also* "Hotels".

Palacios Remondo, Bodegas

r w dr (p) res ☆☆→☆☆☆ 94 95 96 98

Mendavia (Rioja Baja). An old-standing family firm known for pioneering young varietal wines. When at their best the red Herencia Remondo *reservas* are both elegant and complex.

Paternina, Federico

r (p) w dr res ☆→☆☆

Haro (Rioja Alta). Founded in 1896 by Don Federico Paternina Josué, this was one of the largest and most successful firms in the Rioja, before its purchase by the RUMASA group and subsequent sale to Don Marcos Eguizábal. It has moved successively from the original cellars in OLLAURI to a larger bodega bought from a HARO co-op and to the present great, modern plant, with its 40,000 BARRICAS capable of maturing twenty-five million litres of wine. The red BANDA AZUL CRIANZA is one of the best-known wines in Spain, but standards are not as high as before the takeovers. Probably the best wines are the white Banda Oro and the red Viña Vial *reservas. See also* CONDE DE LOS ANDES. The glory of Paternina is its rare old vintages, kept in the deep cellars of the old bodega at Ollauri, now also home to a visitors' centre and restaurant. No system of stars could do justice to such beautiful old wines as the 1902, 1910, 1920, 1935, 1947, and 1959.

Primicia, Bodegas

r res ☆☆→☆☆☆ 94 95 96 97 98 99 02

Laguardia (Rioja Alavesa). A range of good red wines including a 100 per cent Gran Diezmo Mazuelo, Tempranillo blends labelled as Julián Madrid, Viña Carravalseca, and Viña Diezmo, and the elegant Curium (98), of which only 3,000 bottles were produced.

Ramón Bilbao

r res ☆☆

Haro (Rioja Alta). Its modern-style wines are much improved and include Viña Turzaballa *gran reserva* and first-rate Mirla Tempranillo (00), rich and luscious.

Real Divisa, Bodegas

r (p) w dr ☆☆ *94 95 96 98*

Abalos (Rioja Alta). A bodega of some note in a small enclave of RIOJA ALTA to the north of the EBRO, producing some worthwhile red wines made mainly from the Tempranillo and sold as Marqués de Legarda.

Remelluri, Granja de Nuestra Señora de

r (w dr) res ☆☆☆ *91 93 94 95 98 00 01*

Ribas (Rioja Alavesa). This small, family-owned bodega was founded by Don Jaime Rodríguez in 1968. With 105 hectares of vineyards planted high up on the slopes of the Sierra Cantábrica, it is one of the few in Rioja to make its wines entirely from its own grapes – a typical *coupage* being ninety per cent Tempranillo, five per cent Garnacha, and five per cent Mazuelo and Graciano. Made by traditional methods, the wines are soft and fruity with a long finish and among the very best Riojas. Gifted oenologist Telmo Rodríguez, who established the reputation of the wines, has now left, but the bodega continues to make excellent wines, like the Colección Jaime Rodríguez Salis (00).

Remírez de Ganuza, Bodegas

res ☆☆☆→☆☆☆☆ *92 94 96 97 98 99 02*

Samaniego (Rioja Alavesa). The wines from this small bodega, founded by Fernándo Remírez in 1989, are already among the choicest and most sought after from Rioja. The wines, including a superb Erre Punta (02) made by carbonic maceration, are made exclusively with hand-sorted grapes from old vines (ninety-two per cent Tempranillo and eight per cent Graciano).

Rioja Alavesa

DO ca r (w dr) ☆☆→☆☆☆☆

The smallest of the three sub-regions of the DO Rioja, Rioja Alavesa is located in the province of Alava and extends north of the River EBRO, from near the Conchas de Haro to a line a little east of Logroño. Because of the temperate climate, the southerly exposure of the vineyards, and the composition of the soil, which is almost entirely calcareous clay, Rioja Alavesa produces some of the best wines from the whole region – in the opinion of many experts, *the* best. Another factor is the very high proportion of Tempranillo used in making the red wines. The main production centres are at LABASTIDA in the west, and ELCIEGO, LAGUARDIA, and OYON towards the east. In general, the red Alavesa wines are big, fruity, and soft (though one or two are very light) with a pronounced and characteristic Tempranillo nose, somewhat resembling that of Cabernet Sauvignon, but they mature more rapidly than those from Rioja Alta and do not last as long. Rioja Alavesa also produces smaller amounts of white wine with a good acid balance, made mainly from Viura and Malvasía.

Rioja Alta

DO ca r (p) w dr sw ☆☆→☆☆☆☆

Together with RIOJA ALAVESA, the sub-region of Rioja Alta produces the best Rioja wines. It lies within the province of La Rioja, extending (apart from a small northern enclave around ABALOS) south of the EBRO from the Conchas de Haro in the west to just beyond LOGROÑO in the east. The soils are more mixed than those of the Rioja Alavesa, comprising calcareous clay, ferruginous clay, and alluvial silt. On the basis of this and of the microclimate, oenologists have subdivided the area, from west to east, into the zones of Cuzcurrita, HARO, San Asensio, and CENICERO-FUENMAYOR.

The wines from the wetter and hillier area of the west tend to be more acidic and lower in alcohol that those from Cenicero, where there is a transition in climate from humid to semi-arid and a change to predominantly calcareous soils, particularly suitable for growing the Tempranillo grape.The main production centres are Haro in the west, Cenicero and Fuenmayor in the centre, and NAVARRETE in the east. Although the Tempranillo is the basic grape of Rioja Alta, as of Rioja Alavesa, traditionally its red wines contain a higher proportion of Mazuelo, Graciano, and Garnacha, and tend to be brisker and fresher on the nose, a little more acidic, and longer lasting. The whites are made mainly from Viura and Malvasía, with some Garnacha Blanca. It is difficult to be more specific about the proportions, since the large bodegas sometimes use a blend of wines made from grapes grown both in the Rioja Alta and Rioja Alavesa.

Rioja Alta, SA
r (p) w dr res ☆☆☆→☆☆☆☆ *87 90 92 94 95 96 97 98*

Haro (Rioja Alta). A large family concern founded in 1890, and one of the first to build a bodega in the hallowed area near the railway station in HARO, La Rioja Alta has consistently maintained the quality and prestige of its wines. It owns 330 hectares of vineyards, both in RIOJA ALTA and RIOJA BAJA, and has recently expanded into Ribera del Duero. It has 52,000 BARRICAS for ageing its wines, all red, and made by strictly traditional methods. These include a characterful CRIANZA, Viña Alberdi (actually aged in oak for as long as many bodegas' *reserva*, and now sold as a *reserva*); the fruity, full-bodied, and velvety red VIÑA ARDANZA (named after one of the five families which founded the bodega); a lighter, very stylish Viña Arana; and the excellent 904 and 890 *reservas*.

Rioja Baja
DO r (w dr) ☆→☆☆☆

The largest of the sub-regions of the DO Rioja, Rioja Baja extends from just east of LOGROÑO along the EBRO to ALFARO in the southeast. The larger part of the area lies in the province of La Rioja, south of the river, but there is also a narrow strip in Navarra to the north. The soils of Rioja Baja are almost entirely composed of alluvial silt and ferruginous clay; the climate is semi-arid, of the Mediterranean type, and the predominant grape is the red Garnacha Tinta, which yields musts high in alcohol and extract, but quick to oxidize.

For these reasons the typical wines are coarser than those of the cooler and hillier RIOJA ALAVESA and RIOJA ALTA, and are often used for blending, to confer alcoholic degree and body. Nevertheless, the planting of Tempranillo and Viura in calcareous soils in the higher part of the area, particularly at Monte Yerga near Aldeanuevo del Ebro, has proved very successful. The main centres of production are San Adrián, ALFARO, ARNEDO, and Aldeanuevo del Ebro, a sun-baked town which produces better asparagus and peppers than wine and is curiously named – it is not, as the name implies, a hamlet, new, or near the Ebro. The typical wines are full-bodied reds, high in alcohol and more akin to those of Ribera Baja (*see* "Navarra", page 114) than the delicate growths of Rioja Alta or Rioja Alavesa.

Rioja Santiago, Bodegas

r p w res ☆→☆☆☆ *97 98 99 02*

Haro (Rioja Alta). Old-established firm with bodegas in HARO, just across the bridge over the EBRO, recently taken over by Bodegas LAN. The firm developed a large market in the USA for its bottled *sangría*, labelled as Monsieur Henri; it was eventually taken over by its American distributor, Pepsi, but has since reverted to Spanish control. Its best wines are the red Vendimia Seleccionada and Vizconde de Ayala *reservas*.

Rioja Vega

r res ★★

Reliable red wine from Bodegas MUERZA.

Riojanas, Bodegas

r (p) w dr s/sw res ☆☆→☆☆☆ *64 73 81 91 94 95 96 98 99*

Cenicero (Rioja Alta). This large and old-established bodega was founded in 1890 and built in a flamboyant style with a castellated keep. Advice from Bordeaux was taken and French technicians worked there until the early years of World War II. The bodega draws its grapes from both RIOJA ALTA and RIOJA ALAVESA, from some 200 hectares of vineyards owned either by the company or its shareholders and also from private farmers. Small amounts of selected Garnacha grapes from RIOJA BAJA are also used. Its wines include a dry white Canchales, barrel-fermented Albina, and an inexpensive and very basic young red Canchales. It also makes excellent VIÑA ALBINA *reservas*; and among the most interesting wines of all are the red MONTE REAL *reservas* which are made with a sizeable proportion (eighty-five per cent) of Tempranillo from Rioja Alavesa. Among the best of the older vintages were 1890, 1915, 1922, 1934, 1942, 1950, 1956, 1964, 1966, 1968, and 1970.

Roda, Bodegas

res ☆☆→☆☆☆☆ *92 94 95 96 98 99 00 01*

Haro (Rioja Alta). Founded in 1989 by a Catalan couple, who decided that only in the Barrio de la Estación in HARO could they create their dream wines. The bodega makes only superb and costly *reservas*, all from hand-picked and sorted grapes from old vines vinified in French oak vats. Roda I has the edge on Roda II, but both are dark, concentrated, and hugely fruity. A premium Cirsión (01) was introduced in 1998 and has established itself as one of the best of all Spanish wines.

Rumasa

At its peak this great Spanish conglomerate, with extensive interests in banking, hotels, and property as well as wines of all types, had taken over the important Rioja firms of PATERNINA, FRANCO-ESPAÑOLAS, LAN, and BERBERANA. After its expropriation in 1983 the firms were first run by the government and finally sold to private interests, the first two to a Spanish businessman, Marcos Eguizábal, whose family is from the region. *See also* "Sherry and Manzanilla", page 160.

Salceda, Viña

r res ☆☆→☆☆☆ *91 92 95 96 97 98 00*

Elciego (Rioja Alavesa). The bodega, just beyond the bridge over the EBRO on the road from CENICERO to ELCIEGO, is of modern construction, dating from 1974. It is equipped with stainless-steel fermentation tanks, together with the traditional OAK BARRICAS for ageing the wines. Of medium size, Viña Salceda makes only red wine with a high proportion of Tempranillo: a

Viña Salceda CRIANZA and Conde de la Salceda *reservas* and *gran reservas* are of good quality. The bodega has recently been taken over by the large Navarra firm of Julian Chivite.

San Mateo, Festival of

One of many such festivals in the wine-growing districts, the Fiesta de San Mateo begins in LOGROÑO on September 21, rather before the official start of grape-picking on October 10, and lasts for a week, with a uniformed band parading the streets, bullfights, and firework displays in the Plaza del Espolón at midnight.

San Vicente de la Sonsierra

Picturesque village near LABASTIDA dominated by a ruined castle, with magnificent views over the River EBRO and across Rioja.

Santa Daría, Sociedad Cooperativa

r w dr p ★★

Cenicero (Rioja Alta). Well-equipped co-op, one of the best in the Rioja, bottling and selling its wines, ranging from *jóvenes* (young, unoaked) to *gran reservas*, under the label Santa Daría.

Santo Domingo de la Calzada

Just outside the DO Rioja, Santo Domingo, south of HARO, is on the old pilgrim route from France to Santiago de Compostela and its *parador* is one of the most pleasant places to stay when visiting the region. The twelfth-century cathedral incorporates an unusual feature: a live cock and hen housed behind a grille high on one wall, in commemoration of a miracle wrought by St Dominic, patron saint of pilgrims.

Señorío de San Vicente

DO r res ☆☆☆ *97 98 99 00 01*

San Vicente de la Sonsierra (Rioja Alta). Since the foundation of the bodega in 1991, Marcos Eguren has been making some of the best wine to come out of Rioja. Elegant, concentrated, and complex, the 100 per cent Tempranillo San Vincente (00) is no exception.

Sierra Cantabria SA

r res w dr p ☆☆☆ *90 91 94 95 96 97 98 01 02*

San Vicente de la Sonsierra (Rioja Alta). Small bodega known for its excellent young red Murmurón, made by carbonic maceration, fruity and well-balanced red Sierra Cantabria, and a premium El Bosque.

Solagüen, Bodega

See LABASTIDA, UNIÓN DE COSECHEROS DE.

Sonsierra , Bodegas

w dr p r res ★→★★★ *93 94 96 98 99 00 02*

San Vicente de la Sonsierra (Rioja Alta). Large and well-known co-op controlling 675 hectares of vineyard. Good white wines, especially the 100 per cent Viura fermented in barrel. Of the red wines the best, which are very good indeed, complex, fruity, and long, are the Pagos de Sonsierra Reserva (99) and the Viña Mindiarte Gran Reserva (96).

Torre de Oña SA

DO r res ☆☆☆ *90 92 94 96 98*

Laguardia (Rioja Alavesa). Small bodega with fifty hectares located below the old walled town of LAGUARDIA. It now belongs to RIOJA ALTA SA but it maintains its individuality. It makes only one wine: the red Barón de Oña reserva, which is delicate, complex, fruity, and aged in French oak.

Unión Vitivinícola

See MARQUÉS DE CACERES.

United Wineries

See BODEGAS UNIDAS.

Valpiedra, Finca

res ☆☆☆→☆☆☆☆ *94 95 96 97 98*

Cenicero (Rioja Alta). A state-of-the-art winery recently built by MARTÍNEZ BUJANDA in a bend of the EBRO near CENICERO, to produce premium-quality single-vineyard *reservas*. The first (1994) vintage was outstanding – dense in colour, vividly fruity and aromatic, and long on the finish.

Viña Ardanza

r ☆☆☆

Consistently satisfying red Riojas, smooth, fruity, and full-bodied, from RIOJA ALTA SA.

Viña Bosconia

r ☆☆☆

Excellent Rioja from LOPEZ DE HEREDIA, using grapes grown in its Bosconia vineyards on the south bank of the EBRO.

Viña Herminia, Bodegas

w dr p r res ★→★★★ *94 95 96 98 99 01*

Aldeanueva del Ebro (Rioja Baja). The bodega, belonging to sherry firm Luis Caballero, makes good wines from the RIOJA BAJA (but *see* BARON DE LEY), including the inexpensive red, white, and rosé Preferido and sophisticated Viña Herminia CRIANZAS and *reservas*. Best is the first-rate 100 per cent Graciano Reserva 1995.

Viña Pomal

r ☆☆→☆☆☆

Full-bodied red Rioja from Bodegas BILBAINAS made with grapes from its vineyards in Leza in the RIOJA ALAVESA.

Viña Real

r ☆☆☆

Excellent red RIOJA ALAVESA *reserva* from the COMPAÑIA VINICOLA DEL NORTE DE ESPAÑA, made in an outlying bodega in ELCIEGO.

Viña Tondonia

r w dr ☆☆☆→☆☆☆☆

First-rate, long-lasting red and white Riojas from Bodegas LOPEZ DE HEREDIA.

Viña Villabuena

w dr r res ☆☆☆ *96 97 98 99*

Villabuena de Alava (Rioja Alavesa). The wines, including a barrel-fermented white Viura, are labelled Viña Izadi. Best are the beautiful Expression (99), made from ninety per cent Tempranillo and ten per cent Cabernet-Sauvignon, and the Selección (99), containing eighty per cent Tempranillo and twenty per cent Graciano.

Víñedos y Bodegas de la Marquesa

r (w dr) res ☆☆ *91 94 95 96 98 00 01*

Villabuena (Rioja Alavesa). Formerly known as SMS, the initials of three families: Samaniego, Milans del Bosch, and Solana. Founded before 1900 and originally called the Marqués de la Solana, the bodega has a capacity of 700,000 litres and 2,700 OAK BARRICAS. The wines are made mainly with grapes grown in the sixty hectares of vineyards belonging to the bodega. Until 1981 the grapes were not de-stalked, so that the old wines, fermented in oak vats, are dark in colour, and mature more slowly than most from RIOJA ALAVESA. Those currently available are labelled as Valserrano and include a 100 per cent Graciano and 100 per cent Mazuelo. They have a hint of cedar in the nose and are fragrant and full-bodied, with a lot of fruit.

Ygay

Hamlet in the Rioja Alta a little east of LOGROÑO. Since 1872 the cellars of bodegas MARQUÉS DE MURRIETA, a business established twenty years earlier, have stood on its outskirts on the Ygay estate.

Ysios, Bodegas

DO r res ☆☆→☆☆☆ *98 99*

Laguardia (Rioja Alavesa). Better known for its architecture – including a wavy modernistic roofline – than its wines; these are characteristic of the easy-drinking output of its owners BODEGAS Y BEBIDAS (Allied Domecq), but have markedly improved in recent vintages.

WINE AND FOOD

It is perhaps a bit pretentious to talk of Riojan "cuisine". What the area offers is a range of genuinely regional dishes based on the excellent lamb, pork, kid, spicy *chorizo* sausage, and fresh vegetables in season. When André Simon first wrote about Rioja, he was, in fact, more enthusiastic about the vegetables than the wines, and it is still an experience to visit the great open market in Logroño. The meals served to guests in the bodegas themselves, often in a great cellar lined with casks, are simple and well designed to show off the wines. They usually begin with fresh local asparagus or a *menestra* of vegetables, followed by small lamb chops cooked over glowing vine shoots, and ending with the ubiquitous *flan* (cream caramel) or the luscious peaches preserved in syrup. Such simple delights are not to be despised, however. When a few years ago the celebrated chef Paul Bocuse was engaged by the COMPAÑIA VINICOLA DEL NORTE DE ESPAÑA to prepare its centenary banquet, the story goes that, having sampled the *patatas a la riojana* (*see below*) prepared by the bodega's regular cook, he asked why he had been sent for.

Alubias con chorizo A rib-warming stew made with haricot or butter beans, chopped onions, garlic, olive oil, and highly cured *chorizo* sausage, further seasoned with sweet paprika powder and parsley. This calls for a full-bodied two- or three-year-old red, or a *jarra* of the local house wine.

Bacalao a la riojana Dried cod cooked with olive oil, onions, garlic, strips of canned red pepper, and sweet paprika powder. Drink one of the traditional oaky white Riojas with sufficient character to stand up to the rich assortment of flavours: for example, a white Tondonia from López de Heredia.

Cabrito asado Roast kid Rioja style. This is a good chance to show off the qualities of one of the many red *reservas*.

Callos a la riojana Highly spiced tripe, Riojan style.

Cardo Cardoon, a celery-like vegetable, served braised as a first course. Choose from among the many styles of white Rioja, perhaps one with oak, such as Monopole from CVNE.

Chorizo a la brasa *Chorizo*, the famous spicy cured pepper sausage, often homemade, and roasted whole. Since this is an extremely hot dish, a chilled glass of one of the young white Riojas, such as the Marqués de Cáceres or Faustino V, makes a refreshing accompaniment.

Chuletas de cordero al sarmiento Small lamb chops grilled over glowing vine shoots and served in the bodegas to set off the better reds and *reservas*.

Cordero lechal asado Milk-fed baby lamb roasted in a baker's oven. Choose the best red *reserva* you can run to, from Riscal, La Rioja Alta, López de Heredia, Muga, Riojanas, CVNE, etc.

Espárragos Rioja Baja grows some of the best asparagus in Spain, which is served as a starter either with vinaigrette or mayonnaise. Take your choice of the dry white wines.

Malvices Tiny birds (red-wings) fried crisp and eaten whole. A light red Alavesa wine.

Melocotones en almíbar Particularly large and luscious local peaches preserved in syrup. Try a sweet or semi-sweet wine, such as the Diamante from Franco-Españolas.

Menestra de verduras a la riojana A mixed vegetable dish made from whatever happens to be in season, such as broad beans and peas, together with chopped onions, tomatoes, bacon or ham, seasoning, and sometimes hard-boiled eggs. It is cooked in olive oil and light red wine. Try the Viñadrián *rosado* from Bodegas Gurpegui Muga.

Morcilla dulce Morcilla is a blood sausage akin to black pudding, but this version is made with cinnamon, other sweet spices, and a little sugar. It is usually a first course, but anything other than a sweet or semi-sweet white wine would seem tart.

Patatas a la riojana Potatoes in a clear orange-coloured sauce with *chorizo* sausage.

Picadillo A variant of *chorizo a la brasa*, the filling being ground, cooked, and served hot. This calls for a chilled and cooling dry white: try Banda Dorada from Paternina, or the dry Lan.

Pimientos de piquillo rellenos a la riojana Regional variant on stuffed peppers, filled with a mixture of ground pork, beaten egg, nutmeg, garlic, parsley, and a little pepper and salt, fried in hot olive oil and served in a piquant sauce. Order a full-bodied and robust red.

Pochas riojanas Substantial stew made from a local variety of haricot bean, allowed to fatten in the pod but not dried, and cooked with *chorizo*. Best eaten with a *jarra* of the local red house wine or a robust bottle of Rioja Baja.

Quesos (cheeses) The best local cheeses are the soft *Camerano* made from goats' milk and the *Idiazábal* from the Basque Country, semi-hard and made from unpasteurized ewes' milk.

Revuelto de ajos tiernos Eggs scrambled with tender young garlic shoots. An oaky or slightly oaky white Rioja, such as the CVNE Monopole, balances this very well.

Sopa de ajo con huevos A traditional Castilian garlic soup, seasoned with sweet paprika powder and thickened with bread and beaten egg. Better to leave the table wine for later and ask for a glass of fino sherry.

Tapas *Embuchados* (pork sausages), *lecherillas* (sweetbreads), and *champiñones a la plancha* (grilled mushrooms) are typical.

HOTELS

Alfaro *Hacienda la Concordia* operates a hotel in the vineyards of the winery.

Arnedo Its hotels are the three-star *Victoria* and two-star *Virrey*.

Calahorra There is a comfortable *parador* here.

Elciego A spectacular hotel and visitors' centre, designed by Frank Gehry of Bilbao fame, is located in the grounds of the *Marqués de Riscal* winery.

Haro Boasts a good hotel, *Los Agustinos*, housed in an old convent.

Laguardia *Antigua Bodega de Don Cosme Palacio* is an atmospheric hostelry installed in a former bodega, with good restaurant.

Logroño Recommended hotels are the new five-star *Gran Hotel AC La Rioja*, *the* four-star *Tryp Bracos*, *NH Herencia Rioja*, and *Carlton Rioja*, and the three-star *Ciudad de Logroño*.

Santo Domingo de la Calzada *Parador de Santa Domingo* is a converted old pilgrim hospice.

RESTAURANTS

Arnedo *Joselito* offers regional cooking such as roast kid and stuffed red peppers. *Picabea* serves a good choice of fish dishes.

Briones *Los Cuatro Arcos* with home cooking, modest prices, and a sensational *menestra* on Sundays.

Calahorra *Parador de Calahorra* serves regional dishes and wines; *La Taberna de la Cuarta Esquina* is a small restaurant with inventive cooking.

Ezcaray *Echaurren* is probably the best restaurant in the region. The menu includes vegetable soup, monkfish, and clam *potage*.

Fuenmayor *Asador Alameda*, and *Mesón Chuchi* for seabream and roast kid.

Haro *Beethoven I, II,* and *III* all provide good regional dishes, especially sweetbreads and *cocochas; Terete* is the classical Haro restaurant, in simple surroundings, serving marvellous roast baby lamb and with a long list of *reservas*. It also sells take-away food.

Laguardia *Marixa* is the best in Laguardia; *Posada Mayor de Migueloa* is located in an old baronial house.

Logroño *Mesón Egües* is the best in Logroño for roasts of suckling pig, lamb, and kid. *Casa Emilio* serves salads in season and roasts. The prestigious *Cachetero* is not all that it once was. *Las Cubanas* serves typical Riojan food, at low prices with wine included, and is always full. *Robinson's English Pub* for dancing and perhaps a late nightcap.

Ollauri The old cellars of *Federico Paternina* incorporate a restaurant and visitors' centre in the bodega's old cellars.

Oyón *Mesón de la Cueva* serves good regional food in atmospheric surroundings.

San Vicente de la Sonsierra *Casa Toni* serves traditional dishes and specialities – breasts of quail in vermouth, truffles, venison, and salmon.

Santo Domingo de la Calzada The speciality of the extremely popular *El Rincón de Emilio* is *callos a la riojana*.

Sherry (Jerez) and Manzanilla

Sherry is, of course, the classical Spanish wine, and has long had particularly close associations with Britain. The great sherry boom took place with the active participation of British merchants, many of whom settled in Jerez. Further than this, the UK consumes more sherry than Spain and, closely followed by the Netherlands, is still the largest foreign market.

In common with most other fortified wines and spirits, sherry has recently suffered something of a setback – but this is not the first in its long history and the producers are fighting back with marketing campaigns to attract younger drinkers. A glass of chilled fino remains the most satisfactory preliminary to a meal – the least likely to interfere with what follows. For a wine of such character and one so expensive to make, sherry of all types remains extremely reasonably priced.

The wines were well-known even in Roman times, but it was Sir Francis Drake's raid on Cádiz in 1587 and the seizure of some 2,900 pipes (110-gallon barrels) which firmly established them in England. The British presence had begun to be felt after the expulsion of the Jews from Spain by the Catholic Monarchs in 1492; and during the late eighteenth and early nineteenth centuries English, Scottish, and Irish merchants arrived in force. Their names survive in those of such famous sherry houses as Duff Gordon, Osborne, Garvey, Terry, Sandeman, and Williams & Humbert.

The industry is now dominated by three major groupings: Allied Domecq, embracing Pedro Domecq, Harveys, Terry, and Blázquez; González-Byass, also owner of Crofts; and the rapidly expanding José Medina which, in conjunction with the Dutch Ahold group, controls Williams & Humbert and has acquired as its headquarters the former Bodegas Internacionales, together with its huge stocks of wine and the *soleras* of the admirable Don Zoilo.

Other important players are Osborne, with its extensive interests in brandy, gin, and beverage wines; Garvey, now owned by José María Ruíz Mateos of New Rumasa; Sandeman; Barbadillo in Sanlúcar; Caballero (owners of Lustau); and Valdespino, the archetype of the traditional family concern, recently taken over by José Estévez. Rationalization has, however, seen the disappearance of well-known firms like La Riva, Bertola, and Palomino & Vergara, and of well-loved sherries such as CZ, Tres Palmas, Diez-Mérito, and Duke of Wellington.

The sherry district occupies a triangle, with its apex near Cádiz, bounded by the Guadalquivír and Guadalete rivers and embracing the main centres of Jerez de la Frontera, Puerto de Santa María, and Sanlúcar de Barrameda. The whole area, amounting to 10,674 hectares, falls within the province of Cádiz, while the best vineyards lie within a thirty-two-kilometre radius north and west of Jerez. The soils are of three classes: the most highly rated is the dazzlingly white *albariza*, containing some forty per cent chalk, together with sand and clay. This composition enables it to retain moisture throughout the year, in a region where average rainfall amounts to only 550 millimetres and temperatures rise to 40°C during the long, cloudless summers. Other soil types are the darker *barro* and a sandy *arena*, which are planted mainly with Moscatel grapes.

The sherry grape *par excellence* is the white Palomino, which grows best in the chalky *albariza* and is used for all the different types of sherry and almost exclusively for the finos. Next in importance is the Pedro Ximénez (PX), which can, as in Montilla (*see* page 104), produce excellent dry wines, but is principally used in Jerez for sweet dessert wines. Smaller amounts of Moscatel are also grown for sweet sherries.

Sherry owes its individual character to the method by which it is made. Unlike table wines it is matured with free access to the atmosphere, in a loosely stoppered cask with an air space above the liquid. This would ordinarily result in fairly rapid oxidation, were it not that the new wine spontaneously grows a *flor* ("flower") on the surface of the liquid. This layer of yeasts both regulates the access of air to the must and eliminates harmful vinegar-producing bacteria. The growth varies according to the type of wine: it is thickest with finos (and even

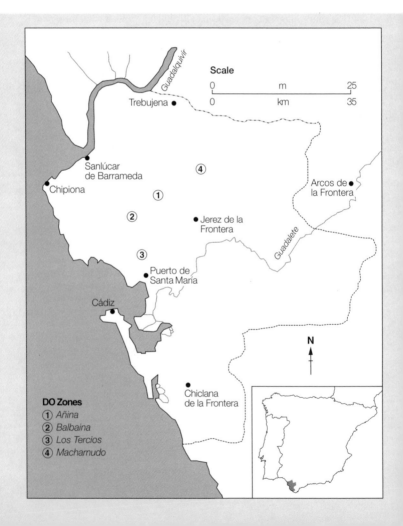

DO Zones
① *Añina*
② *Balbaina*
③ *Los Tercios*
④ *Macharnudo*

more so with the manzanillas from Sanlúcar de Barrameda) and less vigorous with the fuller-bodied olorosos, which are soon fortified to kill the yeasts and to protect the wine during its long physico-chemical maturation.

The other difference between the making of table wines and sherry is that sherry is aged by the *solera* system: the progressive blending of older and younger wines. The *solera* consists of long rows of oak butts which are arranged in the bodega in tiers. Each row of butts, or "scale", contains wine of the same type but of different age. When wine is required for shipment or bottling, it is drawn off from the butts at the bottom containing the oldest wine. The contents are then made good from the "scale" immediately preceding it in age, and so on through the system. In this fashion, there is regular "refreshment" of older wine with younger, and as Richard Ford explained in 1846, "houses are enabled to supply for any number of years exactly that particular colour, flavour, body etc. which particular customers demand".

With few exceptions, then, there are no vintages in sherry, and a description such as "Solera 1847" refers to the year in which the *solera* was first laid down. The *consejo regulador* has, however, recently introduced two new categories of age-dated sherry: VOS (very old sherry, more than twenty years of age), and VORS (very old rare sherry, more than thirty years old).

The basic styles of sherry are the dry and light finos, such as Tío Pepe or La Ina, drunk chilled as an apéritif; the rather fuller amontillados; and the dark, fully bodied olorosos, the most maderized and fragrant of the wines. In their natural state olorosos, such as Río Viejo, are completely dry and are best drunk before a meal; but they are often blended with sweet wine to make a dessert sherry or cream, of which one of the best known is Bristol Cream. This does not exhaust the possibilities, however, and other varieties such as palo cortado, medium, and pale cream are described in the A–Z listing. Manzanilla from Sanlúcar de Barrameda, though made by similar methods and from the same grapes, is no longer officially allowed to be described as sherry.

In the past, it was very much a question of making the wine and then waiting to see how it would develop. Modern methods have enabled the bodegas to take these decisions at a much earlier stage; and in the latest of the continuous vinification plants, wine destined as a fino is drawn off after the lightest crushing of the grapes, which are then more firmly pressed to obtain the must for the olorosos.

In all essentials, sherry continues to be made along strictly traditional lines, but there have been many other innovations in recent years. González-Byass has instituted a programme for eliminating plant diseases by the cloning (vegetative reproduction) of virus-free vines, and the bacchanalian rite of treading the grapes with nail-studded boots has given way to modern horizontal or continuous presses. The wine is increasingly (but not always) fermented in temperature-controlled stainless-steel tanks rather than in butts, and is no longer shipped in cask, but bottled in the bodega first.

Quite apart from visits to the bodegas, the sherry region is a delightful one in which to spend a holiday. There are the Atlantic beaches of Puerto de Santa María, Rota, and Chipiona; the great nature reserve of the Coto

Doñana across the Guadalquivír; the rugged mountains and hunting of the Sierra de Cádiz; the historic buildings of Cádiz and Sevilla; and by no means least, the superb seafood from the Bay of Cádiz.

Jerez is at its best in the late spring, or in the early autumn at harvest time. From the UK there are direct flights to Jerez; from elsewhere the quickest way to reach the area is to fly to Madrid and then on to Jerez by an internal flight or by the fast and luxurious high-speed train; alternatively, one may fly to Sevilla, eighty-four kilometres to the north by the A4 *autopista*, and hire a car. Once there, a car is not a necessity, as there is a local electric train to Puerto de Santa María and bus services to other places.

The larger bodegas, such as Pedro Domecq, González-Byass, and Williams & Humbert, are well-organized for visits, which usually end with a generous tasting. Visiting hours are normally 9.30am–1pm, but it is always advisable to check by letter or telephone beforehand. A letter of introduction from a wine merchant or shipper helps to smooth the way if you are planning to visit smaller establishments.

As to the vineyards, good views (as well as spectacular panoramas) can be found of the famous areas of Macharnudo and Carrascal to the north of Jerez by branching off the A4 from Sevilla at Las Cabezas and following the hilly by-road. Follow this almost lunar landscape of whitish sunbaked clay, by way of Lebrija and Trebujena and into Jerez.

Serving Sherry

Sherry is often ruined by improper serving and storage, especially fresh and delicate finos which are easily spoilt by oxidation. All sherries should be served in a glass tapering towards the top and large enough to be filled only a third or half full to allow for the development of the bouquet (*see* COPITA, page 152). Fino begins to deteriorate after about three months in bottle; and once the bottle is opened, the contents should either be drunk within three days or poured into a tightly corked half-bottle. Many of the complaints about popular finos arise from the habit of keeping half-empty bottles for weeks on the shelves of a warm bar.

Much the same applies to the lighter styles of amontillado, although they deteriorate more slowly. Oloroso, especially the sweetened ones, last much longer in bottle, and the rich dessert sherries sometimes improve because of the slow consumption of sugar, which gives them a dryish finish.

Fino and light amontillado should be served chilled, but not iced. The best thing is to leave the bottle in the refrigerator for a few hours before serving it; and the wine will also keep longer if stored in the refrigerator. In a bar, rather than suffer a lukewarm fino, it is better to ask for it to be poured into a larger glass and drink it "on the rocks" – though chilling is preferable. Oloroso, the fuller-bodied amontillados, and creams should be drunk at room temperature.

Albariza

The best of the soils, white in colour and containing some forty per cent chalk, the residue consisting of sand and clay.

Age-Dated Sherry

Since sherry is a blended wine (*see* SOLERA) no vintage is stated except in the case of rare old single-vintage AÑADA sherries. However, the *consejo regulador* has recently introduced two new categories of age-dated sherries: VOS (very old sherry of more than twenty years average age) and VORS (very old rare sherry of more than thirty years average age). The ages are estimated both by reference to records of the sherries used in the *solera* and carbon dating.

Almacenistas

Small concerns which mature wine from their own vineyards or bought from individual growers. Such concerns do not sell direct to the public, but only to the large shippers for improving their commercial sherries. Fine-quality *almacenista* sherries are now much in demand, especially in the USA. Emilio LUSTAU is the firm that has specialized in bottling and shipping them for retail sale.

Amontillado

Style of sherry, amber-yellow in colour, with a dry, nutty flavour, and about sixteen to eighteen per cent strength. It takes its name from wines formerly prepared in Montilla (*see* page 100), and the genuine article is made by allowing a FINO to age for a further period after the flor has died or been eliminated by addition of alcohol. Only completely dry wines may now be described as amontillado.

Amoroso

Traditional name, in Spanish "loving", not now much used, for a smooth, sweet wine made by adding Pedro Ximénez wine and VINO DE COLOR to OLOROSO.

Añada

A vintage wine as yet unblended in a CRIADERA. There has recently been an interest in unblended, single-vintage sherries, such as the magnificent old GONZÁLEZ-BYASS *añadas* put on sale at Christie's in London.

Añina

District between JEREZ DE LA FRONTERA and SANLÚCAR DE BARRAMEDA, rated fourth of those with ALBARIZA soil.

Arcos de la Frontera

Picturesque town east of JEREZ, perched on a rocky crag above the River Guadalete. One of the region's most pleasant places to stay.

Arena

Reddish, sandy soil, containing some ten per cent chalk and the least favoured, except for the Moscatel vine.

Argüeso, Herederos de

Sanlúcar de Barrameda. Founded in 1822, this old-established firm makes good Las Medallas and San León MANZANILLAS, an Amontillado Viejo, and a sweet Moscatel Fruta.

Argüeso, Manuel de

Sanlúcar de Barrameda. Founded in 1822, this small firm now belongs to AR VALDESPINO and makes excellent Señorita MANZANILLA, Amontillado del Teatro, and splendid PX El Candido.

Arrope

A non-alcoholic syrup, made by evaporating down must to twenty per cent of its original volume and used in making the VINO DE COLOR for sweet sherries.

Balbaina

This district to the west of Jerez is rated third in order of merit of those with ALBARIZA soil.

Barbadillo, Antonio

Sanlúcar de Barrameda. Founded in 1821, Barbadillo is the largest of the operations in SANLÚCAR, with offices in the former bishop's palace and a complex of bodegas facing the church of Santa María in the centre of the town; even its *bodega nueva* ("new cellar") dates from 1850. The firm owns vineyards in San Julián, and has gone into partnership with John HARVEY & Sons in the development of 1,000 hectares of new vineyards, as well as the most modern of vinification plants in Gibalbín, east of the A4 to Sevilla. However, it remains a family concern. The late Don Manuel Barbadillo was the doyen of MANZANILLA wines and wrote the most authoritative book on the subject.

Barbadillo makes an outstanding range of manzanillas, including a fresh and aromatic Solear MANZANILLA FINA; Príncipe AMONTILLADO; a beautiful Cuco dry OLOROSO; and a very round and satisfying Eva Cream. The pride of its wines are the superb Reliquía AMONTILLADO, PALO CORTADO, OLOROSO SECO, and PX. The bodega also produces a fresh young table wine from Palomino grapes, labelled as Castillo de San Diego.

Barro

A mud clay containing up to ten per cent chalk, dark in colour because of its iron oxide, and second in quality of the soils.

Bienteveo

These rough shelters, made of poles thatched with *esparto* grass, can still occasionally be seen in the vineyards and were formerly manned by armed guards to prevent the depredations of thieves helping themselves to the ripe grapes. The literal translation is "I see you well".

Blázquez, Hijos de Agustín

Jerez de la Frontera. Old-established firm now owned by PEDRO DOMECQ, known particularly for its first-rate Carta Blanca fino.

Bristol Cream

A proprietary name belonging to John HARVEY & Sons of Bristol, who decided during the nineteenth century to produce an even richer dessert sherry than the popular BRISTOL MILK by blending it with older OLOROSO. It is now the biggest-selling sherry in the world, with very large sales in the USA.

Bristol Milk

Bristol has for centuries been famous for the shipping of wines and the blending of dessert sherries under the name of Bristol Milk. The best-known labels were those of HARVEY and Avery's of Bristol, now replaced by Avery's Bristol Supreme, a blend of OLOROSO and PX.

Brown sherry

The English name for a dark dessert sherry, one which is usually of only very moderate quality.

Burdon, John William

John William Burdon, who began by working for DUFF GORDON, became one of the most successful nineteenth-century sherry shippers. The firm was eventually taken over in 1932 by Luís CABALLERO, which still markets a well-known range of sherries under the Burdon label. They include a crisp and fresh Dry Fino, a Medium Amontillado, a Pale Cream, and a raisiny Rich Cream.

Butt (bota)

The standard butt used for maturing sherry in the SOLERA is of 500 litres capacity, and is made of American oak. There are also larger butts, less pointed in shape, such as the *bocoy* of 600 litres. Butts have become increasingly expensive and represent an appreciable proportion of the cost of a wine which is more expensive than most to produce. Sherry butts are sometimes used for ageing Scotch whisky, but there is also a demand in Jerez for whisky casks for maturing sherry.

Caballero, Luís

Puerto de Santa María. The Caballero family was making wines in CHIPIONA as long ago as 1795 and shipping them from 1830. In 1932, by way of a takeover, the firm became the successors to John William BURDON, whose firm was one of the most successful of the English enterprises in Jerez during the nineteenth century. Apart from the Burdon sherries and its own well-known Pavón and Puerto finos, the nutty Don Luis AMONTILLADO, and Macarena MANZANILLA, it makes one of the most popular *ponches* (*see* "Spirits, Aromatic Wines, and Liqueurs", page 192). Caballero also owns Emilio LUSTAU, famous for its ALMACENISTA sherries.

Cádiz

Capital of the province embracing the sherry region, Cádiz, south of JEREZ DE LA FRONTERA on a peninsula connected by a stone causeway, is one of the most stylish of Spanish cities. The only city not captured by Napoleon during the Peninsular War, it is a place of white houses, narrow streets and handsome squares, shaded gardens, and a wide promenade with views out to the Atlantic. Its port is now the main centre for shipping sherry. Cádiz also claims to be the gastronomic capital of Andalucía. The waters of its bay and the surrounding coast supply fish and shellfish in great variety, and its *freidurías*, where you can buy them freshly fried to take away, were the forerunners of the British fish-and-chip shop.

Camera

A wooden box containing a candle for judging the clarity of the wine against the light.

Canoa

A wedge-shaped funnel traditionally used for transferring wine from one BUTT to another.

Capatáz

The cellarman at a bodega, his knowledge and experience is all-important in the operation of the SOLERA.

Carrascal

District to the immediate north of JEREZ, whose ALBARIZA soils are rated second in order of merit.

CAYD

Sanlúcar de Barrameda. Founded in 1825 by the Bozzano family, which was of Italian descent, the bodega was sold in 1969 to the local Cooperativa de Campo Virgen de la Caridad, which was by then supplying most of its wine. This embraces 1,000 members with vineyards in the locality; and the combined capacity of the cooperative and the original bodega amounts to some 30,000 butts. The musts were formerly fermented in cement *tinajas* (*see* "Montilla-Moriles and Málaga", page 105), the first of which were in fact constructed by craftsmen from Montilla, but these have now been replaced by stainless steel. Some of the musts develop as typical MANZANILLAS, including Bajo de Guía and Saeta FINAS, and others as the Cayd FINO, AMONTILLADO, MEDIUM, and CREAM.

Chiclana

Village on the border of the sherry district south of CÁDIZ, which produces wine in large quantity, but not of the highest quality. Its finos are sometimes blended with the less expensive sherries.

Chipiona

Seaside town on the coast road from SANLÚCAR DE BARRAMEDA to PUERTO DE SANTA MARÍA. Its arena vineyards are noted for their Moscatel, used in some of the sweet dessert wines.

Copita

The tall glass, narrowing towards the top, used for tasting sherry. It should be filled only a third to a half full, so that the full aroma of the wine may be appreciated. The small Elgin glasses habitually used in bars, pubs, and restaurants, and filled to the brim, are entirely unsuitable for sherry, since the wine needs space and air for the nose and flavour to develop properly. If you are served sherry in an Elgin or small thistle glass, ask for it to be poured into a tulip-shaped brandy or wine glass. When travelling in the sherry area, it is well worth bringing back a set of *copitas* or the larger *catavinos*.

Cream sherries

These sweet dessert wines are of two types. The dark, full-bodied, mahogany-coloured variety is made by sweetening an OLOROSO with a sugary must prepared from Pedro Ximénez and other grapes left to dry in the sun. The base wine for pale creams is a FINO or pale AMONTILLADO, which is blended with a sweet, concentrated must. *See also* AMOROSO, BRISTOL CREAM, and BRISTOL MILK.

Criadera

The literal meaning of the word is "nursery", and it is used to describe the series of BUTTS from which wine is drawn off to "refresh" or replenish a SOLERA.

Croft Jerez

Jerez de la Frontera. Croft is one of the oldest names in the port trade, but has been associated with sherry only since 1970, when IDV (International Distillers and Vintners, now part of Diageo), which had fallen heir to the company by way of WA Gilbey, decided to set up Croft Jerez to supply its large requirements of sherry. It is now owned by GONZÁLEZ-BYASS.

Starting from scratch, the company planted more than 375 hectares of vineyards and in 1975 opened the Rancho Croft on the outskirts of Jerez, whose handsome, traditionally styled buildings, with a capacity of 50,000 BUTTS, house one of the most modern of sherry establishments. Thanks to a new vinification plant and well-organized handling procedures at a time when other firms have found themselves in financial difficulties, it is one of the most flourishing in Jerez. Its largest-selling sherry is the sweet Croft Original Pale Cream; Croft Particular is along similar lines but medium to dry and there is a high-quality Croft Limited Edition containing old OLOROSO. Other labels are a light, dry, and elegant Delicado fino and a first-rate and moderately priced PALO CORTADO.

Crushing

See ZAPATOS DE PISAR.

Delgado Zuletta

Sanlúcar de Barrameda. Prestigious SANLÚCAR firm, founded in 1719 and most celebrated for its fragrant La Goya MANZANILLA PASADA, with which King Alfonso XIII is known to have toasted the crew of one of his submarines while it was submerged in the Bay of Santander.

Don Fino

Popular AMONTILLADO from SANDEMAN.

Don Zoilo

This superior range of sherries was formerly made by Zoilo RUÍZ MATEOS, the flagship of the expropriated RUMASA group in JEREZ; it is now made and sold by Luís PAEZ of the Medina group who took over the SOLERAS. The best known of the range is the round and aromatic FINO, one of the best in its class.

Dry Sack

A medium sherry, the most popular of the wines from WILLIAMS & HUMBERT, sold in a distinctive sack – though the name, of course, is derived from the old English name for sherry (*see* SACK).

Duff Gordon

Puerto de Santa María. The company was founded in 1768 by a Scot, Sir James Duff, who was British Consul in CÁDIZ at the time. The firm flourished and in 1833 his son, Cosmo Duff Gordon, entered into partnership with Thomas Osborne of the sherry firm of the same name. OSBORNE finally bought out the interest of the Duff Gordon family in 1872, but, in addition to its own sherries, continued to market the Duff Gordon wines under that name, though they are sold only abroad, in limited amounts, and are not found in Spain itself. They include the Fina Feria; No 28 Oloroso (popular in the USA, Canada, and Japan); the popular El Cid medium-dry AMONTILLADO, and Santa María CREAM.

Fiesta de la Vendimia

The famous wine festival held in JEREZ DE LA FRONTERA in mid-September to celebrate the beginning of the vintage. Dedicated each year to a different country or city where sherry is popular, this colourful affair embraces flamenco, bullfighting, and horse shows, and culminates in the pressing of the first fruits on the steps of Collegiate Church, a ceremony presided over by the Queen of the Vintage and her attendants in traditional costume, chosen from the prettiest girls in Jerez.

Fina

A light, dry MANZANILLA from SANLÚCAR.

Fino

The lightest, driest, and most delicate sherry, a pale straw colour and of fifteen to eighteen per cent strength – the present tendency is to market lighter, less alcoholic finos. It develops beneath the FLOR until final fortification and is at its fragrant best when freshly bottled. Once opened, it should be served chilled and drunk within a few days.

Fino Quinta

Excellent FINO from OSBORNE.

Flor

A film of yeasts of the genus *saccharomyces* growing spontaneously on the surface of certain types of sherry, especially FINOS, during their maturation in SOLERA. It protects the wine from undue oxidation or conversion to vinegar and develops most thickly on wines aged in old BUTTS.

Florido, Bodegas César

Chipiona. Small firm making the excellent Moscatel Especial.

Fortification

The addition to a wine of alcohol or brandy. When deficient in alcohol, FINO sherries are lightly fortified at an early stage, and OLOROSOS more strongly to kill the FLOR. Finos destined for export are further fortified before shipment or bottling with a fifty per cent mixture of alcohol and mature sherry to prevent the reappearance of the *flor*.

Garvey

Jerez de la Frontera. Famous sherry house founded by William Garvey, who emigrated from Ireland in 1780 and set up business in SANLÚCAR DE BARRAMEDA about 1797. His bodegas were long among the biggest in JEREZ and are impressive even by modern standards, with an OLOROSO SOLERA ranged along the side of an arcaded patio a quarter of a mile long.

The firm was acquisitioned in 1979 by RUMASA, which fastidiously restored the old family mansion and also constructed a new vinification plant and further large bodegas for maturing the wine on the outskirts of Jerez. After the collapse of Rumasa in the early 1980s the firm was government controlled for a while, but it has been re-acquired by the former head of Rumasa, José María Ruíz Mateos.

The wine is now fermented in stainless steel. Of its excellent sherries, the best known is the San Patricio FINO, named by William Garvey after the patron saint of Ireland. Other wines include the aromatic and fully flavoured AMONTILLADO, the dry Ochavico OLOROSO, and outstanding Puerta Real sweet olorosos, as well as the sweet Asalto CREAM sherry and Gran Orden PX. Garvey has recently introduced a quartet of rare age-dated twenty- and thirty-year-old oloroso and PX wines, with the labels Garvey 1780 VOS and VORS.

González-Byass

Jerez de la Frontera. One of the largest and most important of the sherry firms, González-Byass is still family controlled. The company was founded in 1835 by Don Manuel María González Angel, who later took into partnership the firm's London agent, Robert Blake Byass. The head of the firm until his death some years ago, Don Manuel González Gordon, Marqués de Bonanza, was one of the most distinguished figures in JEREZ, and wrote one of the best books on its wines: *Sherry, The Noble Wine* (1972). The Byass family sold its interest in the firm some time ago.

The old bodegas in the centre of the town, alongside those of PEDRO DOMECQ, are vast in size: the famous "La Concha", designed by Gustave Eiffel, houses 12,400 butts, and the more modern "Tío Pepe" bodega, on three floors, a further 30,000; but even these are dwarfed by the modern vinification plant of "Las Copas" on the road to CÁDIZ, with its capacity of 60,000 butts.

TÍO PEPE is the biggest-selling FINO in the world and deservedly so, since it remains one of the driest and most elegant. Other popular wines are the new Manzanilla Rocío, Elegante dry fino, La Concha AMONTILLADO, Alfonso dry OLOROSO, San Domingo Pale Cream, Nectar Cream, and Noë PX.

González-Byass also makes a magnificent old Amontillado del Duque and some superb old olorosos in limited quantity, such as the dry Apóstoles Oloroso Muy Viejo, and two very old dessert sherries, the Matusalém and Solera 1847 oloroso dulce. Both are almost black in colour with a deep, maderized nose and a dryish, bitter-sweet finish, since most of the sugar has been consumed over the years. The company's ultimate sherry is the recently introduced Millennium Oloroso.

Guadalete, River

The Guadalete River, which flows into the Bay of Cádiz, fairly closely follows the eastern boundary of the fan-shaped sherry-producing region.

Guadalquivír, River

The river Guadalquivír flows into the Atlantic at SANLÚCAR DE BARRAMEDA and forms the western boundary of the sherry region, dividing it from the salt marshes of the famous wildlife reserve of the Coto Doñana.

Gutiérrez-Colosia, Bodegas

Puerto de Santa María. The bodega makes a range of sherries, including good FINOS, OLOROSOS, and an AMONTILLADO, but perhaps the best are the first-rate PALO CORTADO, and the sweet PX and Moscatel Soleado.

Harvey, John

Jerez de la Frontera. The old Bristol company of John Harvey & Sons had its origins in an earlier company founded in 1796, with which the Harvey family became associated in the early nineteenth century. Long famous as a sherry shipper and particularly for its BRISTOL MILK and BRISTOL CREAM, it is now part of Allied Domecq. It was not until 1970 that it established its own vineyards and bodegas in JEREZ by buying the old-established firm of Mackenzie & Co and the adjoining large bodegas of the Marqués de Misa (both have now been sold), and in 1973 began developing much larger vineyards in association with GARVEY and BARBADILLO. The continuous vinification plant which John Harvey operates at the Gibalbín vineyards with Barbadillo is one of the region's most modern. Apart from the world-famous BRISTOL CREAM, Harvey's markets a pale CREAM and an AMONTILLADO – the renamed Harvey's Club Classic.

Hidalgo y Cía, Vinícola

Old-established SANLÚCAR firm and makers of the light and graceful La Gitana MANZANILLA, soft and deep Palo Cortado Viejo, and first-rate new Pastrana MANZANILLA PASADA.

Hidalgo, Emilio

Small firm whose labels include Panesa FINO and Gobernador OLOROSO. With their depth and complexity the Privilegio 1860 PALO CORTADO and Santa Ana 1861 PX are among the very best wines to come from Jerez.

Infantes de Orleans-Borbón, Bodegas de los

Founded by the Duke of Montpensier in 1886, the firm is now fifty per cent owned by BARBADILLO. Among its well-made sherries are the Alvaro FINO and first-rate Botánico AMONTILLADO.

Jerez de la Frontera

Jerez (or Xérès) de la Frontera is the capital of the sherry region and, in its corrupted English form, has given its name to the wine. The town was probably founded by the Phoenicians and was much fought over during the period of the Moorish occupation – hence the suffix of *de la Frontera* granted by King John I in 1380 (there is another Jerez de los Caballeros on the borders of Portugal). Its wines were well known in Roman times;

but the trade greatly increased with the settlement of foreign traders, mostly English, after the expulsion of the Jews in 1492 and the massive participation of English, Scottish, and Irish shippers, many of whom remained in the area, during the late eighteenth and nineteenth centuries. With its old castle and walls, narrow streets and attractive white Andalucían houses, its great roofed market, and innumerable bodegas, often set in decorative gardens, it is a most attractive place to stay, especially in late spring or autumn.

La Goya

First-rate MANZANILLA PASADA made by DELGADO ZULETA.

La Guita

Classic MANZANILLA PASADA made by PÉREZ MARÍN.

La Ina

PEDRO DOMECQ's big-selling and excellent FINO, which is a shade less dry than some other examples.

Los Tercios

Reputed vineyard area with ALBARIZA soil, to the southwest of JEREZ and adjoining that of BALBAINA.

Lustau, Emilio

Jerez de la Frontera. Once family owned, but now taken over by Luís CABALLERO, Lustau has moved from its bodega in the old city wall to the spacious Mackenzie bodega bought from HARVEYS. It is one of the concerns which best weathered recession through its policy of selling well-made own-brand sherries. Its branded sherries in various styles are first-rate wines and include Puerto FINO; Escuadrilla AMONTILLADO; very rare Emperatriz Eugenia OLOROSO; Solera East India Cream; and a luscious Emilin dessert Moscatel. What has particularly caught the imagination of sherry drinkers is the ALMACENISTA range of sherries from small, individual stock-holders, rarely seen abroad until Lustau began selecting, bottling, and shipping them for retail sale. Since 1995 Lustau has been selling "single cask" sherries from its *almacenistas*, the first being the dry oloroso from Pilár Aranda.

Macharnudo

Rated the best of the ALBARIZA areas, Macharnudo lies on high ground north of JEREZ. At its centre is Macharnudo castle, familiar to enthusiasts of PEDRO DOMECQ sherries from its picture on the labels. The firm still uses the castle, which was built during the seventeenth century, for receptions.

Manzanilla

A pale, crisp, and very dry FINA with a salty tang from SANLÚCAR DE BARRAMEDA, made in a SOLERA sometimes containing as many as fourteen SCALES. The word is also used in Spain for camomile tea, from which it is probably derived because of a certain similarity in flavour. Manzanillas owe their special characteristics to the atmospheric conditions and the special methods of operating the *soleras* in Sanlúcar. Not all the wines matured in Sanlúcar emerge as manzanillas, and manzanilla musts aged in JEREZ develop as normal FINOS.

Manzanilla pasada

An old and mature MANZANILLA, which resembles a light and very dry AMONTILLADO.

Medina y Cía, José

Jerez de la Frontera. The company was formed fairly recently by the progressive acquisition of bodegas in SANLÚCAR DE BARRAMEDA and JEREZ DE LA FRONTERA by the Medina family. Besides José Medina the group now includes Luís PAEZ, PÉREZ MEGÍA, and WILLIAMS & HUMBERT and is one of the biggest concerns in Jerez. Through its Dutch partners, the Ahold group, it is the largest exporter of sherries to Holland and Germany. As a new base for its growing operations, José Medina acquired from Marcos Eguizábal the extensive installations of the former Bodegas Internacionales, together with most of its stocks of wine. These include the famous DON ZOILO SOLERA. Medina also markets a complete range of sherries under its own label.

Medium sherry

An increasingly popular term for a sherry which is akin to an AMONTILLADO, but a little sweetened and made in a different way – from a blend of wines rather than by ageing FINO. Superior brands, like those from SANDEMAN, are made by blending fine amontillado with Pedro Ximénez.

Mitad y mitad

A mixture of alcohol and mature sherry in equal proportions which is used for fortification.

Oloroso

The darkest, softest, fullest-bodied, and most fragrant of the styles of sherry, containing up to twenty-four per cent alcohol. It is matured without FLOR and in its natural state is completely dry, but is often blended with Pedro Ximénez wine and VINO DE COLOR for making sweet dessert sherries.

Osborne y Cía

Puerto de Santa María. Founded in 1772, still in family hands. The largest firm in PUERTO DE SANTA MARÍA, Osborne bought the important DUFF GORDON in 1872 and has since launched sister concerns in Portugal, Mexico, and the Rioja (see "Montecillo", page 133).

Osborne's old bodega in Puerto de Santa María, built in 1837, is one of the most beautiful in the region; and the modern vinification plant, where the wine is fermented in horizontal rather than vertical tanks to approximate more closely to the traditional BUTT, is among the most advanced. The wines include the excellent Fino Quinta, very dry, with a greenish cast and almond-like taste; the nutty Coquinero AMONTILLADO; the dry Bailén OLOROSO; and Santa María CREAM. The firm is also the largest maker of Spanish brandy and spirits. See also "Spirits, Aromatic Wines, and Liqueurs", page 192.

Paéz, Luís

See MEDINA Y CÍA, JOSÉ.

Pajarete, Paxarete

Pedro Ximénez wine used for sweetening certain styles of sherry.

Palo cortado

Style of sherry between an AMONTILLADO and OLOROSO. Having 17.5 to twenty-three per cent alcohol, it is classified as *dos, tres*, or *cuatro cortados*, in ascending scale according to body and age. Genuine palo cortado is a beautiful wine possessing great depth and fragrance – always expensive.

Palomino & Vergara

Jerez de la Frontera. This family firm, which was founded in 1765, occupied bodegas (now demolished) in the middle of JEREZ. The bodegas' centrepieces were the great glass-domed offices with the original mahogany and gilt counter and fittings. Palomino & Vergara was one of the largest of the firms taken over by RUMASA, and was later sold to John HARVEY and subsequently dismantled. The SOLERAS of its best-known wine, the light, dry Tío Mateo FINO, were sold to REAL TESORO.

Paternina SA – División Jerez

Jerez de la Frontera. Marcos Eguizábal of Paternina in Rioja acquired large interests in JEREZ from RUMASA, but sold off most of its well-known sherries and brandies except for a trio from the former Díez-Mérito. The excellent Fino Imperial, Oloroso Victoria Regina, and sweet PX Vieja Solera are now marketed under the Paternina label. Paterina also sells sherries under the Bartola and Pemartin labels.

Pedro Domecq

Jerez de la Frontera. Pedro Domecq is the oldest of the large bodegas and the biggest single firm in the region, with extensive vineyards in MACHARNUDO and elsewhere, and dozens of bodegas between JEREZ, PUERTO DE SANTA MARÍA, and SANLÚCAR DE BARRAMEDA. In the oldest, 'El Molino', built in 1730, there are BUTTS laid down centuries ago and dedicated to historical figures such as Pitt, Nelson, and Wellington.

The firm was founded by an Irish emigrant in 1730, but greatly expanded by the Domecq family from the Basses Pyrenées in association with its English agent, father of the writer John Ruskin. It was sold in 1994 to the British Allied-Lyons (also owner of John HARVEY) which, in view of the importance of the acquisition, has since been renamed Allied Domecq. Don José Ignacio Domecq, who died in 1997, was one of the great sherry tasters and authorities of his generation; and the family maintains ties with Britain, among other things mounting one of the world's crack polo teams from among its members.

The firm makes an excellent Rioja and has extensive interests in Mexico, where it produces both beverage wines and vast quantities of brandy and tequila. It is in fact one of the largest brandy makers in the world (see "Spirits, Aromatic Wines, and Liqueurs", page 192). Apart from the famous FINO LA INA, Domecq's other sherries include one of the best dry OLOROSOS, Río Viejo; Botaina (old AMONTILLADO); Capuchino (PALO CORTADO); a superb VORS Sibarita Oloroso; the popular Pedro Cream; and an older and richer VORS Venerable.

Pérez Marín, Hijos de Rainera

Sanlúcar de Barrameda. This small firm, founded in 1850, has long been known for making some of the best MANZANILLA. Its Bodegas La Guita took the name from the habit of a former member of the family, Domingo Pérez Marín, of refusing to sell his wine except for cash – *guita* in local slang. Its most famous wine is the delicious La Guita MANZANILLA PASADA, an old and very fragrant FINA on the point of conversion to AMONTILLADO. The other speciality is a *vinagre de yema*, a sherry vinegar made in SOLERA and of quite astonishing fragrance and fruitiness.

Pérez Megía, Hijos de A

Sanlúcar de Barrameda. Dating from 1821, the firm was in the fifth generation of the family which founded it when it was bought by José MEDINA. Jalifa VORS a top-quality AMONTILLADO, made in the SOLERAS laid down by the founder, is now marketed by WILLIAMS & HUMBERT.

Plastering

The light dusting of the grapes with gypsum (calcium sulphate) before vinification, a process strongly attacked in Victorian times, but beneficial and leading to improved acidity in the musts.

Puerto de Santa María

Next in importance of the sherry towns to JEREZ, Puerto de Santa María is particularly noted for its FINOS, AMONTILLADOS, and brandy. It was the main port for shipping sherry until it was supplanted in the 1920s by its larger neighbour, CÁDIZ. It is a pleasant, open place with wide streets, houses with grilles and *miradores*, and an impressive bullring built by the OSBORNE family. There are good beaches in the vicinity, served by resort hotels (*see* "Hotels"), and on the outskirts is the lush Casino Bahía de Cádiz.

PX

Abbreviation for the Pedro Ximénez grape, which is used mainly for sweet wines in JEREZ. There is a legend that the vine originated in the Canaries, from where it was taken to the Rhine and brought to Jerez by one Pieter Siemens, a soldier of the Emperor Charles V, in the sixteenth century. Unfortunately, this seems more picturesque than true.

Raya

A term employed in classifying musts and also used to describe less delicate styles of OLOROSO.

Real Tesoro

Jerez de la Frontera. The firm, formerly known as the Herederos del Marqués del Real Tesoro, takes its name from the first *marqués*, who gained the title ("Royal Treasure") by using his own silver to forge cannonballs while in command of a fleet for the Royal Treasury. The bodega was founded by a descendant of the *marqués* in the late nineteenth century. One of the smaller family firms, it is particularly noted for an excellent MANZANILLA and a good, natural, unsweetened, nutty AMONTILLADO. Real Tesoro was bought by José Estévez who, in a period of recession and with the profits from an enterprise producing sand for glass-making, has constructed an impressive, brand-new bodega and continues the business under the name of Real Tesoro. The biggest-selling of Real Tesoro's brands is the popular Tío Mateo FINO, of which the SOLERA was acquired from John HARVEY after the takeover of PALOMINO & VERGARA.

Refreshment

The replenishment of the BUTTS of a SOLERA with younger wine as the most mature wine is drawn off.

Rota

Village on the coast west of JEREZ, once known for its red Rota Tent wine, but now the site of a great US naval base.

Ruíz Mateos, Zoilo

Founded as a small wine company in ROTA in 1857, Ruíz Mateos was the springboard for the vast RUMASA empire, to which, in abbreviated form, it gave its name. The company moved to JEREZ in 1930 and later acquired the handsome mansion of La Atalaya, formerly belonging to the Vergara family of PALOMINO & VERGARA, as administrative head-quarters both for itself and the whole of RUMASA'S sherry group. La Atalaya also housed the magnificent Museum of Clocks and Watches founded by José María Ruíz Mateos, the president of Rumasa; the mansion is now a municipal museum. The SOLERAS of Ruíz Mateos' magnificent DON ZOILO sherries have been acquired by José MEDINA, which now markets the wines.

Rumasa

The early steps in the formation of Rumasa have been described under RUÍZ MATEOS, and the company embarked on the high road to fortune when it signed a contract with John HARVEY & Sons of Bristol for supplying all its large requirements of sherry. After breaking with Harvey's, José María Ruíz Mateos, the younger brother of the founder, Don Zoilo, moved to Madrid and set about forming the largest grouping in Spain, embracing banks, insurance, shipping, chemicals, hotels, and property as well as foreign business.

However, Rumasa lost none of its early interest in wines and gained control of thirty-five per cent of the bodegas in Jerez: RUÍZ MATEOS, Unión de Exportadores de Jerez, WILLIAMS & HUMBERT, PALOMINO & VERGARA, Marqués de Misa, Pemartín, Varela, Bertola, Otaolaurruchi, Diestro, Lacave, Diez Morales, Valderrama & Gordon, Bodegas Internacionales, GARVEY, and TERRY. In Rioja, the company took over Paternina, Bodegas Franco-Españolas, LAN, and Berberana; in Montilla, Monte Cristo and Pérez Barquero; and in Penedès, the sparkling wine firms of Castellblanch, René Barbier, Conde de Caralt, and Segura Viudas. Among its foreign acquisitions, the company included the Augustus Barnett chain of off-licences in England.

Rumasa overstretched itself and in 1983 was expropriated by the government, which took over the running of the different enterprises, finally selling them. This was the subject of prolonged litigation, with José María Ruíz Mateos seeking refuge abroad for a time. The last of the companies to be returned to private ownership was WILLIAMS & HUMBERT, and José María has since re-entered the trade by buying José de SOTO and GARVEY.

Sack

Old name for sherry (and also for Málaga and Canary wines), probably originating in the fifteenth century and derived from the Spanish *sacar* ("to draw out").

San Patricio

One of the best-known FINOS, made by GARVEY.

Sánchez Romate Hermanos

Jerez de la Frontera. This old-established firm is supplier to the Spanish royal family. Its sherries, which have long been noted for their quality, include the NPU AMONTILLADO, an unblended SOLERA wine of great quality; Romate FINO; Don José OLOROSO; and La Sacristía de Romate CREAM. Sánchez Romate is, however, most famous for its Cardenal Mendoza brandy (*see* "Spirits, Aromatic Wines, and Liqueurs", page 188).

Sandeman-Jerez

Jerez de la Frontera. The firm was founded by a Scot, George Sandeman, who started business as a shipper in London about 1790, acting as agent for DUFF GORDON and later setting up his own establishments in Oporto and JEREZ. Until its takeover by Seagram and recent resale to the Portuguese SOGRAPE group, it remained a family firm. One of the largest concerns in Jerez, it makes its wines scrupulously and by traditional means, although they are no longer vinified in cask as they were. Big-selling wines are its

DON FINO; Character AMONTILLADO; and Medium Dry, made by blending amontillado with PX; and Armada CREAM, a good dessert wine. It also makes some quite exceptional wines in limited amounts, such as the Royal Ambrosante PALO CORTADO and the dry and sweet Imperial Corregidor and Royal Corregidor OLOROSOS.

Sanlúcar de Barrameda

Town west of JEREZ at the mouth of the GUADALQUIVÍR estuary, famous for its dry MANZANILLAS. A picturesque place with a wide beach opposite the wildlife reserve of Las Marismas, it has several good seafood restaurants and a few small, characterful hotels.

Scale

Term used of a SOLERA to denote a row of BUTTS containing wine of similar type and age.

Sobre tabla

Young wine which has been racked free of the lees and is ready for use in a CRIADERA.

Solera

Derived from the Latin *solum*, or Spanish *suelo* (meaning "a floor"), the word in its narrower sense applies to the BUTTS at floor level from which sherry is withdrawn for bottling or shipment. More loosely, the word is used for the whole assembly of butts in which sherry is matured, including those of the CRIADERA from which the *solera* proper is replenished. The butts are arranged in tiers of SCALES containing wine of identical type, but progressively younger in age. In limited amounts, and from time to time, the wine is taken from the last row of butts, or *solera* proper. As wine is drawn off, the butts are topped up with rather younger wine, and each scale is in turn "refreshed" or replenished from that immediately preceding it in age. This procedure is known as "working the scales", and is feasible because the younger wine rapidly takes on the characteristics of the older. *Soleras* for producing FINO require more scales, perhaps five, than those used in making the fuller-bodied OLOROSO; and the most complicated are those used in SANLÚCAR DE BARRAMEDA for making MANZANILLA, which can have up to nineteen.

Soto, José de

Jerez de la Frontera. Apart from its sherries, which include the MANZANILLA Juncal, Soto FINO, AMONTILLADO CREAM, and PX, the old family firm was the first to make a *ponche* (*see* "Spirits, Aromatic Wines, and Liqueurs", page 192), and its brand remains one of the best: drier than the others, with hints of chocolate and herbs. Soto was recently bought by José María Ruíz-Mateos, formerly of RUMASA.

Sunning

In the past, it was standard practice to lay out the grapes on *esparto* grass mats and to sun them briefly. Thanks to improved methods of judging the optimum time for picking, sunning is now mainly used for grapes intended for sweet wines and the effect is to concentrate the amount of sugar in the must.

Terry, Fernando A de

Puerto de Santa María. This large firm, which is also a brandy maker on a big scale, was founded in 1883 by the descendants of an Irish family which had settled in Spain as long ago as 1500. In 1981 the founding family sold both the bodegas and famous establishment for raising the white

Cartujano horses to a Catalan finance house, in fact acting for RUMASA; the company, with its huge complex outside PUERTO DE SANTA MARÍA, was later acquired by John HARVEY and now belongs to Allied Domecq. Of its various sherries, only Maruja MANZANILLA survives. It makes brandy on a large scale (*see* "Spirits, Aromatic Wines, and Liqueurs", page 193).

Tío Pepe

The world's largest-selling FINO, made by GONZÁLEZ-BYASS, and one of the driest, of consistently high standard.

Valdespino, AR

Jerez de la Frontera. Old-established Spanish sherry house, whose bodegas and patios are among the most beautiful in JEREZ – the older bodegas were once part of an ancient monastery. This is one of the oldest of the sherry firms, which until recently belonged to the Valdespino family, who have been making wine in the area since the fourteenth century. However, the concern has been sold to José Estévez of REAL TESORO.

Its methods are strictly traditional, the wines are still fermented in OAK BUTTS, and their quality is testament to the care with which they are made. The sherries include a classic single-vineyard Inocente FINO; a dry macho Tío Diego AMONTILLADO; an older and superb Don Tomás amontillado; and a raisiny El Candado PX Solera Superior. In the USA, where the firm's wines are sold under the name of Hartley & Gibson, the range comprises MANZANILLA, FINO, AMONTILLADO, dry OLOROSO, and CREAM.

Venencia

An instrument used for withdrawing samples of sherry from the BUTT. In JEREZ, it consists traditionally of a small silver cup on a long whalebone handle; in SANLÚCAR DE BARRAMEDA, where it is even more important not to disturb the FLOR, the cup is smaller and the *venencia* is made in one piece out of a bamboo cane. *Venencias* are now made with plastic handles and stainless-steel cups.

Vino de color

A dark-coloured wine used for blending with certain brown and dessert sherries and made by fermenting a sugary boiled-down must (*arrope*) with a proportion of new must.

Williams & Humbert

Jerez de la Frontera. The firm was founded in 1877 by Alexander Williams, until then working as a clerk for WISDOM & WARTER. It subsequently became one of the most important in JEREZ. Once a jewel in RUMASA's crown, it was the last of the sherry companies acquired by the expropriated colossus to be returned by the government to private ownership. It now belongs to José MEDINA. Its bodegas are among the most picturesque in Jerez, and points of interest for visitors are the splendid coaches and harnesses. Until 1979 the office of the British Vice-Consul was located within the bodega. Its most popular wines are the DRY SACK FINO and MEDIUM; it also makes the well-known Canasta Cream, Alegria MANZANILLA, and a first-rate VORS Dos Cortados PALO CORTADO.

Wisdom & Warter

Jerez de la Frontera. The company was founded in 1854 by two Englishmen, of whom Punch once wrote, "Wisdom sells the wine, Warter makes it". The firm, now controlled by GONZÁLEZ-BYASS, markets a wide range of sherries, including Fino Los Buhos, Manzanilla la Canoa, very rare Solera Centenario AMONTILLADO, Merecedor Oloroso, and Wisdom's Choice Cream.

Zapatos de pisar
Old-fashioned cowhide boots, studded with flat tacks and formerly used for crushing the grapes. Crushing is now carried out in horizontal presses, either mechanical or pneumatic, or in yet more modern vinification plants by a continuous process, in which a first light crushing produces musts or FINOS and later, heavier pressing for the fuller-bodied OLOROSOS.

WINE AND FOOD

On gastronomic maps of Spain, Andalucía is often labelled the *zona de los fritos* or "region of fried food"; and high on the list of such dishes must come the fries of mixed fish, sometimes called *parejas* in Cádiz – this being the name of the dish cooked by the fishermen while at sea in their boats. Cooking in the sherry region is very much oriented towards fish and seafood, available in great variety from the Bay of Cádiz and the nearby Atlantic coastline. In places such as Sanlúcar de Barrameda the shellfish is magnificently fresh and the lobsters, for example, are large enough to serve a party of six. Another great speciality is the *gazpachos* or cold soups. Sherry vinegar is one of the best and fruitiest of vinegars – it is a great adjunct in salad dressing and other dishes. Apart from the delicious iced cakes and fruit tarts from the sweet trolley, by far the most popular sweet is *tocino de cielo*. Sherry is, not surprisingly, often used in cooking, and it is also usual to drink a chilled fino throughout the meal rather than a table wine.

Acedías fritas Fried baby soles.
Barbujitos Small fresh anchovies, fried.
Bistec salteado al Jerez Steak sautéed with sherry.
Boquerones de la Isla Fried fresh anchovies, locally caught.
Cañaíllas de la Isla A sea-snail typical of the coast. It is lightly boiled and eaten cold, the sharp tail of one snail being used to extract the meat from the others.
Cazón Baby shark, marinated with paprika and vinegar.
Consomé al Jerez Consommé with sherry, usually "fortified" with an extra dose at the table!
Coquinas al ajillo Cockles in garlic sauce.
Dorada a la sal Gilthead baked in a thick paste of sea salt, which is removed by the waiter at the table.
Fritura gaditana A mixed fry of small fish.
Gazpacho andaluz Cold, uncooked soup containing chopped tomatoes, cucumber, and green peppers, together with olive oil, vinegar, and garlic. Breadcrumbs may either be used in making it or served on the side.
Helado de pasas con PX A particularly delicious ice cream made with raisins and served with sweet Pedro Ximénez sherry poured over it.
Jamón de Jabugo The best and most fully flavoured type of the highly cured *jamón serrano*, from a village near Huelva. Like Bayonne or Parma, it is either eaten on its own or served with melon, usually as a first course.
Macedonia de frutas naturales Fresh fruit salad served in the fruits' own juices, laced with sherry.

Naranjas acaramelizadas Fresh oranges, cut up and served in a syrup containing caramel.

Paire Scabbard fish, cut into steaks and grilled.

Pijotas A tiny fish fried crisp in olive oil.

Pipirrana con gambas Prawns cooked in a sauce of tomatoes and peppers.

Puntillitas Minute inkfish, dipped in a light batter and fried in olive oil.

Riñones al Jerez Calves' kidneys, sliced and sautéed in olive oil and served in a tomato sauce containing sherry.

Salchichas al Jerez Fried sausages, flavoured with sherry and served with squares of fried bread.

Salpicón de mariscos Cold fish and shellfish salad with scampi, monkfish and lobster, dressed with a sauce which contains sherry vinegar.

Sopa de pescado gaditana A rich fish soup akin to bouillabaisse.

Tortilla suflé A sweet soufflé omelet.

Urta a la roteña Urta is a fish for which there is no translation. It feeds on shellfish, acquiring great flavour, and is a speciality of Rota, on the coast west of Jerez, where it is often cooked with a rich sauce of tomatoes and red peppers.

HOTELS

Arcos de la Frontera *Parador de Arcos*, with splendid views over the gorge; *Los Olivos* in an old mansion; and *El Convento* a former convent with magnificent views of the Guadalete valley.

Cádiz The quietest, most pleasantly situated hotel is the *Parador de Cádiz* also known as the *Hotel Atlántico*, in a garden at the far tip of the peninsula, overlooking the ocean. Its only disadvantage is a long walk through the narrow streets to the centre (and back again!) and it would be an adventurous driver who took the car.

Jerez de la Frontera Recommended hotels are the four-star *Royal Sherry Park* and *Hotel Jerez*, both of which possess large gardens and swimming pools, and the three-star *NH Avenida Jerez*.

Puerto de Santa María *Hotel Duques de Medinaceli* has luxurious accomodation in an old palace; also recommended, *Monasterio San Miguel* in a converted monastery; *Tryp Caballo Blanco*.

Sanlúcar de Barrameda has a few small but characterful hotels including *Doñana* and *Los Helechos*.

RESTAURANTS

Arcos de la Frontera *Parador de Arcos* and *El Convento* with its pretty patio for outdoor dining.

Cádiz *El Faro* is the best in Cádiz, with a splendid range of locally caught fish and sophisticated cooking, such as stuffed cuttlefish and peppers stuffed with *bacalao* or dried cod. *Ventorrillo del Chato* affords period charm, well-cooked Andalucían dishes, such as oxtail in oloroso, and a long wine list.

Jerez de la Frontera The small and sophisticated *La Mesa Redonda* belongs to a member of the Valdespino family who does the cooking and marketing. *El Bosque* provides charming surroundings, international cuisine, some well-cooked Andalucían dishes, and a good wine list.

Also *Tendido* (opposite the bullring) with local fish dishes and a long wine list. *El Abaco* in the Hotel Royal Sherry Park.

Puerto de Santa María *El Faro del Puerto* is a branch of the famous El Faro in Cádiz. *La Terraza*, a luxurious restaurant of the Casino Bahía de Cádiz, serving international cooking. *Reina Isabel* in the Hotel Duques de Medinaceli serves good Mediterranean food. Also *Guadalete* near the Club Nútico.

Sanlúcar de Barrameda Try *Mirador Doñana*, a beach restaurant serving tapas and the excellent local seafood or *Bigote*, once small and select and serving superbly fresh seafood, but now greatly enlarged and something of a *caravanserai*.

Valencia and Murcia

The eastern area along the Mediterranean coast, known as the Levante, embraces the three DOs of Utiel-Requena, Valencia, and Alicante within the autonomy of Valencia, and Jumilla, Yecla, and Bullas in Murcia. For bulk production the Levante is second in importance only to La Mancha. The city of Valencia is home to a number of large wineries with the very latest equipment, drawing from the region in general for grapes or wine. Clean and drinkable light table wines are supplied to the world and the bodegas specialize in blending wines to their customers' specification.

The traditional wines are Mediterranean, full-bodied, spicy, and high in alcohol. The alcoholic strength of the wines from Yecla and Jumilla may in part be explained by the fact that the black Monastrell grape, so typical of the regions, was largely unaffected by phylloxera, and the vines are not always grafted on to American stocks as in other parts of Spain and the rest of Europe. Monastrell, which in recent years has been "rediscovered" and is enjoying increasing prestige, is also the grape *par excellence* of Alicante, though a certain amount of white wine is made from Verdil.

Perhaps the best of the Levante wines are the *rosados* from the upland region of Utiel-Requena, made from the black Bobal grape. On top form, these are among Spain's most attractive rosés: pale, very light, fruity, fragrant, and refreshing. The commercial bodegas in Valencia draw largely on the wine from Utiel-Requena for their blends – the Swiss firm of Schenk, for example, maintains a bodega there and buys from the cooperatives – and there is a gentlemen's agreement that wine from any of the three demarcated regions of the autonomy of Valencia may be labelled and shipped as DO Valencia. Not surprisingly, in a part of the country famous for its dessert grapes, there is also some luscious Moscatel from the coastal area.

Tourists in resorts such as Alicante, Benicasím, Benidorm, Calpe, and Javea will certainly profit from choosing the local growths and the house wine in the restaurants, rather than Rioja.

Agapito Rico, Viñedos
DO r ☆☆→☆☆☆☆ *98 00 01*
Jumilla (Murcia). DO Jumilla. Founded in 1989, this small bodega makes some of Spain's best *vinos jóvenes* in the unlikely region of JUMILLA, especially the 1998 Carchelo wines (100 per cent Merlot, 100 per cent Syrah, and a blend of Merlot with Monastrell and Tempranillo). Also produces excellent *crianzas* and *reservas*.

Alicante
Alicante, with a mild climate and marble-paved promenade, lined with palms and facing the port, is the best base for visiting the local bodegas and also those of the somewhat inaccessible regions of YECLA and JUMILLA in the mountainous hinterland of Murcia.

Alicante
DO r p (w dr sw) ☆→☆☆
Demarcated region, extending to 14,254 hectares and producing 10.4 million litres of wine in 2002. It is divided into two sub-regions. The maritime zone on the coast around Calpe, Javea, and Denia, makes sweet Moscatel. The

larger, more important central zone lies in the hills around Villena, Pinoso, and Monóvar and produces a light rosé, a VINO DE DOBLE PASTA, and full-bodied reds high in alcohol, made with ninety per cent Monastrell. Small amounts of white wine are also made from eighty-five per cent Verdil.

Alicante, Bodegas Cooperativas de BOCOPA

DO r p w dr ★★

Petrer (Alicante). DO Alicante. Large co-op formed in 1987 and accounting for half of the DO wine from the region, made by its 3,000 members. Of its reliable wines, the best are the Monastrell/Tempranillo Viña Alone red (Alone was the Roman name for Alicante); a luscious Sol de Alicante; and a very good Marqués de Alicante, made from Tempranillo, Monastrell, and Cabernet Sauvignon.

Alto-Turia

w dr ☆→☆☆☆

Subdivision of the DO VALENCIA located in the high northwest of the province, and producing white wines of some quality. Fruity, lightly acidic with a greenish cast and containing some 11.5 to thirteen per cent alcohol, they are made with the Merseguera grape.

Balcona, Bodegas

DO r ✩→✩✩

Cehegin (Murcia). DO Bullas. The wines from this small bodega with twelve hectares of vineyard and 128 *barricas* are the best from the new DO. They comprise a red Partal and Partal Selección, both made from blends of Monastrell, Tempranillo, and Cabernet Sauvignon.

Benicarló

VC r ✩

A prime favourite in the nineteenth century for lacing less robust French wines, the red wine of Benicarló has virtually disappeared, owing to the expense of replanting with grafted vines after PHYLLOXERA. The small town of Benicarló, which has a comfortable seaside *parador*, is close to the picturesque and sea-girt Peñíscola, whose castle was the refuge of the last of the Anti-Popes, Pedro de Luna.

Bleda, Bodegas

DO r p w dr g ★★★ *98 00 01 02*

Jumilla (Murcia). DO Jumilla. The bodega was founded in 1917 by the father of the present owner and was the first in the region to bottle its wines (in 1936). The white Castillo Jumilla, made from 100 per cent Macabeo, and the rosé containing 100 per cent Monastrell are worthwhile young wines for early consumption, as are the red blends of Monastrell and Tempranillo. The Divus Barrica (01), a blend of Cabernet Sauvignon and Monastrell, is outstanding.

Bullas

DO r (w dr) ✩✩→✩✩✩

Small DO west of the city of Murcia with 2,550 hectares and eight bodegas, making mainly red wines from Monastrell and Tempranillo. The largest winery is the Cooperativa Agri-Vinícola Nuestra Señora del Rosario. The best is Bodegas Balcona, with a good meaty Partal Selección.

Carcelén NCR, Asensio

DO r p w dr ✩→✩✩

Jumilla (Murcia). DO Jumilla. Maker of sound, but typically full-bodied JUMILLA wines high in alcohol, labelled as Sol y Luna, Pura Sangre, Bullanguero, and Acorde.

Casa de Calderón

DO r p g

Requena (Valencia). DO Utiel-Requena. This small bodega, which is attractively set islanded among its vineyards, is owned by the Mompó family and makes some superior Requena wines, among them a port-like *generoso*. *See also* VINIVAL.

Casa de la Ermita

DO r (w dr p) ★★★ *00 01 02*

Jumilla (Murcia). DO Jumilla. This young bodega, founded in 1999 makes some of the best and most reasonably priced wines in Jumilla. Excellent *crianza* (01) made from Monastrell, Tempranillo, and Cabernet Sauvignon; and Monsterio de Santa Ana range comprising 100 per cent Monastrell, Merlot, Syrah, and Cabernet Sauvignon (all 01).

Castaño, Bodegas

DO r p w dr ★★→★★★ *99 00 01 02*

Yecla (Murcia). DO Yecla. This is a very well-equipped bodega, the best in YECLA. Most of the wines produced are light for the region, made with

Tempranillo, Monastrell, Merlot, and Cabernet Sauvignon, and around twelve to 12.5 degrees of alcohol by volume. The young red Castaño, made by carbonic maceration, is clean, very fruity, and well structured.

Castellón de la Plana
VC r w dr

The province of Castellón de la Plana, north of VALENCIA, was once a prolific producer of wines, including the famous BENICARLÓ. After the PHYLLOXERA epidemic it was replanted with hybrids, yielding coarse, "foxy" wines frowned on by INDO. Because of the expense of replanting with grafted varieties, vineyards have been progressively abandoned. The 1,000 hectares which remain have been demarcated as the VC San Mateo, and they mainly produce a white wine of high alcoholic degree in small wineries where conditions are often anything but sanitary.

Castillo de Liria
DO w dr r p ★→★★

The label used by large-scale exporter Vicente GANDIA PLA for its range of pleasant table wines.

Celler del Roure
Non-DO r ☆☆☆ 00 01 02

Moixent (Valencia). Tucked away in a mountainous enclave of the province of Valencia east of Jávea, this small family estate grows a variety of black grapes including the almost extinct local Mando. The wines are made with the advice of Sara Pérez, daughter of the owner of Mas Martinet in Priorato (*see* "Cataluña", page 69). The wines, Les Alcuses and the premiumn Maduresa, are intense, fruity, and complex.

Cheste
DO w dr ☆→☆☆

Formerly a DO in its own right, Cheste, lying between VALENCIA and UTIEL-REQUENA, has been incorporated in the DO VALENCIA. It is a prolific producer of dry and somewhat earthy white wines of 12.5 to fifteen per cent, neutral and without a great deal of character.

Clariano
DO r w dr ☆

Subdivision of the DO VALENCIA in the extreme south of the province bordering ALICANTE. It produces both red and white wines of eleven to thirteen per cent, the best of which are the reds from the Monastrell grape.

C. Augusto Egli
DO r ☆→☆☆

Venta del Moro (Valencia). DO Utiel-Requena. This Swiss firm was formerly a big player in VALENCIA, but now restricts its Spanish operation to making a decent red Casa lo Alto on its estate of the same name.

Eval, Bodegas
DO r (p g) ☆☆

Villena (Alicante). DO Alicante. Large, modern bodega making reliable López de la Torre reds, matured in oak, from a blend of the Monastrell and Cencibel (Tempranillo) grapes.

Finca Luzón
DO r ☆☆☆ 98 99 00 01 02

Jumilla (Murcia). Founded in 1978 and has 400 hectares of vineyards and 1,500 oak *barricas*. Makes good red wines from blends of Monastrell, Tempranillo, Cabernet Sauvignon, and Merlot. Like the others, the best of them, Castilla de Luzón and Finca Luzón, are slow to mature and repay bottle age.

Fondillón
DO g ☆☆☆

Famous *generoso* from Monóvar, west of ALICANTE. It is aged in *solera* and emerges copper-coloured, aromatic, fairly sweet, and somewhat like a light oloroso sherry. Very little is now made.

Gandía Pla, Vicente
DO w dr sw r p ★★★

Valencia. DO Valencia and DO Utiel-Requena. Large-scale exporter with huge state-of-the-art plant at Chiva, west of VALENCIA, making inexpensive and very drinkable Castillo de Liria wines. Also a top-quality Ceremonia (98) made from Tempranillo and Cabernet Sauvignon. Also Fusta Nova, one of the best Spanish Moscatels.

García Carrión, Bodegas J
DO r p w dr ☆→☆☆

Jumilla (Murcia). DO Jumilla. Private firm making good JUMILLA wines, mainly red. Best is the delicious Castillo de San Simón.

García Poveda, HL
DO r (p w dr sw) res ★→★★

Villena (Alicante). DO Alicante. Sizeable family concern with bodegas at Villena in the hills behind ALICANTE. Costa Blanca red, white, and rosé; Marquesado red, white, and rosé; Costa Blanca Moscatel. The firm also makes a range of vermouths, full-bodied in character like the other wines.

Gutiérrez de la Vega, Bodegas
DO w dr sw p r ☆☆→☆☆☆☆ *00 01*

Parcent (Alicante). DO Alicante. Output is minute and the wines, in big demand, are hugely expensive, but individual and excellent. There are a dry white 100 per cent Moscatel Romano; a Rojo y Negro made from Merlot, Garnacha, and Cabernet; and the intriguing, sweet Casta Diva Cosecha Miel (01) and Cavatina Tender (01), both 100 per cent Moscatel de Alejandría, the latter *pétillant*. Also a 1994 Casta Diva Fondillón.

Huertas, Bodegas
DO w dr p r res ☆☆ *98 99 00*

Jumilla (Murcia). DO Jumilla. Sound white and rosé wines and good red Monastrell Aranzo. The Rodrejo *reserva*, made with eighty per cent Monastrell and twenty per cent Tempranillo, is first rate.

Hybrids

The district around CASTELLON DE LA PLANA, BENICARLO, and Vinaroz supplied red wine to France during the PHYLLOXERA epidemic of the late nineteenth century, but after it had itself been affected, vines were replaced with American hybrids. Many survive on peasant plots, but government regulations forbid their use in new plantations.

Irrigation

Because of the low rainfall, irrigation is permitted in JUMILLA and YECLA, but only on a limited scale and during the winter.

Jumilla
DO r (w dr) ☆→☆☆

The demarcated region extends to 41,700 hectares with a production in 2000–1 of twenty million litres of wine. The traditional wines were dark, full-bodied reds containing up to eighteen per cent alcohol. Apart from the heat of its long summers, the other reason for this high alcohol content is that, because of the high content of chalk and organic material in the soils, the region was largely unaffected by the PHYLLOXERA aphid, and it is one of the few areas in Spain or in Europe where vines are still grown ungrafted. The wines are now being lightened by earlier picking and better winemaking, and Spain has discovered that the Monastrell grape when properly handled can yield dark and fragrant wines, to rival those of Ribera del Duero and the New World. *See* AGAPITO RICO and CASA CASTILLO.

La Purísima, Cooperativa del Vino
DO r p w dr g ☆

Yecla (Murcia). DO Yecla. The livelihoods of the thousands of smallholders in YECLA have long depended on this huge co-op, which vinifies their grapes. In the mid-1980s it exported vast amounts of basic bulk wine, but has undergone a severe crisis as demand fell away and consumers required something better. Modernization is resulting in better wines such as Estio and the Iglesia Vieja *crianzas* and *reservas*.

Levante
Name given to the strip stretching along the Mediterranean coast of Spain from the Cabo de Gato, east of Almería, to the delta of the Ebro in the north.

Mendoza, Bodegas Enríque
DO r res w sw ☆☆→☆☆☆☆

Alfaz del Pi (Alicante). DO Alicante. Good red wines made from 100 per cent Cabernet Sauvignon, 100 per cent Syrah, and blends with Merlot. Also a pleasant Moscatel.

Murviedro, Cavas
DO r p w dr

Requena (Valencia). DO Utiel-Requena. Label for very drinkable Valencian wines from Bodegas SCHENK. The white is made with Merseguera and Moscatel; the rosé with Bobal and Garnacha; and there are different *crianza* reds made with Monastrell and Bobal or Monastrell and Tempranillo (from Utiel-Requena). The bodega is now exporting branded Santerra wines.

Olivares, Bodegas
DO r sw ☆☆☆ *98 00 01*

Jumilla (Murcia). DO Jumilla. This sizeable bodega with 250 hectares of vineyards makes wines of marked personality. The Altos de la Hoya is aromatic and sappy, while the Olivares Dulce is that curiosity: a sweet wine of real quality.

Phylloxera
Certain areas of the LEVANTE (JUMILLA and YECLA) were wholly or partially unaffected by this insect pest of the vine and still grow ungrafted vines, while others, like CASTELLON DE LA PLANA, were replanted with American hybrids and have never fully recovered.

Poveda, Salvador
DO r p w dr g ☆☆

Monóvar (Alicante). DO Alicante. Family concern with bodegas in the hills, making some of the best ALICANTE wine; albeit full-bodied and high in alcohol, notably the red and rosé Viña Vermeta and the outstanding dessert FONDILLÓN 1980.

Quiles, Primitivo

DO r p w sw g ☆☆

Monovar (Alicante). DO Alicante. Founded in 1780, this family firm is famous for its Moscatel and FONDILLÓN. It also produces modern-style wines, but the best are the magnificent El Abuelo *rancio generoso* and Fondillón, made in *solera*, and the Primitivo Quiles Moscatel Extra.

Roch, Julia e Hijos

DO r (p) ☆☆→☆☆☆☆ *99 00 01 02*

Jumilla (Murcia). DO Jumilla. Young bodega founded in 1991, with 192 hectares of vineyard planted with the native Monastrell, as well as Cabernet Sauvignon and Syrah. Makes young wines labelled as Casa Castillo from Monastrell/Syrah, and also first-rate *crianzas*, including a 100 per cent Monastrell.

San Isidro, Cooperativa

DO r (p w dr) res ★→★★

Jumilla (Murcia). DO Jumilla. Huge, well-equipped, and well-run modern co-op. Apart from its fresh, young Sabatacha white and rosé, and a young red Sabatacha Gran Noval made by carbonic maceration for immediate consumption, it also makes good oak-aged reds with 12.5 to fourteen degrees of alcohol under the labels of Sabatacha and Gemina.

Schenk, Bodegas

DO r p w dr sw res ★→★★

Valencia. DOs Valencia and Utiel-Requena. This Spanish arm of the large Swiss concern buys wine from the whole LEVANTE area and from as far afield as La Mancha. Apart from elaborating and shipping wines for supermarkets and own-label purchasers, it bottles good, standard Valencian wines under the label Cavas MURVIEDRO, Estrella, Los Monteros, Las Lomas, and Aldea.

Sebiran, Bodegas

DO w dr p r res ☆→☆☆

Campo de Arcis (Valencia). DO Utiél-Requena. The bodega makes a range of wines labelled Coto D'Artis and Señorío de Arcis, including barrel-fermented whites; best is the red Coto D'Arcis *reserva* (97).

Señorío del Condestable

DO r p w dr ★★ *94 95 96 98 99 00*

Jumilla (Murcia). DO Jumilla. An outpost of Bodegas y Bebidas (*see* "Rioja", page 126) making a particularly fresh rosé and also a pleasant red Señorío de Robles.

Utiel, Cooperativa Agrícola de

DO r ☆ *p* ★★

Utiel (Valencia). DO Utiel-Requena. One of the best of the large co-ops in the region, making a thick, black VINO DE DOBLE PASTA for blending, a normal red wine, and light, pale, and fragrant Castillo de Utiel rosé.

Utiel-Requena

DO r p ☆→☆☆

At the western extreme of the province of VALENCIA, with an area of 40,000 hectares, 120 bodegas, and a production in 2002 of 18.5 million litres. Utiel-Requena is an upland extension of the central plateau. The traditional wines, which are made from ninety per cent of the black Bobal grape with smaller amounts of Cencibel (Tempranillo) and Garnacha, are of three types: a thick, almost black VINO DE DOBLE PASTA for blending (of which progressively less is being produced); a pale, light, and delicious rosé; and a sturdy *tinto*, or red wine. Another increasingly important activity is the large-scale production of grape juice.

Valencia

Valencia, the third city of Spain, surrounded by its orange and lemon groves, is the queen of the LEVANTE, and despite the devastations of the Napoleonic and Civil Wars there still remain parts of the old walls with their gates and turrets, and narrow streets flanked with balconied houses. Its *fallas*, celebrated in mid-March with bonfires and processions of giant effigies in the street, is one of the liveliest Spanish fiestas. Valencia is the headquarters of numerous huge export houses, shipping wine in bulk all over the world; and its Grao ships more wine than any other port in Spain. It is the natural base for visits to the neighbouring vineyards and to those of UTIEL-REQUENA.

Valencia

DO (r) w dr sw ☆→☆☆

The demarcated region, of 18,212 hectares, with eighty bodegas and producing 66.5 million litres of wine in 2002, incorporates the former DO CHESTE and the sub-regions of ALTO TURIA, CLARIANO, and VALENTINO. It produces more white wine than red, mostly of typical Mediterranean type: earthy, full-bodied, strong, and low in acid.

Valentino

DO r dr (w) ☆→☆☆

The largest of the sub-regions of the DO VALENCIA, to the west of the city in the centre of the province and incorporating the former DO CHESTE. The principal white grape varieties are Merseguera, Malvasía, Moscatel, Pedro Ximénez, and Planta de Pedralba; and the best wines are the dry whites made from Merseguera and Pedro Ximénez and the sweet Moscatels. Reds are made from Garnacha Tinta and Tintorera.

Valsangiacomo, Cherubino

DO w dr r p ☆☆

Valencia. DO Valencia. Reputed exporter of regional wines, such as the Vall de Sant Jaume range and the superior Marqués de Caro wines.

Vinival, Bodegas

DO r p w dr sw ☆

Valencia. DO Valencia. Vinival was founded in 1969 to handle bulk wines from across the LEVANTE, from the old-established firms of Garrigos, Mompó, Techendorff, and Steiner. The majority shareholder is now Bodegas y Bebidas (part of Allied Domecq *see* "Rioja", page 126). It operates from a huge, brick-built, cathedral-like building near the port. With its capacity of thirty million litres, it ships huge quantities of sound, spicy, Mediterranean-type wine.

Vino de doble pasta

Much of the wine from UTIEL-REQUENA and ALICANTE is traditionally made in an entirely individual fashion. The grapes are destalked and lightly crushed, and after a few hours in the vat to extract colour from the skins the must is pumped off into a fresh vat, where fermentation continues *en blanc* to produce a light, fragrant, and delicate rosé. The original vat is then topped up with a further load of crushed grapes, and continued fermentation produces a *vino de doble pasta*. This is thick in extract, black in colour, and with up to eighteen per cent alcohol; not for consumption, but for blending with thinner wines such as those from Galicia. With the growing demand for lighter wines, production is decreasing in favour of grape juice.

Yecla

DO r (w) ☆→☆☆

The demarcated region, which extends to 4,500 hectares and produced 3.5 million litres of wine in 2002, neighbours that of JUMILLA in the hills of Murcia, and its vineyards produce very similar wines. As in Jumilla, the impact of the PHYLLOXERA epidemic was far less severe than in other parts of Spain, and forty per cent of the predominant Monastrell grapes are still grown ungrafted. The typical wines are dark, full-bodied reds containing up to eighteen per cent alcohol. With a drop in the demand for bulk wine, exports have fallen in recent years, and attempts are now being made to produce lighter wines. *See* Bodegas CASTAÑO.

WINE AND FOOD

Like all the coastal areas of Spain, the Levante offers a magnificent variety of fish and shellfish; but the region in general, and Valencia in particular, is known above all for its rice dishes, especially the world-renowned *paella*. The fertile *huertas*, known as the gardens of Valencia, are famous for their oranges and also for their vegetables, of which good use is made in cooking. Alicante almonds are used to make nougats or *turrones*. It is one of nature's ironies that hot regions, where one most appreciates lighter wines, produce the strongest, and colder areas the lightest. At least in its rosés from Utiel-Requena the Levante has a wine that goes admirably with fish and light food. Oddly enough, a full-bodied red wine goes better with *paella* than a white, though one of the spicy Valencian whites will also stand up to its mixture of definite flavours.

Arroz abanda Fish and shellfish cooked with onions, bay leaf, saffron, olive oil, and seasoning, and served with rice which takes on the flavour by being boiled in the fish stock. The rice is served first with the fish broth, and then the fish as a second course with *alioli*.

Arroz "Empedrat" Popular with the workers in the *turrón* factories of Jijona, this is also known as *arroz de fábrica* ("factory rice") and is made with haricot beans, garlic, tomatoes, parsley, and rice.

Bacalao a la valenciana Dried cod cooked in the oven with rice, fish broth, tomato purée, onions, grated cheese, butter, and hard-boiled eggs.

Conejo a la valenciana Young rabbit stewed with green peppers, black peppercorns, garlic, parsley, and olive oil.

Empanadillas valencianas Small pasties filled with a tuna and tomato sauce mixture, before being fried crisp in olive oil or baked in the oven.

Faves al tombet Fresh broad beans cooked with lettuce, artichoke hearts, garlic shoots, red paprika, vinegar, and bread.

Guisantes al estilo valenciano A delicious dish of fresh peas cooked with garlic, pepper, onions, thyme, white wine, bay leaf, olive oil, and saffron.

Paella valenciana Saffron-flavoured rice, cooked simply with fish and shellfish or with a variety of other ingredients, such as chicken, meat, and fresh vegetables. It is usual in Spain to drink red rather than white wine with *paella*.

Potaje valenciano A thick soup containing chickpeas, spinach, sweet paprika, lemon, parsley, onions, garlic, and egg yolks.

Sopa a la valenciana A thick soup made with a variety of fresh vegetables, rice, onions, and parsley, cooked in ham stock.

Sopa de mariscos levantina Valencian version of *bouillabaisse* with shellfish, vegetables, saffron, bay leaf, tomatoes, and garlic. It is served in two parts: first the broth with croûtons, and then the shellfish with a cold sauce.

Turrón Nougat. *Turrón de Alicante* is a hard, brittle tablet made of toasted and coarsely chopped almonds, honey, and egg whites. *Turrón de Jijona* is a softer confection containing ground almonds, ground pine kernels, sugar, coriander, and egg yolks.

HOTELS

Alicante The best hotels are the *Tryp Grand Sol, Almirante,* and *Mediterránea Plaza* in the city itself, and the five-star *Sidi San Juan* in the holiday resort of Playa de San Juan on its outskirts.

Jativa *Hostería de Mont Sant* fifty-six kilometres south of Valencia, is a charming hotel and restaurant set in Moorish gardens with twelfth-century castle towering above.

Valencia has many luxury hotels such as the *Astoria Palace, Meliá Valencia Palace,* and *Husa Reina Victoria* – but my own favourite is the old-fashioned three-star *Inglés*, opposite the best ceramic museum in Spain, in the palace of the Marqués de Dos Aguas.

RESTAURANTS

Alicante *Nou Manolín* is the best in Alicante, with good cooking and the freshest of ingredients. *Maestral* serves excellent rice dishes and *Darsena* has seventy-three of them on its menu.

Castellón de la Plana *Rafael* is located at the port, guaranteeing the very freshest fish and seafood. *Tasca del Puerto* uses first-class ingredients for its seafood and rice dishes.

Murcia Murcia is a good-ish drive from Jumilla and Yecla, but worth the trouble as *El Rincón de Pepe* is quite simply one of the best restaurants in Spain.

Requena *Mesón del Vino* serves regional dishes and wines, excellent roast lamb, and good tapas in the bar. Try the *ajorriero* and *charcuterie* at *Méson de la Villa*.

Valencia *Ca Sento* is now Valencia's leading restaurant. *Eladio* is undergoing a revival, with classic Galician cooking. Try *Albacar* for sophisticated modern cooking. *Rías Gallegas* for Galician cuisine, and *El Angel Azul* for adventurous dishes such as monkfish with mushrooms.

Sparkling Wines

Manufacture in Spain of sparkling wines by the Champagne method was begun by Don José Raventós, whose family firm of Codorníu is now one of the world's largest producers of this wine. The wines were initially known as *champaña*, but producers in Reims rightly objected that the name should be applied only to wines produced in Champagne, and they are now referred to as cava. Cava is also used rather than bodega, to describe the establishments in which they are made.

Since February 1986 cava has been the subject of a DO which, in deference to the pundits of the EU and unlike most of the others, demarcates a patchwork of dissimilar regions, municipalities, and villages in different parts of Spain where it may be produced. These include areas, sizeable and small, in the provinces of Girona, Barcelona (including the whole of the area in Penedès demarcated for still wines), Tarragona, Lleida (Lérida), Zaragoza, Navarra, La Rioja, Alava, Burgos, Valencia, and Badajoz. However, ninety per cent of cava – and all the best – is made in Cataluña, with probably over seventy-five per cent in and around Sant Sadurní d'Anoia in the Penedès, where it originated.

The grape varieties used in Cataluña are mainly the white Xarel-lo, giving alcoholic strength and colour; the Macabeo (or Viura), contributing freshness and fruit; and the Parellada, grown up the hill slopes, conferring acidity and delicacy of nose. Chardonnay is increasingly grown and used for cava; outside Cataluña it is generally made with 100 per cent Macabeo. Pink wines (described as rosés in Spain, but never in the UK), are made with a proportion of the black Cariñena or Garnacha Tinta.

In modern installations the must is extracted in horizontal presses and vinified in temperature-controlled stainless-steel tanks; elaboration then follows the classical methods of Champagne. The young wine is dosed with a solution of sugar and with cultured yeasts, filled into stout Champagne-type bottles, temporarily corked, and left for a period of years in deep underground cellars until the sugar has been converted into carbon dioxide and alcohol. The bottles are then, over a period of months, gradually upended, so the fine sediment falls towards the neck of the bottle, which is finally frozen and uncorked, and the plug containing the sediment is forcibly expelled by the pressure of gas inside. A *licor de expedición* containing a little sugar is added; the bottles are then recorked and allowed to rest before being labelled and despatched.

The large cavas have now rationalized the process by using *girasoles* to promote the descent of the sediment, forklift trucks, and pallets for stacking the bottles in cellars, and electronic systems for locating batches of bottles and bringing them to the bottling line for *dégorgement* (the removal of the temporary corks) and labelling. But none of these handling processes affects the elaboration or the quality of the wine – as romantics would sometimes have one believe. Such differences as do emerge between Champagne and cava result from the character of grapes and soil, not from the method of manufacture.

Not all *espumosos* (or sparkling wines) are made by the same method as Champagne, which is now, in EU jargon, described as the *método tradicional*. There are also sparkling wines whose second fermentation takes place, not in individual bottles, but in large pressurized tanks known as *cuves closes* or, in Spain, *gran-vas*. This process produces acceptable wines, albeit with a larger and shorter-lasting bubble, but still vastly better than the *gaseosos*, made by pumping carbon dioxide into still wine. The *vinos de aguja*, or "green wines", which develop a more subdued bubble or *pétillance* as the result of a naturally occurring secondary fermentation, are described in the chapter on Galicia. Certain wines elaborated scrupulously by the Champagne method may not be described as cava, but as *método tradicional* because the region in which they are made does not qualify for DO. *See* CASTILLA LA VIEJA, BODEGAS Y CRIANZA.

Endless discussions compare the relative merits of cava and Champagne. In my experience cava tends to be softer, fuller in flavour, and fruitier in nose; Champagne has more edge and finesse. Conventional wisdom is that no one of any experience fails to tell the difference, but that most discriminating of Spanish winemakers, Miguel Torres, notes that "the cavas of Sant Sadurní d'Anoia have frequently been judged superior to their French homologues". They are certainly less than half the price. The only sensible thing is to enjoy Spanish cava as a sparkling wine in its own right.

In 2002, 150 million litres of cava were made, of which 108 million bottles were exported, making its production an important facet of the Spanish wine industry.

Styles of Sparkling Wine

In increasing order of sweetness, Spanish sparkling wines are labelled as follows. *Rosado*, or rosé, indicates a pink wine:

Brut de Brut	*Very dry*	Seco	*Fairly dry*
Brut Nature	*Very dry*	Semiseco	*Semi-dry*
Brut Reserva	*Very dry*	Semidulce	*Semi-sweet*
Vintage	*Very dry*	Dulce	*Sweet*
Brut	*Dry*		

Agustí Torelló
DO 98 99 00 01
Sant Sadurní d'Anoia (Barcelona). DO Cava. Small family firm whose cavas are among the most reputable in Spain. Top is the very expensive brut natural Kripta Gran Reserva (98) made from Macabeo, Parellada, and Xarel-lo, and presented in a bottle resembling the traditional amphora. The Agustí Torelló Mata brut natural and the brut are also first-rate wines, and reasonably priced for their high quality.

L' Aixertell
Brand name for a big-selling *cuve close* sparkler made by the Unión de Cellers del Noya, a company jointly owned by FREIXENET and Bodegas y Bebidas (*see* "Rioja", page 126).

Ampurdán, Cavas del
DO
Perelada (Girona). Under the same management as the Castillo de PERELADA, well known for its cava wines. Since it makes still wines in

Cataluña (*see* page 63) and sparklers by the *cuve close* method, Spanish regulations require that it be housed in a separate building across a public highway. Its Perelada was the subject of the famous "Spanish Champagne" case.

Bilbaínas, Bodegas

DO

Haro (Logroño). DO Cava. One of the leading producers of Rioja (*see* page 126), Bodegas Bilbaínas also makes sizeable amounts of Royal Carlton Brut Nature by the *método tradicional*, using Viura and Malvasía grapes. The wines are made in deep cellars beneath the bodega by the most traditional methods, clearance after second fermentation taking place in pupitres and *dégorgement* being effected manually. The wines are dry and of good quality, but rather fuller in flavour than those from Cataluña. They are sold widely in the north of Spain, though not in competition with the cavas from its new owners CODORNÍU, in Cataluña.

Castellblanch

DO 99 00 01

Sant Sadurní d'Anoia (Barcelona). DO Cava. When Castellblanch was founded by Don Jerónimo Parera Figueras in 1908, it was a family concern with only three employees and an annual turnover of 100,000 bottles. Expansion took place rapidly under Don Jerónimo's son, and after Rumasa (*see* "Sherry", page 160) acquired the company in 1974, output was boosted to ten million bottles, made by the *método tradicional* or in *cuves closes*. The firm is now part of the FREIXENET group. Its wines are sold as Brut Zero, Dos Lustros, and Gran Castell.

Castilla la Vieja, Bodegas de Crianza

Producers of an excellent Brut Natural Palacio de Bornos made by the Champagne method. It is one of the absurdities of the *reglamento* covering sparkling wines that because it is not made in one of the many delimited areas, this delicious wine may not be called cava, but is labelled *método tradicional*. *See also* "Castilla-León", page 47.

Cava

Meaning "cellar", the word is used to describe both an establishment in which sparkling wines are made by the Champagne method, and such wines themselves – now the subject of a DO.

Champaña

Name long used for Spanish wines made by the Champagne method until, in deference to the French protests, the Spanish government forbade it.

Chandon

DO

Sant Cugat Sesgarrigues (Barcelona). DO Cava. It says much for the name cava (and reflects the difference in price of grapes in Cataluña and Reims) that Moët & Chandon set up shop in the PENEDÈS, and is making good wines with a blend of Chardonnay and traditional native grapes.

Codorníu

DO

Sant Sadurní d'Anoia (Barcelona). DO Cava. It was Don José Raventós of the family firm Codorníu, winemakers since 1551, who in 1872 began the manufacture of sparkling wine by the Champagne method in Spain, after studying practices in Reims. Today, Codorníu is one of the two largest firms in the world to make wines of this type. The *cavas* and family mansion are situated in decorative gardens above twenty-four kilometres of underground cellars. The original buildings, designed in *fin de siècle* style with echoes of Gaudí and including an old press house converted into a wine museum, have been declared a National Monument; and the former labelling hall is now a reception area for the thousands of visitors who descend on the *cavas* each year.

Cordorníu has vineyards of its own but buys large quantities of grapes from 1,000 regular suppliers in the area. These are pressed in a modern band press and vinified in batteries of temperature-controlled, 20,000-litre stainless-steel tanks, with subsequent elaboration by the *método tradicional*. The best wines are the Gran Codorníu Brut; Jaume Codorníu made with Chardonnay, Parellada, and Macabeo; the fresh Anna de Codorníu, with eighty-five per cent Chardonnay; and Non Plus Ultra, from forty per cent Chardonnay and traditional native grapes. *See also* RAIMAT.

Conde de Caralt
DO

Sant Sadurní d'Anoia (Barcelona). DO Cava. This firm was making cava in Cataluña long before it made still wine. Once part of the Rumasa group (*see* "Sherry", page 160), it now belongs to FREIXENET. Its dry, light, sparkling wine is bottled under the label Conde de Caralt.

COVIDES (Cooperativa Vinícola del Penedès)
DO 00

Sant Sadurní d'Anoia (Barcelona). DO Cava. Large co-op making and exporting good cava under the labels of Duc de Foix and Xenius.

Espumoso
Spanish name for sparkling wine.

Ferret, Cavas
DO 97 98 99

Guardiola de Font-Rubí (Barcelona). DO Cava. First-rate wines, including Esequiel Ferret and Altre Nos Reserva from a small firm which has won many awards.

Florit, Mas
DO

Torrelles de Foix (Barcelona). DO Cava. Small firm founded in 1984, maker of a first-rate extra brut Mas Florit from seventy per cent Parellada and thirty per cent Macabeo.

Freixenet
DO

Sant Sadurní d'Anoia (Barcelona). DO Cava. Freixenet, founded in 1915, with its acquisitions of CONDE DE CARALT, CASTELLBLANCH, and SEGURA VIUDAS, is about equal in size to CODORNÍU and, between them, the two concerns are responsible for at least eighty per cent of all the cava from PENEDÈS.

The Freixenet plant at Sant Sadurní is one of the most modern in the Penedès, and the wine is vinified at low temperature in huge stainless-steel tanks of 600,000-litre capacity. Freixenet was also the first of the cavas to introduce GIRASOLES. Thanks to these innovations and the highly advanced handling and bottling equipment, it has been able to hold down the price of its cavas without detriment to quality. The Freixenet group is currently the largest exporter of Spanish sparkling wines to the USA, where it sells around seventeen million bottles. It also makes sparkling wine in Mexico and California, and owns the Champagne house of Henri Abelé.

Apart from splendid vintage wines, such as the Cuvée DS 1997 (named in honour of Doña Dolores Sala, widow of the company's founder Don Pedro Ferrer Bosch), the best of the wines are the Freixenet Vintage Brut Reserva Real, Reserva XXI, the very dry and light Brut Natural (98), and popular Cordon Negro. It also markets the cheaper Carta Nevada and Brut Rosé.

Gaseoso

The cheapest (and nastiest) form of sparkling wine, made by pumping pressurized carbon dioxide into still wines. It also describes "fizzy" lemonade and aerated mineral drinks generally.

Girasol

A large octagonal metal frame on a faceted base that holds 504 bottles. Increasingly used in cavas in place of the traditional PUPITRE, to effect the descent of the sediment after the secondary fermentation takes place. The frame, with its complement of bottles, may be swung round in a few seconds by a couple of men; FREIXENET, which was the first of the cavas to introduce it on a large scale, claims that it gives more consistent results than the *pupitre*. Most of the cavas in Cataluña have begun to use the device, and it has also been tried out in Reims by the French Champagne-makers.

Girona

This province in the northeast of Cataluña produces sizeable amounts of sparkling wine, most of it made by the Castillo de PERELADA and Cavas del AMPURDÁN.

González y Dubosc

DO

Sant Sadurní d'Anoia (Barcelona). DO Cava. This well-known firm is owned by the sherry-maker González-Byass. The cava wines, light, dry, and fresh, and very reasonably priced, are marketed in the UK as Jean Perico.

Goulart, Roger

DO 97

Sant Esteve de Sesrovires (Barcelona). DO Cava. Old-established firm producing brut natural, extra brut, brut, and pink wines, of which the best is the Extra Brut Gran Cuvée (97) made with a blend of Xarel-lo, Macabeo, Parellada, and Chardonnay.

Gramona

DO 96 98 99 00 01

Sant Sadurní d'Anoia (Barcelona). DO Cava. Family firm founded in 1921 and one of the foremost and most respected cava-makers. Its brut natural, extra brut, and brut are made from blends of the native Xarel-lo, Macabeo, and Parellada; the best are labelled Tres Lustros (98), Celler Batlle (96), and Impérial (99). A Rosado is made from 100 per cent Pinot Noir.

Gran-vas

Spanish name for *cuve close*. With this type of sparkling wine, second fermentation takes place in large closed tanks pressurized to eight atmospheres, and lasts for four to five months according to temperature, usually −5°C. The wine is then filtered and bottled under pressure. Although the wines do not possess such a fine or lasting bubble as those made by the Champagne method, they are a great deal more acceptable than GASEOSOS and make pleasant party drinking. To avoid the possibility of such wine being passed off as cava, Spanish regulations require that it may not be made in the same building. Corks from cava wine bear a star on the bottom, and *gran-vas* a small black circle.

Grapa

A metal hook used for securing the temporary cork during the second fermentation. *Grapas* and corks have now been largely replaced by crown caps.

Hill, Cavas

DO

Moja (Barcelona). DO Cava. Apart from its still Catalan wines (*see* page 68), the firm produces a range of good cavas, including Reserva Oro, Brut de Brut (00), and Brutísimo (00).

Juvé y Camps

DO 98 99

Sant Sadurní d'Anoia (Barcelona). DO Cava. A sparkling wine producer of repute, making limited amounts of a superior cava from free-run juice, this is a favourite of the Spanish royal family. The labels used are: Reserva de la Familia (99), Gran Juvé y Camps (99), and 100 per cent Chardonnay Milesimé (98).

Lar de Barros-INVIOSA

DO

Almendralejo (Badajoz). DO Cava. Very drinkable Bonaval cava, made with Macabeo, Chardonnay, and Sauvignon Blanc from the unlikely Extremadura.

Licor de expedición

A solution of sugar in brandy and old white wine. It is used to top up the bottles after completion of the second fermentation and removal of the temporary cork. It is the amount of sugar in the *licor* which determines the style of the finished wine. A dry brut will contain only two per cent, while the sweet sparklers, which tend to be popular in South America, are dosed to the extent of twelve to twenty per cent. As a general rule, the best sparkling wines are the driest, because defects cannot be masked by excessive sweetening.

Licor de tiraje

A solution of sugar in white wine added before the second fermentation. The breakdown of this sugar into alcohol and carbon dioxide by the action of special yeasts gives wines made by the Champagne method their sparkle in the bottle.

Lleida

The province of Lleida (Lérida), set in the northwest of Cataluña, produces sizeable amounts of cava. *See* RAIMAT.

Llopart

DO 98 99 00

Subirats (Barcelona). DO Cava. Well-known family firm labelling its wines Llopart, Imperial, and Leopardi. All are well-made and characterful wines. The stylish Leopardi perhaps has the edge.

Marqués de Monistrol

DO

Sant Sadurní d'Anoia (Barcelona). DO Cava. The *cavas* are at Monistrol de Noya, just outside Sant Sadurní, and are among the most picturesque in the area, with a flagged patio and old wine press overlooked by the parish church. Although the company, which has been making cava wines since 1882, is now controlled by the Riojan Bodegas Unidas, it is still very much a family concern, with families who work in the *cavas* and vineyards living on the estate.

Monistrol owns ten hectares of vineyards and makes three million bottles of wine annually, most of it cava and much of it exported to Italy. The driest and most elegant of its sparkling wines is the Brut Natural Gran Reserva de la Familia. The company also produces a Gran Reserva de la Familia Rosé and an inexpensive Reserva de l'Hereu. *See also* "Cataluña", page 68.

Masachs, Josep
DO 00 01

Vilafranca del Penedès (Barcelona). DO Cava. A sizeable family firm currently producing three million bottles yearly in its ultra-modern plant. The best of the firm's wines are the brut Millennium Cuvée (00), Carolina de Masachs (00), and Gran Vernier (00). It also makes a large range of Louis de Veriner and Masachs wines in various styles.

Mascaró, Antonio
DO

Vilafranca del Penedès (Barcelona). DO Cava. Small and old-established family firm with cellars in the heart of VILAFRANCA, making liqueurs and an excellent brandy (*see* "Spirits, Aromatic Wines, and Liqueurs", page 191) as well as still and good cava wines. Its Brut Natural, Extra Brut, and Brut wines contain a high proportion of Parellada (with small additions of Macabeo and Macabeo/Xarel-lo) and are correspondingly fresh and fruity. *See also* "Cataluña", page 69.

Mestres Sagües, Antonio
DO 96 97 98 00 01

Sant Sadurní d'Anoia (Barcelona). DO Cava. One of the smaller family firms in the PENEDÈS, making good sparkling wine by the *método tradicional*, now available in the UK under the labels Clos Damiana, Clos Nostre Senyor, Coquet, and Mestres Rosado. Also a mature (90) and very expensive Mas Vía Brar.

Método Tradicional

The approved Spanish name for the traditional Champagne method by which cava wines are made.

Mont-Ferrand
DO

Blanes (Girona). DO Cava. Good cavas from Girona. The Nature contains Chardonnay, as well as Xarel-lo/Macabeo/Parellada, and the Rosado is made from Monastrell and Garnacha.

Mont Marçal (Manuel Sancho e Hijos)
DO

Castellví de la Marca (Barcelona). DO Cava. Made only from free-run juice Parellada, Xarel-lo, Macabeo, and Chardonnay, Mont Marçal Brut Natural, Mont Marçal Brut, and Extremarium are first-rate wines, elegant and very dry.

Muga, Bodegas
DO

Haro (Logroño). DO Cava. One of the most scrupulous in its methods of the Riojan bodegas (*see* page 134), Muga some time ago revived an old Riojan tradition by making a cava wine. Made from 100 per cent Viura, Conde de Haro is a bone dry, fruity, and characterful wine in its own right – though nobody would confuse it with Champagne.

Nadal
DO 96

Pla del Penedès (Barcelona). DO Cava. Small family firm with 100 hectares of vineyards, and a well-equipped modern winery making a first-rate Extra Brut Salvatge (97) and a clean and elegant Ramón Nadal Giro (97).

Parxet

DO

Santa María de Martorelles (Barcelona). DO Cava. Sizeable producer of cava within the tiny DO Alella (*see* "Cataluña", page 70), making a fresh and fruity NV Brut from a traditional blend of Macabeo, Parellada, and Pansà Blanca (Xarel-lo), and also premium Titiana from seventy-year-old Chardonnay vines.

Penedès

Penedès as such is not demarcated for producing cava as it is for still wines (*see* "Cataluña", page 70). However, all the individual municipalities within the DO Penedès are also entitled to make cava by the *método tradicional*, and ninety-five per cent of cava now originates from this area. Many of the scores of cavas in and around Sant Sadurní d'Anoia and Vilafranca del Penedès are small family firms selling direct to visitors, who descend upon the area from Barcelona in their hordes at weekends to tour the cavas and taste the wines. Owing to the fact that, in the last decade, the number of cavas with DO has increased from sixty-five to some 270, it is no longer practical to print the names of firms other than those included in the A–Z listing.

Perelada, Castillo de

DO 99 00 01

Perelada (Girona). DO Cava. Winemaking traditions at Perelada, on the verges of the Pyrenees, date from the twelfth century, when the Carmelite monks planted the first vineyards. To this day the cellars lie beneath the fourteenth-century church of Carmen de Perelada, with its delicately arcaded patio, and the crenellated castle built shortly afterwards. The buildings house a splendid library, a museum of glassware and ceramics, and an extensive wine museum. More recently, a casino has been opened in the castle – dare one suggest, to promote the consumption of its excellent sparkling wines?

Like the associated Cavas del AMPURDAN, the Castillo de Perelada also produces still wines. About fifty per cent of the grapes are from its own vineyards (the rest being brought from local farmers), and the wine, carefully made by the Champagne method, is binned away to undergo its second fermentation in deep cellars underneath the former orchard. The best of the wines is the brut natural Gran Claustro (00), which, with five to six years in the cellars, emerges dry, soft, and flowery. Other wines in its range are the Brut Nature, excellent brut natural Chardonnay, Castillo de Perelada brut *reserva* and *rosado*, and Cuvée Especial (01).

Pupitre

In the production of sparkling wine, the traditional method of coaxing both the sediment and the fine suspended matter into the neck of the bottle after the second fermentation is to place the bottles, neck first, into the oval holes of a *pupitre*. This is a large wooden frame in the form of an inverted "V". The bottles are regularly given a shake and a slight angular twist by hand, and the inclination of the *pupitre* is gradually altered, so that the bottle ends up almost on its head, with the solid matter gathered against the bottom of the cork.

Raimat

DO

Raïmat (Lleida). DO Cava. The Raimat Chardonnay made by a subsidiary of CODORNÍU, with the grapes grown on its estate outside LLEIDA, is one of the best of all cavas. The wines also include Brut Nature and Blanc de Blancs, both made from a blend of Chardonnay, Macabeo, and Xarel-lo, and an outstanding Gran Brut made from Chardonnay and Pinot Noir.

Raventós i Blanc, Josep María

DO

Sant Sadurní d'Anoia (Barcelona). DO Cava. Josep María Raventós left the family firm of CODORNÍU in the mid-1980s, to make his own cava on the basis of 100 hectares of inherited vineyards. The Raventós i Blanc Reserva Brut Natural and the other wines are aimed at the top of the market.

Raventós Rosell, Joan

DO 97 98 99

Masquefa (Barcelona). DO Cava. Founded in 1985, the *cava* has rapidly established a reputation for its well-made and elegant wines, of which the brut natural Gradiva (00) and Reserva Heretat (00) are very attractive.

Rioja

In the full flush of the Rioja boom of the late nineteenth century, various of the newly founded bodegas set about making sparkling wine, using the Champagne process, from the local white Viura and Malvasía grapes. Some were more successful than others, but the Compañía Vinícola del Norte de España (*see* page 127) was so successful that it actually started a sister establishment in Reims. Although this lasted only three years, CVNE long continued to supply the French Champagne-makers with Rioja for making their wines during the period when they were suffering from the after-effects of the phylloxera epidemic. There has been a revival in the making of sparkling wine in Rioja, where various areas are demarcated under the DO Cava; in addition to Bodegas BILBAINAS and Bodegas MUGA, Bodegas Olarra and Bodegas Faustino-Martínez are both making brut cava from 100 per cent Viura.

Rondel

DO

Cervello (Barcelona). DO Cava. Huge establishment belonging to CODORNÍU and making inexpensive Rondel brut and Carta de Oro *semiseco*.

Roura

DO

Alella (Barcelona). DO Cava. Good cava made with Xarel-lo/Chardonnay from a winery reputed for its still Alella wines. Best is Brut Natural Roura.

Rovellats, Cavas

DO 97 99 00 01

San Martí de Sarroca (Barcelona). DO Cava. Small family firm making limited amounts of exclusive and expensive cava, stocked by some of the leading restaurants in Spain. Wines are produced under the labels Brut Especial and Brut Imperial and there are two *gran reservas*, Brut Nature and the Gran Cru Masía S.XV, which is produced in minuscule amounts and is one of the best cavas from Spain. There is also a Rosé Brut from Monastrell and Tempranillo.

San Sadurní de Noya (*Catalan* Sant Sadurní d'Anoia)

Now spelt on road-signs in the Catalan form of Sant Sadurní d'Anoia, this little town west of Barcelona is the headquarters of the Spanish sparkling wine industry, with *cavas* on every street.

Segura Viudas

DO

Sant Sadurní d'Anoia (Barcelona). DO Cava. Once the flagship of the companies formerly within Rumasa (*see* "Sherry", page 160), making sparkling wine by the *método tradicional* and now part of the FREIXENET group. The nucleus of the modern winery is an old house picturesquely situated on the road from SANT SADURNÍ to Igualada, with Montserrat (*see* "Cataluña", page 69) as a backdrop. Some of the grapes are grown on the fifty hectares of surrounding vineyards, the rest are bought from local growers. The most delicate of Segura Viudas' wines are dry, light, and fresh, and among the best of Spanish cavas. They include the Brut Natural Reserva Heredad (98), Brut Vintage (99), and Brut Torre Galmany (98).

Serra, Jaume

DO

Vilanova i La Geltrú (Barcelona). DO Cava. Good brut cavas, including a first-rate Brut Vintage.

Sunflower

English translation of *girasol*.

Vallformosa, Masía

DO

Vilobí del Penedès (Barcelona). DO Cava. Family firm making stylish brut cavas. *See also* "Cataluña", page 77.

Ventura, Jané

DO 99 00

El Vendrell (Tarragona). DO Cava. Well-known for its still wines (*see* "Cataluña", page 77), the firm also produces good extra brut, brut, and rosé cavas from the traditional Xarel-lo, Parellada, and Macabeo blend.

Vilafranca del Penedès

Vilafranca is primarily a centre for making still wines (*see* "Cataluña", page 77) but a number of the *cavas* are located there. It is also the headquarters of the official regulatory body for sparkling wines, the Consejo Regulador de los Vinos Espumosos.

WINE AND FOOD

Manufacture of sparkling wines centres on Cataluña, especially Penedès, and details of regional cooking and restaurants are given in the chapter on "Cataluña" (*see* pages 77–80).

Spirits, Aromatic Wines, and Liqueurs

Sherry is so much an image of Spain that foreigners are often surprised to learn that a great deal more of it is drunk outside the country than in, especially in Britain, the Netherlands, and the northern European countries. In Spain itself, brandy, most of it produced in Jerez, is much cheaper and more popular. Sales of sherry have, in fact, declined in recent years, a fall aggravated by the increasing fashion among the younger generation for imported spirits, vermouths, and liqueurs, and brandy has been the salvation of some of the big sherry houses.

The Spanish learned about distillation from the Moors. Alcohol was first used in medicine by the Catalan-born Arnold of Vilanova, and Spanish brandy was first shipped from Cataluña in the seventeenth century. Until the early nineteenth century it was used in Jerez to fortify sherry, and the first Jerez brandies were not sold by the sherry houses until the mid-nineteenth century. They were made by what is now known as the Charentais method, perfected in Cognac, by distillation of wine in a simple pot-still, in effect a copper kettle with a coiled condenser. This takes place in two stages: the raw spirit is then matured in oak casks. It is still the method used for the best and most refined Spanish brandy; but the great bulk of Spanish brandy is made by "continuous" distillation of wine in tall, steam-heated columns in the manner of grain whisky, a more economical and productive industrial process. The resulting *holandas*, or sixty-five per cent grape spirit, made in distilleries all over Spain, are then diluted with water and aged in oak casks.

In Jerez, which produces ninety-five per cent of Spanish brandy, maturation takes place in a *solera* (*see* page 161) and involves the customary periodic "refreshment" of the older spirit with the younger. The aeration and quicker maturation gives rise to brandies quite different in character from those made in Cataluña or France, where there is no such frequent transfer from cask to cask. Jerez brandy has an oaky charm of its own, but it is so distinctive that it is not sensible to make direct comparisons with Cognac or Armagnac.

In 1987 a new DO was set up for Brandy de Jerez, as it is officially known, and a *consejo regulador* established to administer it. The main provisions are that only brandy made in Jerez de la Frontera, Puerto de Santa María, and Sanlúcar de Barrameda qualifies for DO and that it must be made by traditional methods from *aguardiente de vino* (grape spirit) and matured in *criaderas* and *soleras* as in making sherry, or by static maturation in a single barrel, as in making an *añada* or vintage sherry. In ascending order of quality and depending on the time of maturation and on the content of aldehydes, esters, and higher alcohols, the *reglamento* defines three types of Brandy de Jerez: *solera, solera reserva*, and *solera gran reserva*, the last of which must be matured for more than three years and contain more than 300 milligrams of non-alcoholic congeners per 100 centilitres of absolute alcohol. Another popular spirit is *aguardiente*, made by distilling the pips and skins remaining from the fermentation of wine. Akin to the French *marc* or Portuguese *bagaceira*, this is a somewhat fiery liquid best left to those who have learned to stomach it.

Spain also produces a gamut of liqueurs, many of them household names marketed internationally by foreign companies and made under licence in Spain, by the maceration of fruits and herbs in alcoholic solution and subsequent distillation. Firms in Jerez and Cataluña make very respectable gin and vodka by the traditional methods. Vermouth is made in large amounts, much of it under licence, by the preparation of herbal extracts and their blending with white wine. The native *anís* is first rate; and tonic wines and spirits containing quinine extract, of which the best known are Jerez-Quina and Calisay, are something of a speciality and are made in Jerez, Málaga, and Barcelona.

Aguardiente

Aguardiente is defined by the Estatuto de la Viña, del Vino y de los Alcoholes as "natural alcohol with a strength of not more than eighty-five per cent", distilled from vegetable materials. It therefore constitutes a wide variety which includes the HOLANDAS used for the manufacture of brandy and known as *aguardiente de vino*, as well as other varieties distilled from fermented fruits and cereals. However, over the counter of a bar, *aguardiente* means *aguardiente de orujo*, a popular and potent spirit distilled from the grape skins and pips left over from the fermentation of wine in the manner of the French *marc* or Portuguese *bagaceira*. It is made all over Spain and is not normally branded, but poured from an unlabelled bottle – a fact that, combined with its well-deserved reputation for strength, intimidates many tourists.

Alvear

Apart from Montilla (*see* page 100), Alvear produces brandy, made from HOLANDAS and matured in *solera* after the fashion of the Jerez brandies and the fortified wines of the area. The inexpensive Secular is fruity, with a raisiny nose and peppery finish. The more refined Senador and PRESIDENTE are oakier and more aromatic, and the Presidente Alvear Gran Reserva has a very dry finish.

Anís

Aniseed-flavoured liqueur corresponding to the French *anisette*. The best Spanish *anís*, such as CHINCHON and ANÍS DEL MONO, is of excellent quality.

Anís del Mono

One of the best and most popular brands of ANÍS, made by Bosch y Cía, a subsidiary of OSBORNE, in Badalona near Barcelona.

Bénédictine

Famous French liqueur made under licence in Spain.

Bilbaínas, Bodegas

This is virtually the only bodega in the Rioja to produce that *rara avis*, a Riojan brandy that can stand alongside its still and sparkling wines. Its Imperator has a vinous, oaky nose, is completely dry, but it tastes of little except oak, and the finish is short. *See also* pages 125 and 178.

Blázquez, Hijos de Agustín

DO

Well-known sherry firm, makers of FELIPE II, one of the drier and least manipulated of the Jerez brandies.

Bobadilla

DO

Sherry firm taken over by OSBORNE and best known for its brandies. Now sold under the Osborne label: Solera 103 White Label, aged for six months,

pale, and delicate; Solera 103 Black Label Solera Reserva; and Gran
Capitán Solera Gran Reserva, which is a blend of brandies between three
and (remarkably) eighty years old.

Brandy

As explained in the introduction to this section, most Spanish brandy
is made from HOLANDAS, a grape spirit of sixty-five per cent alcohol. This
is produced by distilling wine (in the manner of grain whisky) in a
continuous still and maturing the raw spirit in *solera* (*see* "Sherry and
Manzanilla", page 161). The better Catalan brandies, and also a few of the
premium Jerez marks, are, however, made by the Charentais method in
pot-stills. A large proportion of commercial Spanish brandies are sweeter
and more caramelized than their French counterparts and have therefore
made less impact to date in international markets other than Latin America.

Brandy 103

DO

Popular Jerez brandy formerly made by the sherry firm Bobadilla, and
now sold under the label of OSBORNE, Spain's largest producer of spirits.

Caballero, Luís

Sherry concern located in Puerto de Santa María and maker of one of
the best brands of PONCHE, Caballero, which is sold in eye-catching
silvered bottles.

Calisay

Quinine-based liqueur, a speciality of the Barcelona area, which may be
drunk either as a digestif or, with ice and with or without fruit (such as
lemon, orange, and maraschino cherries), as an apéritif. A dash of Calisay
much enlivens fruit salads. *See also* MOLLFULLEDA.

Capa Negra

DO

Jerez brandy made by the sherry firm of Sandeman in Jerez de la Frontera.

Cardenal Mendoza

DO

Jerez brandy made by the sherry firm of Sánchez Romate and labelled
"Cardinal" in the USA. First produced in 1887, this *solera gran reserva*
brandy is aged in oloroso casks and is one of the best from Jerez,
exceptionally smooth and fragrant.

Carlos I

DO

The most refined of the brandies made by PEDRO DOMECQ in Jerez, and
though very slightly on the sweet side, it is light and spirituous, more
resembling a French Cognac than most Jerez brandies and more suited
to northern tastes.

Centenario

Made by TERRY and sold in bottles with a yellow net, this popular Brandy
de Jerez is one of the biggest-selling in Spain.

Chartreuse

Although many well-known French liqueurs are made under licence in
Spain, Chartreuse was more firmly rooted, since from 1903 to 1940, during
the exile of the monks from La Grande Chartreuse, it was made exclusively
in Tarragona. The distillery was directly supervised by the three fathers
who share the closely guarded secret of its recipe, and who spent January
to May in Tarragona and the rest of the year in Voiron, in the French Alps.

It is said that 130 herbs (many procured locally) were used for making the Green Chartreuse, and rather fewer for the Yellow. The difference between the French and Spanish versions was minimal, though in my experience the Spanish was slightly drier – and also, of course, like all Spanish-made liqueurs, vastly less expensive. I write in the past tense, since the Tarragona distillery was closed in 1991.

Chinchón

One of the best brands of ANÍS, made by a subsidiary of González-Byass in the small town of Chinchón, southeast of Madrid. It was named after a seventeenth-century Marquesa de Chinchón, wife of a governor of Peru, who in 1638 discovered the medicinal properties of quinine, giving her name to the cinchona tree from the bark of which it is obtained and, indirectly, inspiring the fabrication of VINOS QUINADOS, drunk as tonics.

Cinzano

Cinzano, in its different varieties, formerly made under licence in Vilafranca del Penedès is, with Martini, the most widely drunk VERMOUTH in Spain.

Cointreau

This famous orange-flavoured liqueur was formerly made for the house of Cointreau by Antonio MASCARO in Vilafranca del Penedès.

Coñac

To the legitimate discomfort of producers in Cognac, Spanish brandy is widely known in Spain as *coñac*. This is certainly no fairer than the dubious practice – now outlawed – of labelling sherry-type wines from Cyprus and elsewhere as "sherry". The makers of Spanish brandy are therefore careful to label their product as "brandy" or Brandy de Jerez.

Conde de Osborne

A very old mature *solera gran reserva* brandy made by OSBORNE and presented in white ceramic bottles designed by Salvador Dalí.

Cuarenta y Tres

A sweet, light-yellow, vanilla-flavoured liqueur, rather resembling Southern Comfort in taste. Its name means "forty-three". Sweet as it is, Spaniards often drink it as an apéritif.

Don Narciso

Delicate and aromatic brandy, a blend of seven- and ten-year-old spirits and one of the best from Spain, made and matured by the Charentais method by Cavas MASCARO in Vilafranca del Penedès.

DYC

Spanish-made whisky produced in a distillery near Segovia, now owned by PEDRO DOMECQ, where the water and grain are considered to be most like those of the Scottish Highlands. It is not of the quality of the original and has made limited headway against the imported Scotch, which is widely obtainable in Spanish supermarkets and grocers.

Espléndido

DO

The youngest of the range of brandies from the famous and old-established sherry firm of GARVEY, in Jerez de la Frontera.

Felipe II

DO

Pleasant and inexpensive Jerez brandy made by Agustín Blázquez in Jerez de la Frontera.

Fontenac

One of the best brandies from Miguel TORRES in Vilafranca del Penedès, now discontinued. It was made by the Charentais method and aged in French style rather than in *solera*; it is hence less oaky than Brandy de Jerez, and more along the lines of an Armagnac.

Fundador

DO

One of the first Jerez brandies, put on sale to the public by PEDRO DOMECQ in 1874, some twenty years after Don Pedro Domecq Lustau had been so struck with the quality of a batch of HOLANDAS accidentally left in cask that he decided on systematic production of a brandy. To foreign tastes, Fundador remains one of the most agreeable of the inexpensive brandies, since it is grapier and less sweetened than many of its competitors. Perhaps this explains why it is the export leader.

García Poveda, HL

Makers of a range of Costa Blanca vermouths, fully flavoured and spicy in comparison with those from France and Italy. The firm also produces table wines from the Alicante area (*see* "Valencia and Murcia", page 170).

Garvey

DO

Famous sherry house, now owned by José María Ruíz Mateos, and producer of, in ascending order of age and refinement, ESPLENDIDO, Gran Garvey, and RENACIMIENTO brandies.

González-Byass

DO

As well as the famous sherries, González-Byass produces three brandies: SOBERANO, the medium-priced insuperable, and, in very limited amount, the exquisite LEPANTO *solera gran reserva*.

Gran Duque de Alba

DO

Premium-quality *solera gran reserva* Brandy de Jerez formerly made by Diez-Mérito and now by Williams & Humbert.

Holandas

Grape spirit containing sixty-five per cent alcohol and made by the continuous distillation of wine. It is produced in various districts of Spain, especially La Mancha, Extremadura, and Huelva. This spirit is subsequently diluted with water and aged, either in *solera* or cask, to make brandy.

Honorable

An exceptional brandy made by Miguel TORRES in Vilafranca del Penedès, by double distillation in copper pot-stills and a long maturation in French oak, but now replaced by Jaime I.

Independencia

DO

Dark, velvety, and sweet, this is a premium *solera gran reserva* brandy from the sherry house of OSBORNE.

Insuperable

DO

The big brother of SOBERANO from GONZÁLEZ-BYASS, smoother, more aromatic.

Jerez-Quina

Popular tonic wine made with sherry, macerated cinchona bark, and Seville orange peels, regularly administered to Spanish children and convalescents.

Larios

Larios makes good málaga (*see* page 102), but in Spain it is a household word for its gin, sold in bottles with a red and yellow labels that have a marked likeness to that of the export Gordon's. Though not of the same quality as good London gin, it is acceptable with mixers. Also produces the 1866 Gran Reserva brandy, Triple Seco orange liqueur, and rum.

Lepanto

DO

Soft, mellow, and fragrant, but entirely Jerezano in character, this expensive *solera gran reserva* brandy from GONZÁLEZ-BYASS, sold in a cut-class decanter, is exceptional.

Liqueurs

Most of the best-known French liqueurs are available in Spain, sometimes made locally under licence. A number of distilleries, mainly around Barcelona and in the Valencian area, make ANÍS (*anisette*), fruit brandies, crème de menthe, etc. There are also native liqueurs with a foreign following (*see* PONCHE, PACHARAN, CALISAY, CUARENTA Y TRES, TORRES, MASCARO, etc.).

Lustau, Emilio

DO

Sherry firm, now controlled by LUIS CABALLERO, whose *solera reserva* and *solera gran reserva* brandies are sold as Señor Lustau.

Magno

DO

Made by OSBORNE in Puerto de Santa María, Magno is a brandy that spends four to five years in *solera*. Dark in colour, smooth, aromatic, and a little sweet, it commands half of the domestic market in the popular medium-priced *solera reserva* range.

Martini

Martini, especially in the sweet and bitter-sweet varieties, is extremely popular in Spain.

Mascaró, Antonio

Mascaró, a small family concern in Vilafranca del Penedès (*see* page 69), has long provided some of the best Catalan brandy. Made by the Charentais method and aged along French lines, it is more reminiscent of Cognac or Armagnac than the Brandy de Jerez. The regular Mascaró is light, smooth, and fragrant, and is in my opinion much superior to most three-star Cognacs – as well as being a great deal less expensive. The older DON NARCISO is made from a blend of Macabeo, Xarel-lo, and Parellada grapes vinified in the cava itself. A new introduction is the premium Ego, aged for eight years in Limousin oak.

Mascaró also produces a vodka and a superior gin, made with alcohol distilled from sugar beet and juniper berries from the Penedès. For many years, the firm made COINTREAU for sale in Spain and now produces its own Curaçao, the Gran Licor de Naranja, a pleasant liqueur made by steeping dried orange peel from Spain, Algeria, Haiti, and Italy in alcoholic solution and then distilling it.

Mollfulleda, Destilérias

Now closed and converted into a museum, this large distillery in Arenys de Mar near Barcelona specialized in the quinine-based CALISAY. Apart from this, it also produced rum, gin, kirsch, and a range of liqueurs – orange, peppermint, coffee, cocoa, and others.

Montulia, Bodegas

Apart from montilla (*see* page 103), Montulia also makes ANÍS and a range of *solera* brandies.

Orujo

Popular name for the fiery *aguardiente de orujo* distilled from grape skins and pips (*see* AGUARDIENTE).

Osborne y Cía

DO

This famous sherry firm is the largest producer of spirits in Spain, making VETERANO, MAGNO, and INDEPENDENCIA brandies. All tend to be dark in colour and sweetened and caramelized to the Spanish taste. Its CONDE DE OSBORNE *solera gran reserva* is older and mellower than Independencia. Osborne also makes PONCHE and produces RIVES gin and vodka in a plant outside Puerto de Santa María, and ANÍS DEL MONO in Barcelona.

Pacharán

A delicious liqueur with a base of ANÍS which is made from sloes in Navarra. The most widely available brand is ZOCO.

Pedro Domecq

DO

One of the first firms to make brandy in Jerez, Pedro Domecq maintains a huge store for ageing its brandies in *solera* and, taking into account its vast Mexican operation, is probably the biggest manufacturer in the world. In ascending order of age and quality its labels are FUNDADOR, Carlos II, and CARLOS I. Domecq also makes an ANÍS *dulce* and a sweet lime liqueur, the Crema de Lima.

Ponche

First produced by the sherry firm of José De Soto in 1888, *ponche* is a blend of brandy and herbs. Often flavoured with orange, it is enjoyed by those with a taste for something sweeter than brandy but less sticky than a liqueur, and it fills an uncluttered gap in the market – its silvered bottles also stand out on the shelves. The largest-selling variety, claiming some eighty per cent of the market and with a fragrant orange nose, is CABALLERO. De Soto's *ponche* remains one of the best, since it is more aromatic and less sweet than some. Other Jerez producers are OSBORNE, Hidalgo, Valdespino, and Barbadillo.

Presidente

The best of the brandies from the Montilla firm of ALVEAR.

Queimada

Galician speciality made by setting alight AGUARDIENTE in a white chinaware bowl. When the blue flame subsides, the liquid is, surprisingly, stone cold. More elaborate versions are made, especially at Christmas, by pouring the spirit into an earthenware *cazuela*, adding roasted coffee beans, slices of fresh lemon, and maraschino cherries, burning off some of the alcohol and ladling the potent concoction into glasses.

Quinine

Quinine-based apéritifs and liqueurs are widely produced and very popular in Spain. *See also* JEREZ-QUINA, CALISAY, VINOS QUINADOS, and CHINCHON.

Renacimiento

DO

Smooth and very old *solera gran reserva* brandy made by GARVEY of Jerez and sold in a cut-glass decanter.

Rives

A good-quality Spanish gin made by OSBORNE.

Rum

Rum, popular in Spain as *ron*, is made by RIVES and a variety of smaller concerns.

Soberano

DO

The biggest-selling Brandy de Jerez, made by GONZÁLEZ-BYASS in Jerez. Like FUNDADOR, it is less sweetened and caramelized than many and will thus appeal to foreign visitors more than the darker varieties popular with the Spaniards themselves. An honest-to-goodness young brandy, remarkably inexpensive, especially when bought in litre bottles; the taste for it grows!

Sol y sombra

Literally "sun and shade", a mixture of brandy and ANÍS. Often mixed by aficionados as one part brandy to two of *anís*.

Terry, Fernando A de

DO

Less caramelized than it once was, the regular Centenario Terry, in a bottle with a yellow net, is extremely popular in Spain. The older and more refined Solera 1900 is still on the sweet side.

Torres, Miguel

Together with MASCARO, Torres produces the best Catalan brandy. The range, in ascending order of age, comprises Torres 5, made by continuous distillation and the Solera system; Torres 10 "Special Edition", distilled form the traditional Xarel-lo, Macabeo, and Parellada, also matured in *solera*; Torres 20 distilled by the Charentais method and aged in French oak barrels; the intensely grapey *hors d'age* Impérial; and the premium Jaime I, blended from selected distilled white wines, some more than thirty years old, and presented in a bottle based on a design of Gaudí, the famous Catalan architect. You may still come across some of the premium brandies now discontinued: Fontenac, Miguel Torres Black Label, and Honorable. I have attended blind tastings where it proved extremely difficult to distinguish brandies such as these from good VSOP Cognac. Torres also makes an extremely good Gran Torres Orange Brandy Liqueur and a water-white Aqua d'Or distilled from fruity, recently fermented white wines.

Vermouth

Various of the well-known Italian and French vermouths were until fairly recently produced under licence in Spain, labelled identically and differing little from the originals, since the use of a local white wine was a relatively unimportant factor in comparison with the herbal extract. There is a wide variety of purely Spanish vermouths, produced mainly in Cataluña and along the east coast. These tend to be heavier and fuller in flavour.

Veterano

DO

Jerez brandy made by OSBORNE and known across the country, if only because of the roadside hoardings with its large black bull – though the company name is no longer allowed to appear on them. Dark in colour, sweetened, and caramelized, it currently ranks number three in order of sales in Spain.

Vinos quinados

These tonics or medicated wines containing quinine extract are drunk either for pleasure or given to children and invalids. *See also* JEREZ-QUINA.

Vodka

Spanish vodka, like gin, is produced in sizeable amounts in Jerez and the Barcelona area, and is inexpensive and of acceptable quality – certainly when drunk with mixers.

Whisky

It is now more chic among Spaniards to drink whisky than sherry and it has recently outstripped even brandy in sales, with the young tending towards whisky and Coca-Cola. Most of the best-known brands of Scotch, less expensive than in their homeland, are readily available – as also are some American and Canadian whiskeys. The home-produced DYC whisky is also sold in large amounts.

Zoco

Best known of the brands of PACHARAN, the sloe liqueur from Navarra.

INDEX

Page numbers in *italic* refer to the
maps